PRACTICING

practicing

A MUSICIAN'S RETURN TO MUSIC

GLENN KURTZ

Alfred A. Knopf · New York · 2007

THIS IS A BORZOI BOOK
PUBLISHED BY ALFRED A. KNOPF

Knopf, Borzoi Books, and the colophon are
registered trademarks of Random House, Inc.

Out of concern for the privacy of individuals depicted here,
the author has changed the names of certain individuals,
as well as potentially identifying descriptive details.

The musical notation that appears in the text is the
Fugue from *Violin Sonata no. 1 in G Minor*, by Johann Sebastian Bach.
Transcribed by John W. Lowell.

A portion of "Sitting Down" is adapted from the essay "Practicing,"
which was published in *ZYZZYVA* (Fall, 2001).

Library of Congress Cataloging-in-Publication Data
Kurtz, Glenn.
Practicing : a musician's return to music / Glenn Kurtz.—1st ed.
p.   cm.
Includes bibliographical references and discography.
ISBN 978-0-307-26615-6 (alk. paper)
1. Kurtz, Glenn.   2. Guitarists—United States—Biography.
3. Practicing (Music)   I. Title.
ML419.K97A3 2007
87.87'092—DC27
[B]   2006048794

Manufactured in the United States of America
First Edition

For my parents, Milton and Dede Kurtz,
and my sister, Dana,
and to the memory of my brother, Roger.

CONTENTS

PRACTICING

SITTING DOWN

I AM SITTING DOWN to practice. I open the case and take out my instrument, a classical guitar made from the door of a Spanish church. I strike a tuning fork against my knee and hold it to my ear, then gently pluck an open string. During the night the guitar has drifted out of tune. It tries to pull the tuning fork with it, and I feel the friction of discordant vibrations against my eardrum. I turn the tuning peg slightly, bracing it between my thumb and index finger, until the two sounds converge. Another barely perceptible adjustment, and the vibrations melt together, becoming one. From string to string, I repeat the process, resolving discord with minute twists of my wrist. Then I check high notes against low, middle against outer. Finally I play a chord, sounding all six strings together. Each note rubs the others just right, and the instrument shivers with delight. The feeling is unmistakable, intoxicating. When a guitar is perfectly in tune, its strings, its whole body will resonate in sympathetic vibration, the true concord of well-tuned sounds. It is an ancient, hopeful metaphor, *an instrument in tune,* speaking of pleasure on earth and order in the cosmos, the fragility of beauty, and the quiver in our longing for love.

With a metal emery board, then with very fine sandpaper, I file the nails on my right hand. Even the tiniest ridges can catch on a string and make its tone raspy. In 1799 Portuguese guitarist Antonio Abreu suggested trimming the nails with scissors, then smoothing them on a sharpening stone to remove "rough edges that might impede the execution of flourishes and lively scales." Some guitarists disagree heatedly with this advice, preferring to play with the fingertips alone. For support, they quote Miguel Fuenllana, who in 1554 stated that "to strike with the nails is imperfection. Only the finger, the living thing, can communicate the intention of the spirit." But to my ear, the spirit of music speaks with many voices, and a combination of fingernail and flesh sounds best. I run my thumb over my fingertips. They are as smooth as crystal.

I shift the guitar into its proper position, settle its weight, and adjust my body to the familiar contours. And then I look around me. My chair is by a window in the living room; my footstool and music stand are in front of me. The window shade is partly drawn so that the San Francisco sunlight falls at my feet but not on my instrument, which would warp in the heat. Outside, people with briefcases and regular jobs are walking down the hill to work. Students are arriving at the school across the street. I listen to their voices and footsteps. Then I take a deep breath, letting them go. I draw myself in. I'm alone in the apartment, and my work is here. I begin.

At first I just play chords. The sounds feel bulky, as do my hands. I concentrate on the simplest task, to play all the notes at precisely the same moment, with one thought, one motion. It takes a few minutes; sometimes, on bad days, it takes all morning. I take my time. But I cannot proceed without this unity of thought, motion, and sound.

Slowly the effort wakes my fingers. Slowly they warm. As the muscles loosen, I break the chords into arpeggios: the same notes, but now spread out, each with its own place, its own demands. Arpeggios make the fingers of both hands work together in different combinations. I play deliberately, building a triangle of sound—fingertip, ear, fingertip—until my hands become aware of each other.

My attention warms and sharpens, and I shape the notes more carefully. I remember now that music is vibration, a disturbance in the air. I remember that music is a kind of breathing, an exchange of energy and excitement. I remember that music is physical, not just in the production of sounds, in the instrumentalist's technique, but as an experience. Making music changes my body, eliciting shivers, sobs, or the desire to dance. I become aware of myself, of these sensations that lie dormant until music brings them out. And in an instant the pleasure, the effort, the ambition and intensity of playing grip me and shake me awake. I feel as if I've been wandering aimlessly until now, as if all the time I'm not practicing, I'm a sleepwalker.

I calm myself and concentrate. Give the sounds time, let the instrument vibrate. I have to hear the sounds I want before I make them, and I have to let the sounds be what they are. Then I have to hear the difference between what I have in mind and what comes from the strings.

It's easy to get carried away. The grandeur, the depth and beauty of music are always present in the practice room. Holding the guitar, I feel music's power at my fingertips, as if I might pluck a string and change the world. For centuries people believed that music was the force that moved the planets. Looking into the night sky, astronomers saw the harmony of heaven, and philosophers heard the music of the spheres. Musicians were prophets then, and according to Cicero the most talented might gain entry to heaven while still alive simply "by imitating this harmony on stringed instruments." Every artist must sometimes believe that art is the doorway to the divine. Perhaps it is. But it's dangerous for a musician to philosophize instead of practicing. The grandeur of music, to be heard, must be played. When I hold the guitar, I may aspire to play perfect harmonies. But first I have to play well.

I bring myself back to the work at hand. I listen to the strings, while testing fine gradations in the angle, speed, and strength of my touch. I vary the dynamics and articulation, vary the intensity and color of the notes. If I am to play well, I must gather the guitar's many voices, let each one sing out. After a few more minutes of arpeggios, my fingers grow warm and capable. The notes are clear and distinct, and I play the simple chords again, very softly at first, then louder and more urgently. Again, softly, then filling, expanding, releasing. Once more, until gradually the sounds from the instrument near what I hear in my head.

Listening, drawing sound, motion, and thought together, I find my concentration. My imagination opens and reaches out. And in that reaching I begin to recognize myself. My hands feel like my hands and not the mitts I usually walk around with. I recognize my instrument's tone; this is how I sound, for now. I recognize my body; I feel alert and able. I feel like a musician again, a classical guitarist. I feel ready to work, ready to play.

⌒

"For the past eighty years I have started each day in the same manner," wrote the cellist Pablo Casals in his memoir, *Joys and Sorrows*. "I go to the piano, and I play two preludes and fugues of Bach. It fills me with awareness of the wonder of life, with a feeling of the incredible marvel of being a human being."

Try to describe your experience of music, and you'll quickly reach the limits of words. Music carries us away, and we grope for the grandest terms in our vocabulary just to hint at the marvel of the flight, the incredible marvel, the wonder. "Each day," Casals continues, "it is something new, fantastic, and unbelievable." I imagine him leaning forward in excitement, a round-faced bald man in his eighties, gesturing with his hands, then meeting my eyes to see if I've understood. Fantastic and unbelievable. The words say little. But yes, I think I understand.

I'm sitting down to practice, and like Casals, I'm grasping for words to equal my experience. Alone in the practice room, I hold my instrument silently. Every day it is the same task, yet something new. I delve down, seeking what hides waiting in the notes, what lies dormant in myself that music brings to life. I close my eyes and listen for the unheard melody in what I've played a hundred times before, the unsuspected openings.

What are the tones, the terms, that unlock music's power, the pleasure and profundity we experience in listening? I begin to play, leaning forward excitedly and grasping for the right notes, my whole body alive with aspiration. Sounds ring out, ripening for a moment in the air, then dying away. I play the same notes again, reaching for more of the sweetness, the bittersweetness they contain and express. And again the sounds ring out, float across the room, and fall still. Each day, with every note, practicing is the same task, this essential human gesture—reaching out for an ideal, for the grandeur of what you desire, and feeling it slip through your fingers.

Practicing music—practicing anything we really love—we are always at the limit of words, striving for something just beyond our ability to express. Sometimes, when we speak of this work, therefore, we make this the goal, emphasizing the pleasure of reaching out. Practicing, writes Yehudi Menuhin, is "the search for ever greater joy in movement and expression. This is what practice is really about." But frequently we experience a darker, harsher mood, aware in each moment of what slips away unattained. Then pleasure seems like nourishment for the journey, but it is not what carries us forward. When musicians speak of this experience, they often stress the labor, warning how difficult a path it is, how lonesome and demanding. The great Spanish guitarist Andrés Segovia cautioned that "it is impossible to feign mastery of an instrument, however skillful the impostor may be." But to attain mastery, if it is possible at all, requires "the stern discipline of lifelong practice."

For the listener, Segovia says, music might seem effortless or divine. But for the musician it is the product of supreme effort and devotion, the feast at the end of the season.

Like every practicing musician, I know both the joy and the hard labor of practice. *To hear these sounds emerging from my instrument! And to hear them more clearly, more beautifully in my head than my fingers can ever seem to grasp.* Together this pleasure in music and the discipline of practice engage in an endless tussle, a kind of romance. The sense of joy justifies the labor; the labor, I hope, leads to joy. This, at least, is the bargain I quietly make with myself each morning as I sit down. If I just do my work, then pleasure, mastery will follow. Even the greatest artists must make the same bargain. "I was obliged to work hard," Johann Sebastian Bach is supposed to have said. And I want so much to believe him when he promises that "whoever is equally industrious will succeed just as well."

Yet as I wrap my arms around the guitar to play, I also hear another voice whispering in my ears. "Whatever efforts we may make," warned Jean-Jacques Rousseau in his 1767 *Dictionary of Music*, "we must still be born to the art, otherwise our works can never mount above the insipid." In every musician's mind lurks the fear that practicing is merely busywork, that you are either born to your instrument or you are an impostor. Trusting Bach and Segovia, I cling to the belief that my effort will, over time, yield mastery. But this faith sometimes seems naïve, merely a wish. "The capacity for melody is a gift," asserted Igor Stravinsky. "This means that it is not within our power to develop it by study." Practice all you want, Rousseau and Stravinsky say, but you will never become a musician if you don't start out one. Perhaps practice will carry me only so far. Perhaps, as Oscar Wilde put it, "only mediocrities develop."

I shake out my hands. Outside on the street, the morning commute is over. The workday has begun; school is in session. Only tourists pass by my window now, lumbering up the hill in search of

Lombard Street, "the crookedest street in the world." I walk down this tourist attraction all the time, a pretty, twisting street festooned with flowers. Now, from my chair, I watch a family cluster around a map, Mom, Dad, and two red-haired teenage boys, each pointing in a different direction. They're just a block from their destination, but they don't know it, lost within sight of their goal. I feel that way every day.

Practicing is striving; practicing is a romance. But practicing is also a risk, a test of character, a threat of deeply personal failure. I warm up my hands and awaken my ears and imagination, developing skill to equal my experience. I listen and concentrate in an effort to make myself better. Yet every day I collide with my limits, the constraints of my hands, my instrument, and my imagination. Each morning when I sit down, I'm bewildered by a cacophony of voices, encouraging and dismissive, joyous and harsh, each one a little tyrant, each one insisting on its own direction. And I struggle to harmonize them, to find my way between them, uncertain whether this work is worth it or a waste of my time.

Everything I need to make music is here, my hands, my instrument, my imagination, and these notes. For most of their lives Segovia, Casals, Bach, and Stravinsky were also just men sitting alone in a room with these same raw materials, looking out the window at people on the street. Like me, they must at times have wondered how to grasp the immensity of music's promise in a few simple notes, how to hold fast to their devotion against a cutting doubt that would kill it.

⌢

I begin my right-hand exercises. With the metronome set at fifty beats per minute, I hold a C-major chord with my left hand, while plucking the strings with my right thumb and my index and middle fingers.

One and Two and Three and Four and.

Every other metronome beat, I move my thumb to a different string, from the fifth to the fourth to the third and back to the fifth, playing C, E, G, C. After repeating this sequence of notes four times, I change chords to G[7]. Now the same right-hand pattern plays different notes. My thumb moves B, D, G, B.

One and Two and Three and Four and.
Repeat.

I concentrate on striking the strings consistently, so that the passage from note to note is smooth, fluid, a line. I listen to the strings vibrating, and in the last instant before each downbeat, I plant my thumb and the two fingers on the strings they are about to play. Pull and release. Lightning fast, exactly together, and exactly on the beat.

The top two notes remain the same in each measure. But since the thumb is playing a moving line, I want it to be in the foreground, slightly louder, more articulated. I want the chord change to sound like an event. It is a matter of timing, of phrasing, of playing with the beat. If I hit the notes too exactly, the line sounds square:

One two three four,
One two three four.

Square time sounds singsongy, like a child's counting or a poem in which too much lines up:

I shot an arrow in the air,
It fell to earth I know not where.

Playing with the beat makes time more complex, makes the poetry better, as in this line from Shelley's "With a Guitar, to Jane":

Ariel to Miranda:—Take
This slave of Music for the sake
Of him who . . .

This phrase also has four beats per line, yet it moves through them rather than hammering them in place. Phrasing the thumb's line like the poem makes the chord change more engaging, more dramatic. It gives the line momentum. You want it to continue. I shift between chords, changing my articulation, stringing my ear along. How long can I keep the poem, the story, going, playing this same pattern, before it repeats?

There are infinite variations to this exercise. I follow the 120 patterns for the right hand written in 1812 by the guitar virtuoso Mauro Giuliani. I work on twenty patterns each day, so that every week I practice all of them. Then I change the metronome setting and begin again. Played at 108 beats per minute rather than fifty, these exercises demand the same movements but feel very different. Yet the goal is always the same: to keep the music moving. Each of the variations requires concentration and imagination—perhaps months or years of faithful practice—before I know it will be musical, will continue and not repeat.

⁀

"If everyone knew how to work, everyone would be a genius!" said the harpsichordist Wanda Landowska. I turned to her a few years ago, as to Casals and Segovia, because I wanted to become a better musician. I had played the classical guitar very seriously as a child and young adult, working to become a professional musician, if not a genius. I practiced full of ambition and expectation. I heard so much in music, felt it so deeply. These feelings pressed for expression. And I had some success. I studied at a music conservatory; I won competitions. But ambition and expectation are sometimes not enough. In my mid-twenties, disillusioned with my progress and so with myself, I gave up my dream of becoming an artist. Like so many people who practice an art in their youth, I couldn't reconcile my love for music with the demands of adult life or the professional realities of earning a living from art. Perhaps I lacked the talent; perhaps I didn't work hard enough. Whatever the case, quitting was a catastrophe. For ten years afterward my hands and my habits—the whole history of my playing—seemed like obstacles to music. I lost faith in the power of practicing to lead me forward. The one thing I had loved most in life became a torture. It was a devastating loss.

Then a few years ago I began to practice the guitar again. I was older, chastened in my goals. Music was no longer a profession for me but a private pursuit. I set out to recover the pleasure I had once enjoyed in playing. What I found, however, was more disappointment. Practicing felt like the same thing again, the same routine, the same dead-end mistakes. I worked hard. Yet nothing seemed to change my hands, and nothing could lessen the weight of my disillusionment. I cast around for ways to change how I practiced. Even the art of practicing might be improved with practice, I thought. "Guided by his own inexperience, no one can hope to become great," counseled Johann Nikolaus Forkel, Bach's first biographer. The aspiring musician, he wrote, "must profit by the practice and example of others." To avoid repeating my failure, I sought out method books by musicians I admired, hoping to learn from them.

There are dozens of books offering advice on the subject of practicing. Most of them, like Giuliani's, are finger books that approach practicing technically. For them, the goal of practice is finger fluency, because, as piano pedagogue Carl Czerny put it, "in music, nothing is worse than *playing wrong notes*." Finger books teach you to play correctly, advising the student to view mistakes as mere problems to be solved. "Whatever you may have to do in a piece that is difficult can always be reduced to one finger's doing one particular job, followed by another finger's doing something else," writes the guitarist Alice Artzt in *The Art of Practicing*. "And once that sequence of motions can be isolated, it can be made into an exercise." Finger books prize discipline. They are clear-eyed and practical and say things like "listen carefully to your playing all the time" and "always practice with a purpose."

From the finger books I learned new exercises and helpful techniques, and I remembered to focus on each finger individually before considering them as a group.

Yet making music is more than exercising my fingers. The authors of these finger books—the cheerleaders of hard work—are often merely gymnastic. While their suggestions improved my technique, they failed to improve my practice. I kept searching and found more balanced advice in a different category of method, the mind book.

"I believe that learning to play the guitar is inseparable from learning to harmonize body, mind, and spirit," writes Philip Toshio Sudo in *Zen Guitar*. Mind books rarely contain technical exercises. On the contrary, they are openly disdainful of finger books, whose lists and exercises reek of habit and stale repetition. For the authors of mind books, the goal is not finger fluency but mental freshness, even enlightenment. "In this school," Sudo continues, "one acquires technique solely for the purpose of freeing the spirit." According to Madeline Bruser in *The Art of Practicing: A Guide to Making Music from the Heart*, the goal is to cultivate "a clear and relaxed mind, an open heart, free and natural movement, and vivid, joyful listening."

Mind books sense a world beyond the fingers and find in music a reflection of something larger—the spirit, the divine, the unconscious. Some of them, like Bruser's thoughtful study, read like meditation manuals. Others, like Barry Green's *The Inner Game of Music*, have the cloying ring of self-help, promising to unleash "your natural creativity and genius: the composer, the child at play, the spontaneous and musical you." Instead of lists, mind books offer aphorisms, soothing counsel, and extended quotations from philosophers and psychotherapists. "The value of an exercise depends on your state of mind," says the best of this kind. "We must give up excessive ambition and . . . let ourselves feel the pain of our longing."

I turned to method books because I wanted to learn how to improve. My hands and my habits seemed like obstacles, and I already felt a painful longing for the music I loved. From these books I sought insight into how to move beyond this pain and not repeat it. Finger books presented a path to technical mastery; mind books conceived this path as part of a deeper personal journey. Both are essential to improve as a musician. And yet over the course of several months, as I set out each morning to practice, I realized that my technique and my ability to concentrate were not what held me back. Instead, I discovered that when I abandoned my musical ambitions, I had lost my faith in practicing. I no longer believed the story I was telling myself about hard work and gradual improvement. My history contradicted it. Love of music had led me to heartbreak.

Practicing is training; practicing is meditation and therapy. But before any of these, practicing is a story you tell yourself, a bildungsroman, a tale of education and self-realization. For the fingers as for the mind, practicing is an imaginative, imaginary arc, a journey, a voyage. You must feel you are moving forward. But it is the story that leads you on. Method books can advise or comfort you along the way, companions on the journey. Yet the story of your practice is your own. And unless you translate these methods into your own terms, animating them with the stuff of your particular story, their advice and wisdom are just empty phrases. You want to improve. Yet many paths stand open, and you must select just one. You love music. But how do you put your love into practice?

I turned to method books to clear my mind and clean up my technique. But to become a better musician, I realized I had to practice my story, learn to remake my hands and my history as characters in this narrative, instead of obstacles. To make myself better, I'd have to practice my love of music.

From the outside, practicing may not seem like much of a story. If the family out on the sidewalk were to look in my window, all they would see is me sitting alone in my room playing the guitar. Yet practicing is the fundamental story. Whether as a musician, as an athlete, at your job, or in love, practice gives direction to your longing, gives substance to your labor. Every day you go to the gym or sit down at your desk. The work is not always interesting, not always fun. Sometimes it is tedious. Sometimes it is infuriating. Why do you continue? Why did you start in the first place? You must have an answer that helps you persevere. Maybe you don't have a choice; maybe others depend on your labor. But these too are stories that keep you going, ways of gathering the innumerable little chores of your day into a single compelling task. Because without telling yourself some story of practicing, without imagining a path to your goal, the aggravation and effort seem pointless. And without faith in the story you create, the hours of doubt and struggle and the endless repetition feel like torture.

⌢

With the metronome still at fifty beats per minute, I begin my left-hand exercises. I play a C-major scale, one note per beat. Up two octaves, then down. Repeat. It should sound like one scale, not fifteen notes. But my aim is not to play a scale. I am playing a line of music. One thought up, one thought down, like breathing in and breathing out. Repeat.

I vary the rhythm. Two notes quickly in succession, then rest. Then two more, rest, and so on up and down the scale. Then three notes together. Then a syncopated rhythm. Like syrup. Like gunshots.

It takes effort to hear a scale as one motion, but it isn't hard to play the notes. No matter how fast or complex the music, most of the time each finger is at rest. The hardest part of practicing scales is remembering that they aren't finger work.

The G-major scale extends three octaves up the neck of the guitar. The left hand must shift position four times. My hand flies in one motion, landing on the finger that plays. This movement is not part of the sound or the phrase. The listener shouldn't hear it. It is like turning a page in a book; it has nothing to do with the sentence.

I play major scales in all the keys, then play minor scales as well. It's good exercise. But that doesn't matter. The goal of playing scales is to make the notes seem independent of my fingers. No one is interested in my fingers except me.

︵·︶

Practicing is a story, but not one in "square time," not a simple path to perfection. Instead, it is a myth you weave to draw up the many strands of your doubt and desire. When musicians speak of practicing, therefore, the subject is really themselves.

Segovia, late in his life, told his biographer that he never practiced more than five hours a day, "each session of work being divided into one and a quarter hours, no longer, and four such sessions a day being sufficient. The individual sessions are themselves interspersed with relaxation and activities such as walking, reading, talking with friends, or quiet reflection." Segovia didn't tell us how he practiced, but how he lived, what he valued. Interviewed by *Time* magazine in 1952, Wanda Landowska declared, "I never practice; I always play," conveying more about herself than about her work habits. From his biography we learn that Francisco Tárrega, father of the modern classical guitar, practiced one hour of scales, one hour of arpeggios, one hour of trills, and an hour of exercises drawn from difficult passages each day. "Thus passes the morning," the faithful biographer reports, "after lunch, once more the guitar." I read this and try to imagine the life it describes, with its monastic devotion, its rigor and isolation.

Musical performance establishes a relationship between the performer and an audience. But musical practice is solitary, a relationship with yourself. No matter how much I read, or how well I imagine Segovia, Landowska, or Tárrega in their rooms, I remain on the outside of their practicing. I might discover how many hours a day they worked, or what exercises they favored. Yet how they created music amid a swirl of memories, associations, ambitions, and disappointments remains a mystery. I read about their work, but I learn instead about the stories they tell.

Some musicians lie about practicing to give the impression they are above it. Others exaggerate the effort to show how dedicated they are and how difficult the task is. But everyone tells a story about their ideal, a myth that glorifies their labor. "No artist is pleased," the dancer and choreographer Martha Graham professed. "There is no satisfaction whatever at any time." Yet Graham celebrates a "divine dissatisfaction, a blessed unrest that keeps us marching and makes us more alive than the others."

As I sit down again with my instrument, I know that Graham's story is not the one that will help me now. For her, practicing is heroic, as long as dissatisfaction lofts you above the crowd to some better life. But from painful experience I know that an artist's unrest is not always blessed, that dissatisfaction can devastate your art.

Each day you sit down full of fantasy and flaws, a chaos of discordant voices. To others, your playing might sound sweet and lovely. But alone in the practice room, you must contend with friction and disharmony too. The story you tell yourself must include these, must embrace everything you experience when you sit down in the presence of your ideal. Because in the course of one day, you might practice for sheer joy, since nothing feels as good as making music, and you might practice in rage at the clumsiness of your hands or at the futility of all art. Your practice could be a form of prayer or supplication, an expression of faith or a longing for eventual reward. You might practice out of hunger for fame or to prove yourself to others—your parents, perhaps, or your peers. You might practice to avoid humiliation or reproach or to satisfy a teacher's expectations. One of the saddest stories I know is by the Roman naturalist Pliny the Elder, about a circus elephant that was slow to learn his tricks. Whenever he failed, he was beaten with a lash. While the other elephants slept, the tortured animal "was discovered at midnight practicing what he had to do." To keep yourself from the lash, you might practice with terrified caution or while seasoning your lust for revenge. You might practice as a miser, hoarding skill and never spending it, or as a libertine on the prowl for new pleasures, selfishly exulting in each conquest. In the space of a single note, you might lose yourself in fantasies, and suddenly feel that you have only now discovered your true voice. You might practice in order to play, hoping to recover a childlike spontaneity. You might practice to finally grow up, raising yourself to maturity with discipline and sacrifice. You might practice for the love of a challenge, testing yourself against the minds of great composers. Or you might practice each day as a disciple of anxiety, endlessly picking at the flesh of your playing. Your ear becomes a knife, and you sharpen it against your own skin.

"Men have practiced music at all times without being able to give an account of this," wrote the philosopher Arthur Schopenhauer. Yet every time you sit down, you give an account of your practicing, revealing yourself and the composition of your character with the story that you tell, the metaphors that make your effort seem worthwhile and that marry your many competing voices together.

Because practicing is more than exercises and study, the patient minding of your fingers. When you sit down to practice, however casually, you cast yourself as the hero and victim of your own myth. You will encounter obstacles; you will struggle, succeed, and struggle some more. The story of your practice weaves all this together, absorbing what is within you and making it productive. Because when you truly believe your story of practicing, it has the power to turn routine into a route, to resolve your discordant voices, and to transform the harshest, most intense disappointment into the very reason you continue.

⌒

I open the music on my music stand, *The Complete Sonatas and Partitas for Unaccompanied Violin* by J. S. Bach. I take a deep breath, then begin the first movement of Sonata no. 1, the *Adagio*. The movement opens with a G-minor chord, held for a full beat at very slow tempo. The chord forcefully announces the key and creates the expectation of movement. But it dies away almost to silence before the next note sounds. I wait with the chord, letting it sink in.

I know this music well, or I used to, having played it years ago when I was a student at the New England Conservatory of Music in Boston. In the 1920s Andrés Segovia established the classical guitar as a concert instrument by demonstrating the emotion and intricacy of these pieces. Segovia's performance was revolutionary. Though the music was written for the violin, that instrument's four bowed strings can produce the harmony only in fragments. The guitar, with six plucked strings, unified the harmony and liberated Bach's counterpoint. Since then every serious guitarist has performed

Bach's violin music. When I immersed myself in these works as a student in the 1980s, I felt like a revolutionary too. Through Bach, I thought I might express some basic human need that I alone felt and understood. I believed this music would prove my artistry. These things seem plausible when you're nineteen and in the grip of passion. Every day you're on the cusp of profound discoveries. Every day the truth of who you really are seems to grow more tangible.

But now my playing is halting and awkward. In the time since I last practiced it, the music has reverted to its natural state. The needs, the passion, and the truths I heard—once again they are just notes. I still remember how the piece goes, more or less, but the details, the tones themselves, have escaped me. I play the music very slowly, feeling the instrument's body rising and falling with the sound. My head bobs slightly, half-consciously conducting, as the music thins to two closely spaced lines. The notes glide irresistibly toward each other, and their clash rakes my senses. I stay with the line for five full beats until it drifts to silence again, leaving me waiting, wanting more.

Then I stop to look at the page, puzzling over the phrase. I no longer know how to play these notes, how to fit them together into music. In my fraying edition of the score, each line is busy with pencil markings—fingerings, phrasings, harmonic analyses—left over from that rapturous first encounter, now twenty years ago. Reading these old markings is like rediscovering a journal from college. This book of music is a work diary, and the notes I made as a teenager still glow with the urgency and the innocence of that time. Today, however, I greet these marks with skepticism, even embarrassment. Like a diary, the page records thoughts and feelings born of a certain moment in my life. There are flashes of insight, even brilliance, visible only with distance. But their moment is long past, part of a story I can no longer believe. I am not who I was. Playing the *Adagio* again, I wonder what my old decisions, these old marks of inspiration in the score, have to do with me now. Different phrasings and fingerings seem more natural today. I'm drawn to different rhythms and harmonies. But as much as I want to, I can't simply start anew. These old notes, my old flaws and disappointment, are still at the heart of my playing. I hear so much in this music. But when I reach for it, my hands tense with the effort of holding what I experience and want to express. I cannot begin anew. Instead, I have to begin again. I have to practice myself, form a new relationship with these sounds. I have to forge a new image of myself playing the music, a new image of myself as a musician.

"The mastery of any art is the work of a lifetime," wrote the poet Ezra Pound. Practicing is a process of continual reevaluation, an attempt to bring growth to repetition. After twenty years, I'm sitting down with this music again. But this time I'm not just practicing Bach. To become a better musician, I have to overcome my disappointment, learning to tell a story of practicing that includes the loss within my love for music. I am not who I was: my fingers are not as agile; my ears are less acute. Yet once more music has kindled the spirit of revolution in me. I begin the piece again. Perhaps this time will be better.

Musical artistry may seem divine, but practicing is always mundane. Practice immerses you in your daily self—this body, these moods. You sit down to play; you file your fingernails; you shape your reed or rosin your bow. You play scales and exercises. You struggle with mistakes and flaws. The work is physical, intellectual, psychological. It can be exhilarating and aggravating, fulfilling and terribly lonesome. But it is always just you, the instrument, and the music, here, now. Practicing is the truth of who you are, today, as you strive to change, to make yourself better, to become someone new. The goal is always to bring old notes to life. Even so, while you sit down to work every day, it may take years before you know what you've practiced.

setting the strings in motion

aT NOON we had to be in the key of D. Each day at lunchtime the faculty and students of the Guitar Workshop gathered beneath a massive oak tree for a "sing." Two bearded men in their twenties, both named Jeff, strummed their guitars, leading a circle of twenty-five students—a mixture of kids, teenagers, and adults— as we learned work songs, whaling songs, protest songs, old English ballads, and rounds. I still have a notebook full of these songs— "Irene," "The Jolly Roving Tar," Tom Paxton's "Bottle of Wine," and the traditional "Bright Morning Stars." I never play them now, but looking through the sheet music immediately sends me back to my first summer at the Guitar Workshop. It was 1970, and everyone wanted to play the guitar.

The Guitar Workshop had begun in 1963 in Great Neck, Long Island, as a school for classical guitar. Within a few years, however, it had grown into a lively center for the study of traditional American and English folk songs. By 1965, when my mother started taking lessons there, the school had moved to a dilapidated house on Forest Street in Roslyn Heights, a more modest suburb than posh Great Neck and not far from our house. Two blocks from an elementary school, and next door to the neat lawns and swing sets of comfortable middle-class families, the Guitar Workshop briefly became a sweet, ragged outpost of the counterculture. Young men and women with long hair and harlequin patches on their bell-bottom jeans hung around the house making music, while cleaner-cut neighbors smiled warily from over the fence. My mother—in her late thirties then, a housewife with three young children—walked down the school's gravel driveway once a week for a guitar lesson. It was a pastime, not a political gesture. She enjoyed the songs of Pete Seeger, Burl Ives, and Woody Guthrie. And so one hour a week she lent her voice to the great folk music revival of the 1960s. Occasionally she took me with her.

There was always music in our house. My mother was learning the guitar. In the evenings she sometimes sat at the piano and ran through the Chopin and Mozart she'd learned as a child. My brother Roger, six years older than I, was occupied in his room at the other end of the house, arranging posters on the wall and listening to the Beatles, Jimi Hendrix, and the Grateful Dead. My sister Dana, two years ahead of me, took piano lessons on our upright in the den, and she was learning to play the flute at school. Climbing into bed at night, I'd hear Mozart's "Rondo alla Turca" collide with "Purple Haze," as one wafted up the stairs and the other screeched down the hall. No one seemed surprised when I, the youngest child, picked up my mother's guitar. I taught myself a few chords from the diagrams in a Bob Dylan songbook. Pretty soon I could play "Blowin' in the Wind."

A few months later I stood squirming in front of Kent Sidon, director of the Guitar Workshop. I remember Kent standing with a guitar on his hip, the neck sticking out in front of him. He was a frail, stringy man, stooped and restless. As my mother and I walked into the room, he was singing a sea chantey, with a cigarette waving like a conductor's baton from the corner of his mouth.

"Wiggle your fingers," he told me, holding my hands palm up in his. I wiggled my fingers. He looked at me, a shy, spider-limbed kid, then said to my mother, "We usually don't take students younger than ten." But he agreed to take me that summer, when I was eight. My parents got me an inexpensive three-quarter-size guitar, which I carried with me everywhere—to school, to the beach, to my grandmother's apartment in New York City, where we went every Friday night for dinner. I couldn't wait to get started. By the time I was ten, I was a star at the Guitar Workshop.

During the summer the house on Forest Street was stuffy and stiflingly hot. The Guitar Workshop was too poor to run the air conditioner, and electric fans were too noisy or blew the sheet music around the room. Classes and lessons were held in the yard, under the trees. Two folding chairs and a wire music stand were all a teacher needed to claim a spot by the hedge, near the shed, or where the flower garden used to be. For the classical guitarists, a pile of wooden footstools was heaped by the back door. Made from three boards nailed together, these blocks didn't sink into the grass, unlike the folding metal stools, which were used indoors.

I had my first half-hour lesson in a corner near the fence. Accompanied by a cicada chorus in the branches overhead, I played the songs I knew, and Paul, my teacher, played a song he knew. He bounced his head to the rhythm, encouraging me to play along, his round John Lennon glasses jumping up and down on his nose. It was easy. I'd already been playing these chords for a year or more. I watched his fingers. We played it again, and just like that, I had learned a new song. Paul sang harmony, and I laughed because it sounded so good, it felt so good to play music.

When the lesson was over, we walked across the yard to the giant oak tree that towered over the house. Jeff and Jeff were beginning the midday "sing." The thin, taller Jeff passed around mimeographed sheet music, still inky from the machine in the office. The students bunched together on the grass to share—little kids like me, suburban mothers in sun hats with maids to do the housework, and scruffy idealists gently rebelling against the establishment.

Together we sang "I Ride an Old Paint" and then "Put Your Finger in the Air" and "Little Boxes."

At noon, deep in the bass register, the Roslyn fire siren started to purr almost imperceptibly. Mounted on a telephone pole just a block away from the school, the siren was tested every day. As we sang, it whirred and whined, gaining volume and ascending in pitch, until exactly at twelve it achieved an ear-splitting high D. If we'd been singing in any other key, the siren would have drowned us. But Jeff and Jeff had timed it right. We were in the key of D, and the siren soared high above, singing along.

I remember sitting at a wooden lunch table, at the end of my first morning at the Guitar Workshop. The table faced the kitchen, which served as the office. The ladies inside were supposed to keep an eye on me as I waited for my mother to pick me up. Wessleya, who ran the office and who would later marry Kent Sidon, called out the window to me, "What did you learn at your lesson?" I took out my guitar and played the song Paul had taught me, "All Join In," by the folk group Traffic.

Other students stopped to listen to me, a little boy with his adorable guitar hardly bigger than a ukulele. The ladies came out of the office. Soon I was sitting on the tabletop leading my own "sing." Ten people clustered around clapping their hands and singing along. I loved my lessons at the Guitar Workshop. To me, it seemed like a picnic, a big happy family out on the lawn.

⌒

The guitar quickly became my instrument. My mother gave it up after a little while, instead spending her time finding clients as an interior decorator. But I loved playing, and I got better without noticing. After "Blowin' in the Wind" and "This Land Is Your Land," I learned hobo songs, gold-mining songs, and songs I picked up from the radio. In fourth grade I had memorized all the words to "American Pie" and could play the lead part to "Jumpin' Jack Flash." There is a picture of me playing guitar in my brown plaid pajamas, nestled into the corner of my double-decker bed. There is a picture of me with wild, wavy blond hair, strumming "Bad, Bad Leroy Brown" for my friends at summer camp. There is a picture of my brother and me with my three-quarter-size guitar at the Grand Canyon. I'm wearing a blue T-shirt with peace signs all over it. My brother, then fifteen, had begun to cultivate epic sideburns. We were figuring out songs from the Beatles' *White Album*, "Rocky Raccoon" and "While My Guitar Gently Weeps." Music came easily to me. No one ever forced me to do my lessons. It never occurred to me that I was practicing.

At home in the evenings, my sister, brother, and I sometimes held concerts in my room. Our parents sat on my bed listening, while the kids put on a show. My brother was living in the Sixties, a rebellious high school student protesting the Vietnam War. My sister and I, just a few years younger but part of a different generation, were kids of the Seventies, listening to AM radio and competing at board games. But this was how we all played together. Dana performed pieces from the flute book she used at school. Roger and I strummed our guitars, singing the Grateful Dead songs "Me and My Uncle" and "Friend of the Devil." The three of us joined forces at the end for the family favorites, "Proud Mary" and "Ob-La-Di, Ob-La-Da." I constructed a primitive spotlight by taping cardboard blinders to a desk lamp. When I wasn't playing, I crouched on the upper bunk of my bed with the lamp, changing the colored filters I'd devised from scraps of cellophane wrapping paper.

In sixth grade I got a hand-me-down electric guitar and started a band with a gang of friends. Mark was learning the drums, and Debbie, Dave, and I played guitar. We rehearsed after school in Mark's basement, trying to find songs that fit the two different beats he knew. After a few months we were confident enough to perform at a school fair. "Johnny B. Goode" and "Eight Days a Week," over and over until we blew a fuse in our one little amplifier.

By this time, though, playing the guitar was changing for me. I'd been singing songs for years, learning barre chords and right-hand patterns like the Travis pick, named for the country guitarist Merle Travis. With finger-picking patterns, you pluck the strings instead of strumming, playing notes instead of whole chords. Once you start plucking, however, the guitar becomes a serious instrument. From the Travis pick to the beginner's études for classical guitar is just a matter of degree. By the end of sixth grade I wasn't just singing songs with a band but had begun playing easy pieces by some of the guitar's better-known composers—Fernando Sor, Francisco Tárrega, Mauro Giuliani, and Robert de Visée. There was more to playing the instrument than just strumming.

At the same time, band rehearsal at Mark's devolved into an after-school party. A clique of giggling groupies started showing up, and soon Mark lost interest in keeping the beat. There was more to being in a band than just playing drums. But a few kids, boys and girls, still wanted to make music. Maybe I started practicing to impress this little group.

At the Guitar Workshop I was still one of the youngest students. I had two teachers now, one for classical and one for popular music. Edgard, a quiet, dour Israeli, played dark, energetic Spanish-sounding music. Peter, a pudgy young man with a wispy mustache, smoked cigarettes and knew how to play blues and rock. I wanted to learn everything they knew: Baroque dances and riffs by Eric Clapton and Jimi Hendrix.

Two years earlier the Guitar Workshop had finally been forced to move from its dingy house on Forest Street and now occupied a former school building where I'd gone to kindergarten. My lessons were held in the classroom where I'd once played with blocks. I remember waiting alone in the room before a lesson on one of the first warm, fragrant days that spring. The doors and windows were open, looking out onto the playground and the jungle gym. Guitar playing spilled from every room. Walking down the hall, you might hear a thousand twanging strings and sometimes music. I was playing my big piece, "Weeping Willow Rag" by Scott Joplin. "Weeping Willow" uses the whole neck of the guitar. There are jazz chords and syncopation and dramatic mood changes. When played well, it swings. This was grown-up music. The folk music revival had long since given way to newer fads. It was 1974 now, and the movie *The Sting* had popularized ragtime. When I finished playing, Paul, my former folk teacher, came into the room. A cheerful man, now with a well-trimmed beard, he looked like a skinny Santa Claus. He'd been listening by the door.

"I didn't know you could play like that," he said seriously, startled.

"I didn't either," I answered, startled myself by his response.

I realized I could play something he couldn't. Was this the moment when I first began to practice? Up until that time I had played guitar every day, but I'd played baseball just as much. If I wasn't at band rehearsal, my afternoons were spent at Little League games or in brutal backyard football skirmishes with my friends. But now I began to worry about injuring my hands. The guitar—and what I could achieve or imagine with it—became more important than the things I had previously enjoyed. Music caught hold of my imagination, and it no longer seemed as worthwhile to spend time playing sports, playing games. The guitar had changed for me, gathering momentum. At twelve years old, I didn't feel I was learning to play the instrument anymore. I knew how to play. Now, I thought of myself as a musician. I wanted to get better.

⌢

"What were you just playing?" my mother asked. She had come into the room with a pleased, puzzled look on her face. I played it again, Duke Ellington's 1942 hit, "Don't Get Around Much Anymore." My mother laughed.

"I loved that song when I was a little older than you," she said. "Uncle Stanley and I would sing it while we washed the dishes at night."

Her expression was new to me, a little sister's look of delight. It taught me in an instant more about my mother's childhood than I had ever learned from the family stories she told. This song had harbored her fifteen-year-old's love, and now I was learning to play it.

I taught the chords to my brother when he came home from college for a visit. He was still playing songs by Bob Dylan and the Grateful Dead. But Duke Ellington uses jazz harmonies, rich sevenths, ninths, and thirteenths. I spent the afternoon helping him find the notes. Then we performed it that night at a family concert in my room. The upper bunk bed was gone, as was the red-white-and-blue wallpaper that had been there a few years before, replaced by a dignified tan burlap. Our parents still sat together listening. But the songs my brother and I played that night had been part of their lives long before we were born. They tried to remember all the words—to "All of Me," "Night and Day," and "Autumn Leaves"— as I improvised a solo, imitating the new sounds I'd heard from Charlie Christian and Wes Montgomery, Charlie Parker and Dizzy Gillespie. My playing interlaced with their laughter. Music was at the heart of the family.

This must have been one of our last family concerts. Disco was becoming the fashion, and that summer my father and I had watched the tall ships entering New York harbor in celebration of the country's bicentennial. Music still brought the family together on these evenings. But the times were changing. My sister sang a song by Loggins and Messina. She still played the flute, along with the piano and a little guitar, more instruments than I played. But she was interested in photography now, taking pictures of her favorite bands and sometimes getting to meet them. My brother was living in Washington, D.C., with his girlfriend and wasn't home very often. And my parents, freed from a household full of young children, were spending more time out at the theater and having dinner with their friends. The next year my sister went to college, leaving me the last child still at home. I was a sophomore in high school, playing in the school jazz band and with a new jazz quartet of my own. We listened to Chick Corea and Return to Forever, Frank Zappa, and fusion jazz, sounds that opened our ears and led us to other styles, deeper influences. I wasn't interested in sing-alongs anymore. I was grasping for the right notes, the freeing leap into bebop.

On a Sunday morning a few months later, I was still lying in bed at eleven o'clock, utterly rapt in the first movement of Beethoven's Third Symphony. My brother had let me take down his old Led Zeppelin posters and move into his room at the end of the hall, the farthest away from my parents. I could listen to music when I wanted; I could practice until late at night. There was a window that led onto the roof of the garage, and I imagined I could sneak out, Tom Sawyer style, to meet my friends. Mostly I listened to music. I'd learned a little music theory at the Guitar Workshop, but I didn't know about musical structure, sonata form, or modulation to distant keys. I had started digging around in my parents' LP collection in the den and found Beethoven sandwiched between Herb Alpert and the Kingston Trio. In my new room I listened to the first movement of the Third Symphony over and over, leaping up to grab the needle before the next piece started and ruined the mood. I didn't realize that symphonies had movements. I thought a symphony meant music played by an orchestra. It would be six months before I discovered the second movement, the third, and the fourth.

But the first movement was enough. Lying in bed, I heard enormous blocks of sound, solid and yet in constant metamorphosis. I pictured a kind of molten architecture, surging in my mind, a palace dancing. Each time I listened, the image grew more refined and intense. I heard new relationships, new tensions. Within this immense and active architecture the music unfolded an emotional drama. The lines resolved into figures that separated and coalesced, intimately and forcefully. The figures felt drawn from my own imagination yet were infused with a meaning I could hardly conceive. I listened closely and deeply until the architecture I first envisioned dissolved, and the music seemed to be shaping me as it shaped itself.

I rushed downstairs, bewildered and bursting, to the dining room, where my parents were reading *The New York Times*. It was a regular Sunday morning in the rest of the house. Coffee, bagels, the newspaper—the reassuring rituals of domestic harmony.

"I've discovered something!" I blurted. "There's a passage where the violins and cellos play the same thing, but staggered, like a round." And I tried to sing it, then dragged my parents upstairs to listen on my secondhand stereo.

They listened; they agreed it was incredible. But they'd heard the symphony before, of course. It was wonderful that I enjoyed this music so much, they said. But then they wanted to finish reading the news. My parents returned to the dining room, and their Sunday continued unaltered.

I was mystified. Couldn't they hear the grace, the violence that Beethoven expressed? Didn't they feel the ache of this music, its urgency and explosiveness? With a sixteen-year-old's dramatic disbelief, I wondered if I was the first to discover it. There had always been music in the house. But now, suddenly, it seemed that no one had been listening. It was just there, like the pictures on the wall. How could they hear this music and not feel that everything had changed?

I closed the door to my room and listened to the symphony again from the beginning. And again the boiling energy of Beethoven's passion poured forth, igniting my own. This music might leave my parents unmoved, but it changed everything for me. It gave me a sense of unlimited possibility; it showed me the limits of my parents' understanding.

My father ran a business that manufactured boys' shirts. He had joined his father's company after World War II and built it up, kept it growing. He left the house each morning at seven to make the commute into Manhattan and came home again around seven at night, having battled the traffic on the Long Island Expressway. He'd been doing it since 1957, when my parents moved from Forest Hills to our Roslyn home. Sometimes at night my father would come into my room as I practiced.

"You've gotten better," he'd say, standing in the doorway as I played a little piece by Bach. He praised my discipline and devotion. He appreciated the hard work. But now I thought his praise showed his ignorance. He couldn't hear the difference between discipline and passion. He couldn't hear what lay beneath the work.

My mother ran the household. Now that I was the only child left at home, she was increasingly busy with her interior decorating projects. She too had studied music as a child, and her mother had been a fine pianist. But music wasn't what occupied her.

"A musician's life is a hard one," she said to me one afternoon, when I'd come down to the kitchen to talk about studying music more seriously. "We're just concerned about the kind of living you'd make."

My parents had always encouraged my enthusiasm for music. They attended theater and the Philharmonic regularly; they loved to watch Leonard Bernstein on public television, exclaiming over the joy on his face, the inspiration. There was even a precedent for a career in music in the family. My mother's cousin, Ken Lane, was a pianist. For a few years when I was very young, we would watch him every Sunday night on television, on *The Dean Martin Show*. Ken was Dean Martin's accompanist and had written the music to one of Dino's most famous songs, "Everybody Loves Somebody Sometime." Clearly it was possible to succeed as a musician.

But my parents were concerned. The thought of an artistic life was unsettling to them.

"It's important to have something to fall back on," they said.

Music was a wonderful pastime. But they worried that it wasn't a stable career, wasn't a comfortable life. In this way, they explained what they valued. But to me, who had only known a comfortable life, this sounded like willful mediocrity. I listened impatiently. A stable career was nothing to strive for. I had begun to imagine something quite different for myself.

I sat for hours in my room listening to Beethoven, Mozart, and Bach, to blues guitarists like Muddy Waters and Duane Allman, or to jazz standards by Django Reinhardt and Miles Davis. Then for hours more I'd try to reproduce what I'd heard. And each day as I practiced, I sank deeper into the notes, past their pitch and duration into their intangible yet palpable content. Music *said* something. And though I could not explain what it was, I knew the message was penetrating and profound. Music ignited bursts of anguish, longing, and ecstasy in my imagination that I had not experienced in life. I practiced scales and études. I practiced ear training and music theory, groping to understand how music achieved this power over me. I played increasingly serious and complex pieces—individual movements from Bach's lute and cello suites, a sonata by Domenico Scarlatti, preludes by Heitor Villa-Lobos—music with subtle harmonies, fine gradations of feeling. The shading of love into bitterness, the dark joyousness of desire deferred—music warmed an endless swarm of unexpected emotions into being. And slowly as I practiced, I absorbed the texture of sounds, their inner expressiveness, and acquired the delicate touch that sets the strings in motion.

My parents spoke of comfort and stability. But I dreamed of living the life I heard in music. It would be an artist's life, full of pleasure, discovery, and an edifying sort of suffering. I would tour the world's concert stages, performing the transformation of feeling into sound, and of sound into vibrating emotion. I imagined the love and the gratitude my audiences would show me for resolving their fears and desires into musical form. It might be lonely and difficult work. But it would be a vibrant, joyous, and inspired life.

In the evenings, instead of holding concerts in my room, I occasionally brought my guitar downstairs to the den, where my parents were sitting on the couch, my mother reading a decorating magazine, my father doing the *Times* crossword puzzle.

"Listen to this," I insisted. All afternoon the way two notes crossed each other at the quietest moment of a Bach *Andante* had lashed and laced through me. So simple, just two notes, yet triumphant, melancholy, and inevitable at once.

"Very beautiful," my father said.

Beautiful? Yes, of course. But past the beauty, couldn't they hear the anger, the sacrifice and mourning? It was as if they *chose* not to feel it, chose to keep music confined in a corner of their lives where it wouldn't upset them. What had I expected? I had never seen my parents displaying bitterness or melancholy, never heard them speak of anguish or longing. As I carried my guitar back up the stairs to my room at the end of the hall, I thought their lives seemed frozen, a solid block of stability and comfort. I struggled to explain this contradiction, the throbbing vitality of music, which they seemed to admire so much yet refused to experience.

At high school my friends were hanging out, meeting girls, and getting stoned to *Romantic Warrior* while deriding the Bee Gees. The newspapers were full of crises. Energy shortages gave way to American hostages in Iran. I went to parties; I read the news. But what I really cared about was elsewhere. During study periods at school I scoured the library for artists' biographies, artists' letters and memoirs, eager to learn what they knew. I was searching for words to describe the intensity of what I experienced and aching to share what I heard. Musicians, painters, and poets were my closer kin, I felt. And like so many artsy-awkward kids, I found what I needed in the essays and *Letters to a Young Poet* by Rainer Maria Rilke.

Rilke spoke of the artist's sensitivity and privileged insight. The poet, he wrote, is "destined to set in motion supreme forces within his own heart, forces that others hold at bay in theirs and reduce to silence." "Yes!" I trembled. My parents couldn't hear it, couldn't feel it. They silenced their emotions, delegated them to others. They sacrificed what was most important in order to preserve their comfortable lives. But I was part of a select society, with music and poetry as our secret language. It was startlingly clear: artists expressed exquisite emotional truths in tones that everyone heard but few had the courage to feel and understand. To speak these truths, to be an artist, was the ultimate calling, the antithesis of school and partying and repetitive family rituals. Of course it was difficult and lonely! How could it be otherwise? To be an artist demanded an unsettled life. "What kind of peace could he hope for," explained Rilke in "The Young Poet," "when, within, he is suffering the assaults of his god?"

Music seemed to offer me an irresistible exchange. If I worked, if I practiced and practiced, then ever-new worlds of sound, of feeling, would open, worlds that made visceral sense to me, though they seemed closed to others. To my parents, to my teachers, I might have appeared the picture of a good student. The high school librarian thought I was precocious and highly motivated. Perhaps I was just pretentious. But I didn't feel precocious or pretentious. I felt impatient and unformed, with everything still to learn. Listen to Bach! Listen to Beethoven! I was assaulted by these gods. And I wanted to be an artist like them. I was in an ecstasy of potential.

Shortly after my seventeenth birthday I heard Andrés Segovia perform at Carnegie Hall. Segovia was an old man by that time, in his eighties, a figure from a different world. He had created the profession of concert classical guitarist seemingly by himself. Born in 1893, in Andalusia, Spain, he grew up at a time when the guitar was seen as a peasant instrument, fit for folk songs and flamenco but for little else. By the age of sixteen he had given a solo concert in Granada. His Madrid debut in 1917 established him as the leading guitarist in Spain, and his Paris debut in 1924 was an internationally acclaimed event, attended by Madame Debussy, Manuel de Falla, and Europe's intellectual and musical elite. Reviewing Segovia's first American concert in January 1928, the *New York Times* music critic Olin Downes had written, "He belongs to the very small group of musicians who by transcendent power of execution, by imagination and intuition create an art of their own that sometimes seems to transform the very nature of their medium."

All through my childhood Segovia's name hovered in the air, the gentle god of the classical guitar. At the Guitar Workshop, when I learned classical technique, I didn't just play scales but "Segovia scales," since Segovia had been the one to standardize their fingering for the instrument. The music I learned, from Renaissance airs to modern sonatas, was not the guitar's repertoire but the "Segovia repertoire," since he had transcribed or commissioned it, then published it in the "Segovia Guitar Archive" edition. To this day, pieces from the "Segovia repertoire" are an audition requirement at music conservatories. Seeing him in person was more than a concert, it was a pilgrimage.

I had just gotten my driver's license, and I drove into New York City with my friend Stephen. Stephen wasn't a musician, but we shared an ability to listen and the longing to escape our privileged suburban upbringing. That summer, when the Knack became popular and Donna Summer's "Bad Girls" was on the charts, we had stayed up late in his attic room listening to *Don Giovanni*. Sometimes we analyzed the music; sometimes we plotted strategies for compiling our own lists of conquests. Mostly we dreamed different lives for ourselves, indulging our adolescent resentment by blasting Mozart instead of "My Sharona." In a perfect world we would travel, swagger, change nerdy into suave. The music made anything seem possible. We drove into the city in my parents' 1974 orange Datsun station wagon, giddy with our freedom.

Segovia's annual New York concert was a pilgrimage for many people. Carnegie Hall was sold out, and as we arrived, elegant music lovers in formal evening dress stood glittering in the entry. Next to them hundreds of reverent, rumpled men and women milled around, guitarists like me, who clasped their delicate fingers protectively, as if afraid to lose them. We owed our dreams—some owed their careers—to Segovia. Several had even brought their guitars with them, as if presenting them to be blessed. As Stephen and I climbed the stairs to our seats, I felt like part of a holy order. We took our places jittery with anticipation. And when Segovia stepped onto the stage, we joined two thousand people leaping up to greet him, shouting, Bravo Maestro!

As a young man conquering the world's concert stages, Segovia had demanded respect for the guitar, which was always more popular than it was understood. In crowded halls previously reserved for violinists and pianists, he had leveled a withering stare at anyone who dared shift in a squeaky seat or clear a winter-dry throat. In 1934 the Argentine musician Domingo Prat wrote that Segovia "exacts a religious silence" from his listeners. But at the performance that night this silence was automatic, and Segovia's famous glare was unnecessary. The paunchy man on stage with thick glasses and an uncertain step barely looked up, and the audience fell utterly still.

He performed a program of music that I played, Robert de Visée, Mario Castelnuovo-Tedesco, Isaac Albéniz. He lost his place several times, covering his lapses with sudden repeats and sheer authority. I could hear the mistakes. They startled me, and yet somehow they didn't seem to matter. Segovia commanded attention, if not with the music, then with the weight of his achievement. His presence was everything. His thick, sausage fingers still stamped *Segovia* on every phrase. He sat alone on the enormous stage, playing student pieces, and the audience held its breath for every note. I might play these pieces differently, I thought, but is it possible to play them as well?

At intermission I heard a man saying it was sad.

"He should stop performing," the man asserted. "Let younger guitarists have the spotlight."

There was jealousy in his voice, along with sadness and respect. He was in his forties, stocky and balding, and had the sculpted fingernails of a guitarist. But he and his companion were collecting their coats to leave. Stephen and I begged for their ticket stubs, and after intermission we claimed their seats in the orchestra section. I was thrilled to be in Segovia's presence while I still had the chance.

From our new vantage I could hear the movement of Segovia's fingers, the sharp articulation of each tone. He drew us in, filling every phrase with some secret knowledge that we desperately wanted to possess. Standing and applauding at the end, we raced ahead to grab seats even closer. And after the first encore, like teenagers at every concert, we rushed the stage.

An old couple in evening dress smiled wryly at us as we huddled in the aisle by the first row in our blue jeans and down jackets. We fidgeted with excitement. Segovia didn't even notice us. He played two more encores, ending with a jaunty étude by Fernando Sor that I had learned when I first started classical guitar. From the foot of the stage, I could feel the entire room straining forward as every person leaned in to catch the least vibration of Segovia's strings. Then the audience lurched upward in adulation as the old man stood and an assistant led him from the stage.

I turned to look at the crowd, taking in the euphoria from the balconies, absorbing the heat rising from all this applause and the love it expressed. Segovia had created this hall of cheering guitarists, and I had sat at his feet, filled with awe. But I had also watched him falter. I was just three steps from center stage, maybe light-headed from all the cheering. At seventeen, how could I not dream this ovation was—or would someday be—for me?

⌒

The Guitar Workshop held its annual student recital that May. After almost ten years as a student, I had started teaching, offering classes in technique in exchange for my lessons in jazz and classical. After Kent Sidon's death in 1976 the school had relocated once more, this time to several buildings attached to a church. Now it was 1980 and only a few people there still remembered the house on Forest Street. John, the new director, shifted the emphasis back to classical guitar, though he had kept Kent's open, inclusive spirit alive. The halls were full of people following a trail of candles to the auditorium, where I stood with the faculty, the Guitar Workshop's homegrown wunderkind, greeting students and their friends and families as they entered.

This was my last performance at the Guitar Workshop. I was about to graduate from high school. In the fall I'd move to Boston to attend the New England Conservatory of Music.

"As long as you understand the risks," my mother had said when the letter from Boston arrived. My parents remained worried about my future. But they'd accepted my determination to become a musician.

During intermission I warmed up in an empty classroom. My old three-quarter-size guitar had long since been given away to a younger student. Now I was playing a full-size instrument, a Japanese factory-made guitar, an exact replica of Segovia's famous Ramirez. I pictured Segovia's hands as I played the tricky passages of my piece. An instrument just like this; hands not very different from my own. I listened carefully to each note, trying to find my signature in the sounds, the personal presence that could fill a hall.

"You know," said John, the music director, late in the evening as I waited backstage, "I just read that Harpo Marx loved to play Bach on the harp." People in the audience laughed. John had been supplying jokes and stories between each performance. "But since he couldn't read music, he learned the pieces by listening to Segovia's recordings. If only he'd been here tonight to hear our very own Segovia."

I walked on stage quietly and took my seat before the fifty or sixty people who remained. I checked my tuning, then drew a deep breath and began. I was playing the prelude to Bach's first cello suite. The guitar's lowest string was tuned down a step to reach the resonant bass notes. The instrument hummed against my body.

The prelude opens simply. An arpeggio strides majestically through the pillars of the key—tonic, subdominant, dominant, tonic. Gradually the harmony grows more complex. I could feel the audience tightening in their seats as lines intertwined and pulled taut. They drew forward with the phrases, and I felt as if the tension, their attention, were growing hot. It made my hands feel liquid, and the pleasure of this sensation spread through me. I was playing the music, not just the instrument, and as the tone darkened, moving into the key's recesses, the mood in the room darkened too. And then the harmony turned, emerging suddenly just a step from where it started. The moment came as a shock to me, though I'd practiced it for months. The shock rippled in the room, and I felt like a member of the audience as the long, chromatic climax built toward its peak, and a flicker of shivers licked at the back of my neck.

"Bravo!" someone shouted. The rest of the audience picked it up, and in a moment everyone was on their feet.

I was stunned, hardly aware that John had come back on stage and was giving me a playful shake of the shoulder.

"You want to do an encore?" he shouted in my ear. Before I responded, he'd asked the audience, and almost instantly there was silence as people took their seats again and sat listening. I played the deceptively simple, energetic étude by Fernando Sor that I'd heard Segovia perform. I took a very slow tempo, not jaunty at all, but reflective, almost mournful. I'd never heard this piece played so slowly. It felt as if I were recomposing it on the spot.

A sigh preceded the applause. Then once again the audience was standing.

"Great job!" said John as he hugged me backstage. "The best way to finish your career here."

I was elated by the response and pleased with how I'd played. It was a start, a first step toward bigger stages, larger audiences, proof to myself that I could follow Segovia to Carnegie Hall.

When John resumed his role as emcee, he thanked me for my years at the Guitar Workshop. "If you want to hear more," he said before introducing the next performer, "be sure to watch *The Merv Griffin Show* next week."

Many in the audience laughed. People kidded me about it afterward, as the concert was breaking up. But it was true. Just a few days later I would be performing on national television.

In my junior year of high school I had auditioned with guitarists from all over New York state and been selected for the Tri-State High School Jazz Ensemble, sponsored by the McDonald's Corporation. Now, in my senior year, I was the only guitarist in the all-star band, culled from New York, New Jersey, and Connecticut. We'd performed at the Newport Jazz Festival and at Gracie Mansion for Ed Koch, the mayor of New York City. But *The Merv Griffin Show* was our biggest gig.

The show had been taped in April at the Vivian Beaumont Theater in Lincoln Center. Along with Marvin Hamlisch and Merv's other guests, we were brought backstage to have our foreheads powdered, then sent out to warm up the audience. Twenty-one high school students—trumpets, trombones, sax, and rhythm sections—all wearing red polyester blazers, sitting in the glare of lights and cameras, almost famous. They told us fifteen million people might watch the show when it was broadcast in May. We all thought we were launching careers.

I watched the show at home in Roslyn, sitting in the den with my parents and a group of friends from school. Stephen was there with his new girlfriend, Kate, as were some members of my high school band. It was four-thirty in the afternoon on a brilliant spring day. We were noisy and restless, eager for the show to start. We heckled the commercials for a Catskills resort and President Carter's attack on Ted Kennedy in the presidential primary. Everyone hushed when the title appeared and the announcer intoned the opening.

"From Hollywood—from Las Vegas—this week, from New York City—it's *The Merv Griffin Show!*"

Though the performance was past, I felt stage fright as my friends sat up to listen. We played Merv's theme song, and the camera panned across the band. Then Merv bounded onto the stage, a tubby, gleeful man wearing a gray blazer with a red handkerchief in the pocket. He kibitzed with the audience. My face jutted up just over his shoulder. Finally he cooed in awe of us.

"Do you believe what's behind me?" he asked. "This is the most extraordinary group of musicians."

He mentioned the show's other guests, then said, "I can't stand it any longer. I have just got to sing with this group." He'd fished out "How Little We Know," a tune from his early days, first made popular by the Tommy Dorsey band. Jack Sheldon stood by to play the trumpet solo.

The cameramen swerved around us, and the overhead lights blinked in a rainbow of colors. I caught the bass player's eye as Merv took a confiding tone with the audience. Our smiles made it onto the screen. The lights gleamed on my freshly polished guitar, a hollow-body Gibson jazz guitar that I'd bought earlier that year, the same model Wes Montgomery had played.

The band applauded Merv when he finished singing. He'd done a credible job. But we'd played with better musicians. We were saving our excitement for our other big number. Later in the program we were playing a tune with Dizzy Gillespie, the bebop legend, billowing cheeks, bent-up horn, and all.

Dizzy had given us "Manteca," a wildly funky chart from the 1960s, written in collaboration with the Cuban percussionist Chano Pozo. It brought out all the band's exuberance and skill. We'd rehearsed the tune at a recording studio in New York the week before. Dizzy came in wearing black jeans and a black turtleneck, with a heavy, peaked woolen cap that he kept on all afternoon. He greeted each of us personally.

"You're the guitar player?" he asked as he slapped me on the shoulder. I nodded nervously. "Yeah!" he growled, making me leap.

At rehearsal Dizzy had shown us how he planned to count off the tune. But when he stood in front of us on the show, with the cameras' red lights blinking, he launched into something unintelligible. He made a grotesque face, crossed his eyes, and inflated his cheeks. The whole band cracked up, and then Dizzy started counting. The piece was great for the rhythm section. Although I didn't have a solo, the guitar was part of an extended vamp. I laid down a syncopated groove with Chris, our bass player, while Dizzy jumped and swayed and hit all the high notes.

When we finished the piece, my friends sitting in the den joined the audience at the studio in an enthusiastic roar. My parents smiled proudly. I remembered seeing them in their seats at the taping, shaking their heads. I think they were amazed that I'd gotten this far just by playing the guitar. They didn't understand how I'd done it. But I knew. It felt natural to me: I was one of a special kind, not like them. Art and music had already taught me things they would never know, taken me places they couldn't imagine. It had given me this taste of success, even celebrity. I was ready to graduate, ready to begin my career. And while I could hardly imagine what would come next, I thought I was on my way, gliding from triumph to triumph. It seemed so clear: I understood music; I was going to be a musician. Maybe I'd be a jazz guitarist, maybe a classical guitarist. But in any case I'd be a musician, an artist.

When the performance was over, Dizzy thanked each of us again, shaking our hands and wishing us luck. Then he left quietly. We clustered around Merv for autographs. One of the trumpet players suggested he hire us to replace his usual band. Merv laughed and twinkled his eyes, then pointed to me and said, "I saw you up there. I'll remember."

Adagio and Fugue

aN HOUR HAS PASSED since I sat down. My hands are loose and vibrant, and the guitar feels solid and secure against my body. There is a rhythm to practicing, a tempo that accelerates or slows as my work and the morning progress. Now I feel the movement speeding up. I turn the page of Bach's violin music, eager to cover new ground.

The second movement of Bach's Violin Sonata no. 1 is a fugue. After the languid, flowing lines of the *Adagio,* the fugue is a brisk, angular composition, built up from a single phrase, the theme. Three different lines—high, middle, and low—begin from this theme, then develop simultaneously in different directions. The counterpoint is intricate and demanding, three voices speaking at once, each with its own identity, each saying something important.

Before beginning, I look at the printed notes, preparing them in my mind. On the page the theme has a place and a function; it is the basis for all that follows. In my head, other dimensions emerge. The notes have a particular character, a unique emotional aura. The sound is palpable. I can almost touch it. But the music in my head is not real, just something to strive for. Notes take on life only when I strike the strings. In the air, the sounds have qualities the page cannot describe and that the mind cannot share without an instrument.

The theme has just nine notes. Four D's, two C's, a B-flat, and an A in the first measure, then another B-flat on the downbeat of the second measure. Nine notes, just four different tones. The first four notes are all the same tone, but they are not the same. The first three are like the windup to the fourth, which bursts open to reveal the rest of the piece. They gather momentum; they accumulate urgency.

Like this.

No.

Like this?

No.

I sense what I want. Notes are physical sensations. I can feel how they ought to sound. But I can't play them yet. Like this? Or this? I work with the whole theme again and again, turning it over in my hands. There are endless possibilities, but only one sounds right. Just nine notes. Just four tones. But not these four; not these.

There are two things that people frequently say about practicing that have always puzzled me. The first I must have heard a thousand times as a child from well-meaning friends of my parents. When a kid plays an instrument, adults gush with enthusiasm in an utterly predictable way. No matter how you sound, they say, "How wonderful! How beautiful!" Then they recall their old piano teacher with a laugh, or lament their unfulfilled desire for lessons. For some reason the conversation invariably ends with the cheerful reminder that "practice makes perfect." As a child, I never knew how to respond to this. What can you say, except "thanks" or "I hope so"? As I got a bit older and began to work harder at playing what I heard, the phrase changed in my ears. Now it stung like a criticism: so much practicing—and *still* not perfect? Finally, like all kids who actually practice, I learned to ignore it. "Practice makes perfect" was just something adults said, as if they were perfect already and knew from experience. The next time you hear someone invoke this misleading adage, watch for the knowing nod, followed by an awkward pause. It never fails to end the conversation.

The second phrase that I hear all the time now, as an adult, makes even less sense. When I tell people I practice the guitar, even accomplished professionals—people who spend half of their lives at an office—will ask, "How do you get yourself to sit down every day? It takes such discipline!" This truly puzzles me. As if their work were not also practicing.

For me, sitting down to play has very little to do with discipline. "It isn't just education and discipline that makes one so devoted to work," Rilke wrote in a 1907 letter to his wife, the painter Clara Westhoff, "it is simple joy. It is one's natural sense of well-being, to which nothing else can compare." Love of music brings me to the practice room. Nothing can compare with the joy of playing a Bach fugue. Yet each time I sit down, I grasp only a fragment of what I hear and feel in the notes. Bach's music is better than it can be played, and this taunts and teases and often tortures me. Grasping, shaping these sounds, I breathe faster, I juice up. When the lines intertwine, I feel an exquisite delicacy of expectation: maybe this time I'll get it! Maybe now! Doesn't everyone feel this in relation to something? It doesn't matter if it's your golf swing, playing with your children, baking a cake, or closing a deal. All of this too is practicing. You reach beyond yourself for some imagined beauty. Discipline is just the outward shape of this hopeful desire.

Still, it matters a great deal for your practicing what you do with your desire. Do you crave to be perfect? Do you long to feel like you're in love?

As I struggle to find the right phrasing for the fugue's theme, I can't help comparing what I play with Segovia's famous 1928 recording of this piece. He was thirty-five years old then, younger than I am now, and already the most famous guitarist in the world.

At the time, playing Bach on the guitar was still considered a daring gesture. Music critics responded as if they'd never heard anything so audacious or appalling. Evaluating Segovia's performance, a reviewer for the prestigious British journal *The Gramophone* inclined his nose and opined, "The result, interesting as it is, is hardly Bach." The reviewer was wrong, of course. Segovia's Bach became legendary, an essential part of his revolutionary mystique. For years as a young musician I dreamed of succeeding Segovia, claiming his mystique for myself. He seemed to possess what I wanted, and I struggled and cursed attempting to get it. Now I can't play this fugue without feeling the Maestro standing over me, sadly shaking his head. He dismisses me because I don't play the fugue as well as he did. I'm disappointed in myself because I'm still imitating him.

Listening to the theme in my head, I play it again, accenting it oddly, just to hear how it sounds. I'm experimenting, trying to free the notes from the page, and free myself from my former ideal. The music never became mine because I played it to be Segovia.

In fact, Segovia was not the first to play Bach on the guitar. By the time he recorded this fugue, it had been in the guitar's repertoire for at least twenty years in a transcription by Francisco Tárrega. Fifteen years before Segovia was born, Tárrega had graduated from the Madrid Conservatory with honors in piano and composition and was earning his living as a concert guitarist. In 1880 he gave recitals in Paris and London, and during the following years he toured extensively in Spain and Italy. At these concerts he performed Bach, Granados, Albéniz, and other composers whose work Segovia would later seem to conjure up from nowhere. But Tárrega was a quiet, humble man. Although he performed throughout Europe, he was uncomfortable as a performer. And like most musicians of his era, he considered the guitar a salon not a concert instrument, preferring to appear before a small circle of friends. Yet Tárrega, and not Segovia, is truly the father of the modern classical guitar. Quietly, patiently, he established the technical fundamentals that are still taught today. He determined how to hold the instrument, how to train the fingers of both hands. He established the core of the guitar's modern repertoire, and most important, he shared his discoveries with a group of devoted pupils. The success of his students was proof of his greatness.

Tárrega's most accomplished pupil was Miguel Llobet, who had already toured the world when Segovia held his Madrid debut in 1917. A year earlier, on January 17, 1916, Llobet had performed at the Princess Theater in New York City, where he was billed as "the world's greatest guitarist." In 1910 he had worked with engineers at the Bell Lab in Brunswick, New Jersey, and so became the first guitarist to make recordings. But Llobet was dissatisfied with the sound quality of these recordings and refused to release them. His too-demanding ear prevented him from achieving greater fame. These performances are now lost.

Segovia was dismissive of both Tárrega and Llobet. He called Tárrega "more saint than musician," and although he studied with Llobet briefly in 1915, Segovia acknowledged this debt only grudgingly. In his autobiography Segovia pronounced Llobet "a serious, noble interpreter of Bach" but added that "he always faltered in the same passages, even in relatively easy ones—probably because of lack of discipline or more likely due to laziness. . . . Second, his tone was rasping and metallic."

Once he became famous, Segovia rarely had anything nice to say about other guitarists. What distinguished him was the scope of his ambition. Tárrega and his followers were satisfied with the guitar as a drawing-room instrument, while Segovia dreamed of the concert hall. For the first twenty years of his career Segovia depended on Tárrega's transcriptions to fill out his programs. Yet the force of Segovia's personality made Tárrega and his students into minor figures. It was Tárrega who revolutionized the instrument. But Segovia fantastically enlarged the guitar's public image. Recording, touring, and promoting himself continuously, he became the only guitarist worth remembering, the one all other guitarists had to emulate and strive to surpass.

I relax my hands for a few moments, letting them hang by my sides. I look out the window at the quiet street. A few students from the school opposite my apartment are sitting on the curb, smoking cigarettes. Half watching them, I listen to the first two measures of the fugue in my head. Then I close my eyes and listen more carefully. I watch my fingers in my mind as they make the sounds I want to hear. Without allowing the vision to dissipate, I play the first two measures for real.

It's fair, not bad. It's not perfect—it's still infinitely far from perfect.

Perhaps this is what I have to learn from Segovia now. He was more ambitious than Tárrega. What does this mean, other than that he was not satisfied with Tárrega's ideal but strove to achieve his own? For him, to play "perfectly" meant to perform in concert halls formerly reserved for pianists. This was the goal that drove him to work so hard.

To be Segovia is not what I want now, even if I dreamed of it as a child. Imitating Segovia, I never learned what I could achieve. Now, freeing myself from his ideal, I'm forced to conceive a new one for myself. What would it mean for me to play perfectly now? This is the goal of my discipline. I keep experimenting with the theme, building on what I've played. Like this? Like this?

When you play an instrument, and playing comes easily, playing is enough. But slowly, as you play more, what you hear outpaces your ability. This music beyond you, as you are, leads you on, and you ache to lay hold of it. You sit down, you look at your hands, you hold the instrument. You listen to the musicians you admire, who have this same equipment, hands and instruments. Then you look at your own hands again, and it doesn't seem possible. How do they do it? What you want to play shimmers ungraspable in the air, or in the hands of others. I think this is when your story as a musician begins. Playing, you've begun to practice. And practice has made "perfect." Now you'll never play the way you wish you could. Now one lifetime is not enough. You'll never be finished practicing.

perfecting my mistakes

f LUTE PLAYERS have beautiful contoured lips, always poised to kiss. Violinists develop a dark, ugly mole under their chins from squeezing the instrument to keep it steady. Brass players all seem to have big noses—the deeper the instrument, the bigger the nose. Perhaps the pressure of the mouthpiece against their faces causes other features to protrude. Guitarists, of course, obsessively tend their fingernails. But they also carry their hands more gingerly than other instrumentalists, knitting their fingers together at chest height like nervous servants or hungry squirrels.

I sat on a worn padded bench outside one of the New England Conservatory's practice rooms, waiting for my first lesson. Sneaking a glance through the window of the practice room door, I spied a student I didn't recognize. He was playing intently as Aaron, our teacher, paced slowly across the room, his head angled to one side and his eyes pointed abstractedly toward the ceiling. He gestured with his hands, half conducting, half fanning himself. It was the first week of September. Boston was still sweltering and humid. I straightened in my seat on the bench and waited. It was five past. Ten past. Wind players tended to scurry rather than walk. Voice majors, with their expansive diaphragms, seemed to take up more space than other people. I looked at my watch again. What were they working on? Who was this student?

My parents and I had driven up from Long Island a week before, the old Datsun station wagon weighted down with my things. We exited the Mass Pike in downtown Boston, followed Massachusetts Avenue for a few blocks, then turned onto Huntington Avenue, at the corner dominated by Symphony Hall. Eight-foot-tall posters advertised upcoming concerts by Seiji Ozawa and the Boston Symphony Orchestra. A few weeks later I would join a late-night salvage operation, rescuing several of these posters from a Dumpster to decorate the dorm. As we passed by in the car that day, the concert hall seemed grand and untouchable.

Our destination was just a block away. We made a left onto Gainsborough Street and were greeted by pandemonium. The New England Conservatory is the oldest independent music school in America, founded in 1867, thirty-eight years before Juilliard. Jordan Hall, the school's ornate and regal centerpiece, was built in 1902, and it remains at the heart of Boston's musical life. But the stately and dignified facade was merely a backdrop to the morning's frenetic activity. The narrow street between Jordan Hall and the Conservatory dormitory was clogged with station wagons. Dozens of new students were shuttling instruments and luggage into the dorm, watched over by an impromptu brass band clustered on the balcony of the music building. While we unloaded the car, the band above improvised unconventional arrangements of Sousa marches.

Inside the dorm a neatly handwritten sign was posted on the elevator door: THE ELEVATOR, SHE NO WORK. My parents and I stood in the lobby with twenty other teenage musicians and their parents patiently watching the elevator doors open and close. Then Melissa, the dorm director, came over and angrily tore the sign from the door.

"You can use it," she said. "Someone's been posting 'out of order' notices on everything today."

The elevator worked fine, as did the lights, telephones, and toilets throughout the building, despite warnings to the contrary. This was just the first indication that at music school you couldn't always trust your eyes. But you quickly learned to trust your ears.

On my floor alone we had trumpet, trombone, saxophone, French horn, percussion, violin, viola, cello, bass. There was a harpsichordist and a composer; my roommate, a soft-spoken, fastidious boy from Louisiana, played clarinet. I was one of four guitarists, including Marcus, the RA, who was working on his master's degree. Even as we unpacked my things, music began to spill out of the tiny rooms into the hall.

I wanted to join in, jump into my new life. But my parents lingered, fussing with the squeaky closet door, arranging a spider plant on my windowsill. This was their third and final trip delivering a child to college. They were returning to an empty nest for the first time in twenty-four years. We signed up for an afternoon tour of the music building, even though we'd explored it that morning. We strolled down the street to look at Symphony Hall. Finally they made one last inspection of my room, and I escorted them to the elevator.

"Wicked!" shouted Kevin, the trombone player who lived next door, as we walked past. He was listening to Dave play the alto saxophone.

"This kid's a monster!" he gasped, and people on the hall gravitated toward his room.

My parents smiled at the expression. A few years later Dave would be one of the top studio musicians in New York, playing with B. B. King, Tower of Power, Paul Simon, and Sting. But then he was just the kid who lived across the hall. My parents and I said good-bye in the lobby. I raced back upstairs to join the party in Kevin's room.

Eight or ten boys were strewn on the beds and the floor trading stories. There was a cellist from California, a plump boy with a pageboy haircut, named Robin. He was a wizard on his instrument and also a devoted fan of the Grateful Dead. He had given Jerry Garcia a recording of Dead songs arranged for cello ensemble. Hank, a jazz trumpet player who lived at the end of the hall, was a delicate boy with a thick Brooklyn accent. He and Dave were playing jazz standards in the corner as the rest of us combed through Kevin's tape collection, getting to know each other by comparing tastes.

"Hank Markopolous?" Dave asked, making sure he'd gotten the trumpet player's name right.

"He's a regular Chops Bebopolous," chimed Jim, a percussionist who was busy unpacking his marimba.

This went on until around three in the morning, when Marcus, the RA, came by to quiet us down. He was tall and very thin, with a gentle, haunted manner. He coughed politely at the sweet-smelling smoke that hung in the air, then suggested it was time to go to sleep. I went back to my room with the world spinning, thinking I'd finally found my proper home.

But the first night's revelry was deceptive. The truth of the Conservatory was practicing. At dawn the next day violinists stole past the six-ton statue of Beethoven that dominated the lobby of the music building. They dispersed into the practice rooms that ringed the main concert hall and began the day playing scales like calls to prayer. Pianists showed up next, scrambling for the rooms with the Bösendorfer grands. Living in the dormitory across the street, I didn't need an alarm clock. By seven, there was enough Chopin and Rachmaninoff in the air to waltz the dead from their rest. Around ten, the voice majors were audibly clearing their throats, plunking a note or two on the lesser pianos and do-mi-sol-do-ing the major keys. By eleven, the brass had moved in and were blasting their more sensitive neighbors out of the building and down to lunch.

This racket kept up until sometime after dinner, when the jazz players stumbled in. They practiced all night.

As I sat in the music building a week later waiting for my first lesson, I already understood that no matter how much we partied in the dorm, the colossal spirit of Beethoven ruled the music building. In every room deeply committed musicians were aspiring to concert careers. The whole structure vibrated with intensely focused ambition and the insidious undertone of competition that came with it. Every hour of the day we were immersed in one another's practicing, each contributing our part to the din. The sound was inescapable, a great, chaotic counterpoint. Everyone wanted to be the best, to be the one who would make it.

The practice room door swung open with a crash, smacked into motion by a fiberglass guitar case. Damien, the older student, backed out of the room, still talking with Aaron. The conversation was familiar and collegial. They must have been working together already for several years. I listened for anything that might help me place the other student in the Conservatory hierarchy. Already I was jealous of their relationship, impatient for my turn.

Aaron held the door open for me and motioned toward a ratty couch in the corner. He was an athletic, balding man in his thirties, one of the finest players in the guitar's third generation, after Segovia and his immediate followers. He had achieved what his students were dreaming of, that mysterious apotheosis: a solo career. I noticed his hands, much larger than mine, and the threads fraying around the collar of his blue Oxford shirt. One hour a week for the next four years, he would be my mentor and taskmaster, my teacher. At the Conservatory the first question new students asked each other was not "Where are you from?" but "Who are you studying with?" I would have classes in music history, music theory, ear training, composition, and conducting. But the essence of my education, the real work of becoming a musician, would be done in private lessons with this man.

Aaron asked about my background and training and the guitarists I admired. As I answered, he watched me blankly, responding with an inscrutable wrinkling of his forehead. The room was close and still, just large enough for a baby grand piano, a few chairs, and the grimy couch. High windows looked out onto an alley, and sunlight cut between the buildings in a sharp angle onto the floor. I told him about the Guitar Workshop, *The Merv Griffin Show*, and my experience hearing Segovia. I was sweating, stammering a little, and smiling too much. Finally Aaron pursed his face conclusively.

"Okay," he said, getting up from his chair and wandering toward the window. "Let's hear something."

I played the fast movement from a Bach lute suite, a technical tour de force.

"Very nice," he said when I'd finished. "But too hard. Play something else."

I launched into a sonata from 1928 by the Mexican composer Manuel Ponce, a dark, jazzy piece that showed off my versatility.

Aaron waved his hand at the end of the first section. He put his fingertips to his mouth and pressed them there until his head began to droop.

"Let's hear something easy. What about an étude?"

I tried one of Matteo Carcassi's student pieces, a light, romantic study from my early years at the Guitar Workshop.

"Good, good," Aaron nodded, thinking. He stood at the window looking out, then took a folding chair and sat facing me, his legs crossed, an elbow on his knee, and his chin in his palm. He focused intensely on my hands, just a few inches from his face.

"Play a scale."

Very carefully and slowly, on my best behavior, I played a C-major scale. I looked up, anxious for his response.

"All right," Aaron said, smiling warmly, as if he'd only now recognized me as an old friend. "Let's stick with scales for a little while."

That was my first lesson.

In fifteen minutes I'd sunk from concert guitarist to beginner.

⌒

At the Guitar Workshop, when I was a child, I'd taken technique classes to build strength. Eric, a painfully thin man with shaking hands, presided over a room of eager guitarists as we pounded away at scales and exercises. We put a dustcloth under the strings just behind the sound hole to mute the instrument. Instead of ringing, the strings gave a percussive thud. It sounded like the march of commuters up subway steps. The cloth mute made the strings less pliable. Increasing resistance, we were taught, strengthened our fingers.

Strong fingers were good, and mine were among the strongest. As older students plodded along, I ripped up and down the neck of my guitar. My teachers sometimes played a cruel prank on unpleasant, arrogant pupils, placing me strategically in the classroom, a little kid-bomb, poised to go off.

Now, at the Conservatory, Aaron showed me how my strength worked against itself.

"You're bullying the strings," he said at a lesson a few weeks later. "Use the least possible force, the least effort."

Alone in a practice room I returned to basic technique to see more clearly how I had always played. What I saw horrified me. With each fingerstroke I tensed my forearm or shoulders or neck or palm or wrist. Training for strength, it seemed, was a terrible way to teach technique. It had taught me to work too hard. The tension in my arms was just a substitute for the cloth mute, an unconscious attempt to reproduce the resistance my fingers had been taught to expect. Worse still, the mute had prevented the strings from vibrating, teaching me to play the strings without playing notes. I'd learned to focus on the finger, not on the sound. The strings of a guitar are delicate. If you blow across them, they will vibrate.

Sitting in a tiny practice room as the morning roar rose around me, I gathered all my attention and played a C-major scale. Not one right note! I had hit them all, but I hit them badly, imprecisely. The sound wobbled instead of ringing, a clang instead of a bell tone. On some notes my right-hand finger rebounded wildly, and my fingernail snared the vibrating string. On others my left hand landed too close to or too far from the fret, and the note hissed and sputtered. I tried again with the same result. I had been playing Bach; now I couldn't even play a scale. I took a deep breath, looked out the window, then tried once more. The same thing again.

I gave up on the scale and played only open strings, without using my left hand. I played every note slowly, so that each sound was distinct. In the context of a piece, these notes might be lost in a blur. But independently, under scrutiny, they had a complexity that normal hearing skated over. Listening closely, I heard that the tones were like pebbles, like minerals. They might be hard or soft, rough or polished, their consistency conglomerate or pure. I listened carefully and heard that not one note was clear. They were like loose stones clotted together with mud. I closed my eyes and tried again. But the more clearly I listened, the muddier my playing sounded.

I packed up my instrument and stepped into the busy hallway. A hundred young musicians were shouldering by one another, expertly maneuvering their instrument cases through the crowd. Flute players, violinists, brass, and winds, all darting into tiny rooms to practice. I felt ashamed, disoriented, as if I'd been hard of hearing all along but had only just noticed. Scales had been an exercise for me, an opportunity to show off. Now they were an indictment. At the Guitar Workshop I had leaped ahead of the other students, playing folk music, blues, jazz, and classical. My playing reflected this

hodgepodge of styles; it was laced with flaws. I didn't know anything about how my fingers worked. I'd have to start again from the
beginning, discarding all I had so eagerly practiced when I was a
young prodigy and everyone made a fuss over how good I was.
Meanwhile, all around me, everyone else was moving forward.

I jolted down the main stairs to the lobby, past the scowling
Beethoven, that Ahab of music, rapping my knuckles against the
composer's metal boots as I went by. The statue had been standing
guard over Jordan Hall since it opened, a gift of the Boston Handel
and Haydn Society. Now it served as a message board. Students
taped notes to each other on the bronze hem of Beethoven's cloak,
the trivial things of daily life—"We're in room 201"; "Let's meet
for lunch." It was a playful, domesticating gesture, a sign of defi-
ance. To be the best at the Conservatory meant a competition of
each against all, and of everyone against this oppressive statue of
Beethoven.

⌒

At music school you hear the seasons change. Boston's Indian summer ended with the long, low rumble of thunderstorms that made
the windows of the music building rattle. Fall arrived with leaves
scraping, then squishing against the sidewalk downstairs. The
weather was a sound outside the practice room.

So much attention to sound changes the proportions of your
senses, not just in the practice room but everywhere. You develop
an extraordinary sensitivity to noises in the environment, the rhythmic crumpling of a dinner napkin at the table behind you, the specific squeak of each dormitory door. Living between the ears, music
students are apt to be absentminded, dangerously absorbed in a
mental music that no one else hears. Walking across the street from
the music building, I'd barely notice the cars accelerating toward a
yellow light. But I'd jump in terror when someone's high heels

clacked into consciousness, so much louder than the orchestra that filled my head.

One dark, miserable Saturday night in late October, ten of us were scattered on the floor of the dormitory lounge listening to the rain. It echoed in the street between the music building and the dorm, and we could hear three or four distinct layers to the sound: the swish of it falling, the *thwap* of its impact, a splatter on the street, and then a hissing echo that washed all of these together.

Someone passed behind us whistling on her way upstairs to the girls' floor. Patrick, a violist, was lying closest to the stairwell. He cupped his hands and sent a counterpoint melody up the stairs after her. The tone was rich and resonant.

"It's like a cathedral," said Doug, a cellist, whose father was a church organist.

A few moments later we had reassembled in the stairwell with our copies of Bach's four-part chorales. Bach composed this music as part of his Sunday cantatas to texts by Martin Luther. At the time, Bach was criticized by his employers for his "strange and difficult harmonies." In the nineteenth century, however, the formal rules for four-part vocal music were derived from these pieces, and our textbooks were based on them. None of us was a trained singer, but the stairwell's wild acoustics flattered us. Susanna, Kevin's girl-friend that week, held us together with a theatrical soprano. While the wind howled outside, we began howling inside, filling the whole building with Bach's eerie majesty.

We must have inspired the other residents of the dorm. Early the next morning a trombone choir roused the school from sleep, per-forming a medley of television theme songs at top volume. I craned my head out the window to see fifteen slide trombones protruding from upper floors of the dorm, facing another fifteen across the street in the windows of the music building. *Hogan's Heroes, The Flintstones,* and *I Dream of Jeannie* careened off the walls in stereo.

Student life was rife with this playful jostling, the bizarre, often breathtaking expressions of concentrated talent. One afternoon after music history class I heard Alice, a piano student, sight-read an orchestral score, then improvise ragtime variations on the theme. To settle a bet, my ear-training teacher, who had studied in Paris with Nadia Boulanger, sang a Charlie Parker solo in solfège, using the appropriate do-re-mi syllables for each note. For a joke, Robin entertained my dormitory hall one night, playing guitar music on the cello, perfectly reproducing pieces he'd heard us practicing through the wall.

Yet even these playful performances, this reveling in ability, had an edge of competition, an assertion of status. At the Conservatory we were all gifted. But we woke up every morning to violinists blazing through the Mendelssohn violin concerto, and each note was a pointed question, a challenge. Can you do this? Are you this good? These questions, these comparisons, rippled the air in every corner of the school.

On a brisk November morning I hurried across the street to the music building. With uncommon luck, I found one of the spacious second-floor rooms available. Practice rooms lined the music building's two upper floors. But the four rooms on the second floor facing the dorm were the best, with picture windows and French doors leading onto a balcony. It was rare to find one empty. These rooms also had the best pianos, and pianists lined up in the hall to wait for them. Usually I had to settle for one of the closet-size cubicles on the third floor in the back of the building. These had only space for an upright piano and two chairs, and there was no window except on the door. The walls were made of some unidentifiable material, designed to dampen sound. But the fluorescent lights provided a continuous, exasperating hum, hovering between A and B-flat.

Luxuriating in the second-floor room, I paced the distance between the door and the windows. The new carpet gave a spongy exhale with each step. I warmed my hands over the radiator. Out-

side, the sky was a flat, ominous gray. I tried to focus on the blank-
ness, to clear my head of the commotion around and inside me.
Then I arranged my chair, footstool, and music stand in the center
of the room and tuned my instrument.

Is there a hierarchy of gifts, I wondered, a natural, immutable
order that decrees I am this gifted but no more, that I will be this
good but no better? I've worked my way into this practice room,
but is my gift sufficient to get me out again, to carry me beyond the
practice room and onto the stage? I settled my arms around the guitar and brought my hands to the strings. The sounds of a pianist
seeped through the walls. The cascade of notes fell like glass shards
on the floor. Am I as good a musician, or am I a fraud? I let my arms
hang by my sides and took a deep breath. I began playing scales.
The pianist next door was practicing Brahms.

Some students at the Conservatory possessed perfect pitch, an
ability that cannot be achieved with practice. Mikiko, an oboe
player, could identify every note you'd played if you turned around
and sat on a piano keyboard. But perfect pitch didn't make her the
best musician. She rushed through phrases and never made it into
the Conservatory orchestra. If the most gifted were not the best
musicians, perhaps the best musicians were not necessarily the most
gifted. There were many different kinds of musical ability. Leonard
Bernstein didn't have perfect pitch; nor does Paul McCartney.
What enabled them to become so great?

I played slowly, paying close attention to the muscles in my fingers. Each movement should be independent, one finger then
another, without overlap or interference. The motion should begin
at the elbow, not in the finger or the knuckle. Swift and direct, with
just enough force to produce a tone.

The pianist next door crowded into my room. Fast passages in
octaves. A powerful crescendo. I wanted to play like that. Brahms
pulsed in my stomach, rose into my chest and arms. I wanted to play

great music. Ambition poured into my fingers. But it garbled the scale I was playing, tightening the ligaments and making my joints rigid.

I got up and went to the window. I looked at the sky and again tried to make my mind go blank. The temptation to perform rather than practice was overwhelming. There were so many ways to bring an audience into the practice room, to turn my work into a display. As I stood there, faces kept appearing at the door, peeved pianists hunting for a room. Though I was alone, it felt as if everyone was watching, everyone was listening.

I sat down again and opened a book of études. Aaron insisted that I begin at the beginning, playing the simplest pieces by the guitar's classical composers, Fernando Sor and Mauro Giuliani. A single melody line, with no chords, no place to hide. I played the first piece slowly. I listened, corrected myself, and played it again. Then I tried it quickly, changing the mood, working to find as much music in the notes as I could. The sound was dense, compressed. My fingers were grabbing for the notes. Once more. I closed my eyes and imagined I was downstairs on the stage of Jordan Hall giving a recital. For a moment the music arced gracefully over the orchestra seats to the balcony, to the back row, 150 feet away. The sound seemed full and resonant, not cramped.

The pianist next door woke me from my fantasy. She had taken a break but was back now, playing Schumann. I squelched the fantasies of magical success, of leaping over my fingers and landing on stage. Hard work, concentration, conscious attention were the only way forward. Each day a single step. I opened my eyes and watched my hands, monitoring each motion. Simple music is still music. It demanded the best of my ability.

For an hour, for two, then three hours, I held myself in the proper posture, accepting only correct movements. The pianist kept practicing too. Beethoven, then Schubert. These little études by Sor and Giuliani were like flies tapping against the window.

I stalked around the room, working the tension out of my neck and shoulders, still feeling the crush of music in my limbs, aching to get out. Finally I gave up. Lying on the floor with my feet on a chair, I listened. The pianist next door had returned to Brahms. She played slowly, repeating each phrase, varying the articulation and the tone color. I balanced my guitar on my chest and picked out the melody she was practicing, experimenting with phrasing and sonority. After disciplining my fingers with chirpy études, it was a relief to hold this music in my hands, great music. We never spoke, this pianist and I, and I'm sure she couldn't hear me and my quieter instrument through the wall, as I heard her. Yet for half an hour, we held a conversation over a few lines of Brahms, each of us asking, What raises certain notes, certain lines or phrases, beyond themselves into expressive music? Is it this fingering, this change in shading that evokes a sense of joy or anguish? Is it a slight *rubato* or an *accelerando* that produces a catch in your throat or makes the skin on the back of your neck suddenly want to march down your spine?

I resumed my place in the center of the room and began my lessons again from the beginning. I concentrated on making the clearest tones possible. But the pianist next door kept drilling Brahms into my ears. Great music. Brahms, Beethoven, Schumann, Schubert. No matter how well I played, I couldn't compete with them.

This was my second lesson. Even if I could play the melody by Brahms as beautifully as the pianist next door, Brahms didn't write for the guitar. I had thought I was a musician. Now, for the first time, I realized that I was just a guitarist. Nothing had changed. I still had to practice. But suddenly these études felt like a kind of exile. I was quietly mastering music that only guitarists cared about.

If I had chosen to pursue jazz guitar, none of this would have mattered. The electric guitar can stand up to any other instrument in a jazz ensemble, and its rock-star aura even adds a whiff of danger and allure to its every note. But I had chosen to major in classical guitar. It wasn't a choice, really, but an acknowledgment. This was how my imagination spoke most clearly to me, most urgently. Although I loved to improvise, my strength, I thought, was interpretation. I understood classical music better, felt it more deeply. Walking past Beethoven the next morning, however, it hit me that pianos and violins rule classical music. A pianist would win the Conservatory's annual concerto competition. She might even win the Van Cliburn competition. A violinist would be chosen for first chair of the Conservatory orchestra, on the way to a seat with the New York Philharmonic, the Philadelphia Orchestra, or the Boston Symphony. But the classical guitar exists in its own little world. The Conservatory was progressive in having a guitar department at all. Although Juilliard now has a program, the woman on the phone had laughed when, as a high school junior, I'd naïvely asked for an application. At the time I hadn't grasped the significance of her laughter. But listening to the orchestral fury emanating from practice rooms in every direction, it belatedly sank in. Even at the Conservatory, the guitar was not one of the serious instruments. We weren't going to be in the orchestra. We weren't going to appear as featured performers with the orchestra.

It had never before occurred to me that my instrument might be a limitation, an obstacle. It hadn't struck me as odd that Segovia filled Carnegie Hall but no other guitarist holds solo recitals there. Now I heard the truth. Pianists would drown me out forever. We were competing for the world's limited musical airtime, and pianos always win. Even the best guitarist had only the slightest chance at a solo career. And for the first time, even among guitarists, I wasn't the best.

⌒

Repertoire is destiny. An instrument aspires to the world that composers create for it. For the guitar, however, it seemed the best composers had remained silent. I was stuck with music by Sor and

Giuliani, interpreting the world through their ears and imagina-
tions. It now became terribly important to me to understand who
these men were, how they fit in. I stepped into their worlds, looked
around, listened as carefully as I knew how. I researched their
lives. But I couldn't escape the fact that the guitar's greatest classical composers, while interesting, were hardly Beethoven. In a fate-
ful moment of panic, I drew a third lesson: the guitar itself—*my
instrument*—would always hold me back.

Fernando Sor was a musical prodigy. Born in Barcelona in 1778, the
son of a prosperous merchant, he composed his first opera, *Telema-
chos on Calypso's Isle*, when he was nineteen years old. It made him
a celebrity in Barcelona. In triumph, he moved to Madrid, the center of Spanish musical life, where he came under the patronage of
the Duchess of Alba, who also supported the painter Francisco
Goya. (Goya was said to have been in love with the duchess, and he
used her as the figure in his famous works *La Maja Desnuda* and *La
Maja Vestida*.) Sor remained with the Duchess of Alba for five years
until her death in 1802. He composed symphonies, quartets, and a
large quantity of songs.

When Napoleon invaded Spain in 1808, Sor fought against the
French. But once Madrid fell, he found the invader's Enlightenment
ideals appealing. When the French were defeated in 1813, Sor left
Spain and never returned. He settled in Paris for two years, then
moved to England in 1815.

In London, Sor achieved unprecedented success as a guitarist
and composer. An English critic greeted a collection of his songs by
writing, "Mr. Sor's vocal compositions have gained such favour
among the higher order of musical dilettanti, that a new set of ari-
etts from his pen causes almost as much sensation as the publication
of a new novel by the author of *Waverly*." On March 24, 1817, Sor
gave a recital with the Royal Philharmonic Society, the only gui-

tarist in its history to do so. The program included Sor's *Sinfonia Concertante* for guitar, violin, viola, and cello, now lost. George Hogarth, in his *Memoir of the Philharmonic Society*, wrote that Sor "astonished the audience by his unrivaled execution."

Sor remained in London until 1823. Toward the end of his stay, he became involved in the production of ballets, including his highly successful *Cendrillon* in 1822, which was also performed at the Paris Opera in 1824. His association with the ballet seems to have been a success in other respects as well, because that same year, Sor married Félicité Hullin, one of the company's première dancers.

In 1823, Hullin received an invitation to be prima ballerina at the Moscow ballet. On January 6, 1825, she danced at the grand opening of the Bolshoi Petrovsky Theater. The ballet was Sor's *Cendrillon*.

In Russia the guitarist won the admiration of the imperial family. But after Tsar Alexander and Empress Elizabeth died, things appear to have changed for both Sor and his wife. When he returned to Paris in 1827, Félicité chose to remain in Moscow.

Back in Paris, Sor lived at the center of a vibrant musical society that included Liszt, with whom he is said to have performed, as well as Chopin, Paganini, and Berlioz. At this time Sor published the bulk of his compositions for solo guitar, most of which had been written earlier. In 1830, the same year that Berlioz premièred the *Symphonie Fantastique*, Sor published his *Method for Guitar*, which is still one of the most thoughtful and valuable methods for the instrument.

Fernando Sor was a great popular success during his lifetime. But when I read his biography that first year at the Conservatory, it was his posthumous fate that seized my attention. Sor failed to create a lasting musical legacy for the guitar, as Chopin and Liszt did for the piano and as Paganini did for the violin. After his death in 1839, he fell into obscurity. Between 1840 and 1920, when Segovia rekindled interest in the composer, much of Sor's music went out of print and many manuscripts were lost. Sor's name was omitted when he was buried in a friend's crypt in Montmartre. The site of his grave was rediscovered only in 1934. He was one of the finest guitarists of the age. But his compositions did not stand up to history. Even Segovia admitted it. "We must be honest," he wrote in 1948, "Fernando Sor, the best, and perhaps the only guitar composer of his epoch, is . . . tremendously garrulous."

Today Sor's complete works for guitar are published in a scholarly eleven-volume edition. Yet he remains a marginal figure, more important to the guitar than to music.

Mozart never wrote for the guitar. The closest he came was in 1787, when he had Don Giovanni play the mandolin in the aria "Deh Vieni." Beethoven wrote nearly twenty pieces for the mandolin. At his death a mandolin was among Beethoven's possessions. But he never wrote for the guitar either, though he was certainly familiar with it and was friendly with the other of the instrument's great classical virtuosos.

Mauro Giuliani was born on the Adriatic coast of Italy in 1781. He moved to Vienna in 1806. A few years earlier the chief music critic for Vienna's *Allgemeine musikalische Zeitung* had commented that "the standard by which virtuosos are judged is high—and rightly so, for we have known so many among the very greatest." Giuliani was enthusiastically received. In 1808 he premiered a guitar concerto with full orchestral accompaniment. The *Allgemeine musikalische Zeitung* reported, "He has become, at least for the time, the musical hero of the day."

A musical hero in 1808 Vienna! What musician could hope for higher praise? And yet Giuliani too remains just a footnote in the world beyond the guitar. The footnote is provided by Elisabeth Röckel, a beautiful young singer whom Beethoven had unsuccessfully courted. Instead of Beethoven, she ultimately married the pianist Johann Nepomuk Hummel, a pupil of Mozart's. To show that there was no animosity between the two great musicians on her account, Frau Hummel recalled an afternoon when Beethoven, Hummel, and she dined together "with the famous guitarist Giuliani." The anecdote does not involve Giuliani but rather Beethoven's propensity for "nudging and teasing" Frau Hummel during the meal.

Lunch with Beethoven. This is the great guitarist's part in music history. He was a recognized and respected member of the Viennese musical establishment, playing cello in the orchestra at the première of Beethoven's Seventh Symphony. Beethoven himself publicly thanked the guitarist, among the other famous musicians who made that performance possible. "Ober-Kapellmeister Salieri . . . beat time for the drummers and salvos," he wrote. "And Hr. Siboni and Giuliani also occupied subordinate positions." In 1814 Giuliani became "virtuoso onorario di camera" to Empress Marie-Louise, Napoleon's second wife. And in 1815 he was engaged with the violinist Josef Mayseder and the pianist Hummel to provide a series of six musical soirees in the Royal Botanical Gardens of Schönbrunn Palace in the presence of the royal family and the nobility. Sometime between January and March 1821 he may have performed in Rome with Rossini and Paganini.

But like Sor, Giuliani's great personal success did not establish the guitar as a significant instrument in the musical mainstream. When he died in 1829, the *Giornale delle Due Sicilie* wrote, "The guitar was transformed in his hands into an instrument similar to the harp, sweetly soothing men's hearts."

Then he too was forgotten.

☉

I awoke every morning to the sound of violins. They burned my ears. I gulped down a tasteless breakfast in the dorm cafeteria and raced into the music building. Gripping my guitar case tightly, I barreled up the stairs in search of a room. Could I compete against these musicians? Could my instrument stand up next to theirs? I had lost so much time as a child playing folk songs while others were learning fundamental technique. I could hear them through the walls. The sound squeezed the practice room into a tiny cell. It made me practice fiercely.

But no matter how hard I worked, I seemed to be getting worse. Even the simplest pieces grew into ordeals as old habits fought to remain unchanged. I played études by Sor, Carcassi, and Dionisio Aguado. Easy pieces for beginners; pieces I'd played when I was ten. But now my ears were razors. I could find the flaw in every note. I wanted to play tones that were perfect and pure, to cut away at mistakes until my fingers disappeared. But all I heard was the lisp of flesh against the strings.

"Slow down," Aaron said at a lesson in December. My right elbow cradled the guitar. As I played, I tightened my hold, pulling the instrument closer to me. He made me get up, touch my toes, take a walk around the room. "You're turning musical tension into physical tension," he said.

If only I could become conscious of what my body did, I could fix it, I thought, I could remake my playing. I devoted all my ability to clearing out old habits. I was addicted to exercises, fanatical about scales. I had to play perfectly if I was to become the best. But habits were at the heart of my playing. The moment my mind returned to the music, the tension reappeared.

"Everything feels like a mistake," I complained to Aaron.

"Mistakes are never serious," he responded. "The danger lies in repeating mistakes, practicing them."

Back in the practice room, I spoke to myself calmly, patiently. If it isn't right, I told myself, don't repeat it. But hardly anything was right. My fingers were always getting in the way. All those years at the Guitar Workshop, doing the same thing over and over while expecting to get better. It was a kind of madness. To root out the tension in my playing, I had to change how I sat, how I held the instrument, how music traveled through my body. By the end of the day, I was shouting, *Can't you do anything right?!* I left the practice room exhausted, having played only a few notes.

Climbing the stairs one morning, I noticed that my shoulders rose with each step, just as they did when I played a scale. I went up and down the stairs, practicing climbing, and the same thing happened each time. I gripped my guitar case; I clutched my silverware when I ate. Did I chew too hard, swallow too forcefully? I didn't know how I breathed. Did I work at breathing when work was unnecessary? Did I use the least possible effort? Each gesture, each motion and activity, ought to express the same clarity and directness I wanted to hear in my playing. I had to overcome myself if I was going to rise above the guitar. I wanted to stop time and hold each moment up for examination, so I could get inside it and correct the flaws buried there. It was not just music I had to practice, but everything. I put myself under constant vigilance.

At the end of the first semester, I was back at my parents' house for winter break, frustrated and angry with myself. In my notebook from that time, I wrote, "Every minute that I don't practice or do something constructive I'm wasting my time. By the time I'm twenty or twenty-two, I have to be the best, or there is no hope of a career." No, I couldn't go to the movies with my sister. No, I couldn't go out for a drink with high school friends at night. I had to practice, keep my mind clear, make up for lost time. I shuttered myself in my room.

Late one night my brother disturbed my work to compliment me. He'd been listening at the door.

"You're so good," he said.

"How would you know?" I hissed.

Study in G

SHIFTING THE GUITAR so that it stands upright, strings pointing to the ceiling, I wrap my arms around the instrument's waist.
This is an old habit, hugging my guitar. It reminds me that the
instrument has a body, and that practicing is a physical relationship.
I let my chin droop against the curve of the guitar's shoulder and
nuzzle my cheek against its neck.

I'm still hearing how Bach's fugue should sound. As I sit here
holding the guitar, my hands pulse with readiness. They'll do whatever I ask of them now, or so it feels when I'm not playing. The
reality, of course, is different. My hands are not ready to hold what
I hear. Some flaw deep in my playing keeps getting in the way. To
move forward, I'll have to dig it out. First, though, it's time to take
a break.

Outside, a light breeze has come up, and it ruffles the leaves of
the plane trees by the school across the street. A gardener is busy
pulling down the vines that grow over the building's walls and windows, obscuring the facade and darkening the rooms. Just like me,
she has a never-ending task.

I let out a deep breath, relaxing my concentration. Few things
are as pleasant as sitting like this, leaning against the instrument and
looking out the window. If all I wanted was to dream about music, I

could stay this way forever. It's a comforting and frightening thought: *to stay this way forever.* Part of me doesn't want to move forward, wants to just hug the guitar all day. And part of me will never be satisfied until what I hear, what I dream, becomes real. I take another deep breath, letting the guitar support my weight. This is a crucial moment. If I relax for too long, I might not begin again. Refocusing my attention, I close Bach's violin sonatas and open a book of études. My playing is stuck, and to unstick it, I return to basic technique.

Fernando Sor's Opus 60, no. 16, in G Major is a beautiful piece, one of the most musical of all the guitar's easy études. There are no especially fast passages, no big reaches or awkward shifts. With a little effort, students can quickly achieve something that sounds like children's classical music. Still, the music is not simple. Like much of Sor's work, it's easy to underestimate. Superficially, the notes are soothing, almost a lullaby. And the notes are all there is. But Sor was a thoughtful musician. He may not have been Beethoven, but he was a genius of the guitar. If you listen carefully, his music reaches into the heart of the instrument. As I play, a series of sustained notes catches my ear, resonating in the instrument's body, creating a ringing, sonorous swell. When the harmony progresses, these ringing tones begin to clash, opening a kind of musical wound. This is no lullaby. There's a deeper story in these sweet sounds.

The first time through I play badly. The fingers of my left hand swallow the ringing tones. I play the étude once again. It is important to know what is a mistake, an accident that might happen to any guitarist, and what is a flaw in my technique, something I repeat unconsciously each time and that prevents me from getting better. Sor's study is ideal for improving technique because it has no hiding places. The music's graceful, translucent texture can't survive the buzzes and squeaks that signal fuzzy finger work. I have to know what I want at each moment, making swift, direct movements. If I don't, the study will show it.

The problem occurs in the opening passage. I play it several times, very slowly, watching closely, lying in wait. And then I see it, a wobbling in my muscles. Every time I pull off the string with my fourth finger, my hand tenses and the other fingers bunch together. The flaw is very subtle, but it constricts my movement, distorting the music. I play the same passage again to isolate the tension. Then again. I need to trace its cause, to make it conscious so I can correct it. There is so much in these notes. But everything depends on how I play them.

If playing an instrument is a physical relationship, then technique is the body of your playing. Technique is how you *do* things, the way you handle the notes, how fast or slowly you can play, how varied your tone and dynamics. Natural ability makes up a great part of it. But as in all physical relationships, what you've got is less important than how you use it, how you move. Whether you're an athlete, a surgeon, a hairdresser, or a circus clown, technique defines the scope of your ability. It is both the refinement in what you do and the barrier to doing more, doing it better. When you want to improve at anything, therefore, you must develop your technique. It is the battleground between your habits and your ideal.

I've played the same passage for ten minutes now, and the tension in my fingers is gone. The ringing tones resound. The problem has been fixed. I begin the study again from the top, pleased with my playing. Immediately, the ringing stops, replaced by a stifled grunt. The problem remains. It's infuriating. My hands are in the way of what I hear so clearly in my head.

If only I could play the guitar with my mind!

I look out the window to calm myself. Outside, a hummingbird hovers by a trumpet flower tree. It senses my gaze and flits away. I picture my hands moving like that, light, precise, and incredibly swift. I turn to Sor's study once more, dreaming of hummingbird wings. But wishing and dreaming are part of my problem. When you dream, you stop paying attention to what you're actually doing. The hummingbird doesn't move its wings magically, just efficiently.

If my hands aren't moving well, it's not their fault. My fingers play exactly the way I've trained them. This is how I've always done it. Technique, like the body's memory, is gloriously reliable and stubbornly resistant to change. Try to alter the way you hold a fork, or the way you face your spouse when angry. If you really concentrate, then it isn't hard to do. But the moment you are distracted—the moment you begin to rely on your habits, your technique—you slip back into established patterns. Fixing mistakes is easy. Correcting your technique means undoing all your previous practice. You have to replace one habit with another, better one.

Although this étude has revealed the flaw in my technique, it's not just this one passage, this one movement, that I need to change, but a whole lifetime of movement, my whole history. Playing the étude very slowly, I'm able to correct the mistake. But this is just the surface of the problem. It's not my fingers but me, my relationship with the guitar, that stands in the way. I begin the étude again, trying to reach into the heart of my playing. There is a deeper story in these stifled sounds. As a musician, my first time through, I played badly.

"The guitar," Segovia said, "is like an orchestra, distant and mysterious, its sound coming to us as if from a world much smaller and subtler than ours." Whether writing or playing, Segovia made the guitar sound dreamy. This was his great gift. Yet dreams inhabit some distant and magical realm, far removed from daily life and the mainstream of musical culture. To me, as a young musician striving for acceptance, this magical distance felt like an exile, excluding the classical guitar from serious music and keeping me from what I wanted. In his review of Segovia's 1928 New York debut for the *New York Herald Tribune,* Lawrence Gilman rubbed it in. "The elfin wizardry of his playing is in a musical world by itself," he wrote. Maybe he thought this was a compliment. A less sympathetic critic didn't leave room for doubt. Olin Downes of *The New York Times* acknowledged Segovia's mastery, but concluded that he "did not and cannot succeed in removing the limitations which will always surround his instrument. He has stretched these limitations to the utmost. He has far outdistanced . . . the ordinary twanger of strings. Nevertheless, the guitar remains the guitar, with limits of sonority, color, dynamics."

"The guitar remains the guitar." What does this mean? Certainly the guitar has its limitations. But so does every instrument. Even in the hands of Yo-Yo Ma, a cello remains a cello too. Yet no reviewer ever faulted this instrument for being what it is. When I read Downes's review as a student at the Conservatory, it opened a deep wound. What's wrong with the guitar? I demanded angrily. Perhaps Downes just didn't understand the instrument. But if this was the case, he was hardly alone. A hundred years earlier, in 1832, the French music critic François-Joseph Fétis had reviewed a concert by Fernando Sor in almost the same terms. "M. Sor does very pretty things on the guitar," Fétis conceded, "but I confess that I have always regretted that this artist, whose musical intelligence is far from ordinary, does not devote himself to an instrument which would offer greater resources to his ability. On hearing M. Sor one recognizes a superior artist; but, I repeat, why does he play the guitar?"

What makes this instrument inferior to others? I wanted to know. Why should playing the guitar condemn me to mediocrity?

In fact, the guitar has been one of the world's most popular instruments for more than two hundred years. Sor and Giuliani are the classical era's best known guitarists. But they were not the only ones. Between 1800 and 1840 Europe was crisscrossed by traveling guitar virtuosos. Matteo Carcassi was a native of Florence who achieved local fame very young. He toured Germany in his teens and debuted in Paris in 1820. His spectacular playing created such a stir there that he knocked the reigning guitar virtuoso, Ferdinando Carulli, out of fashion. Carulli, who was born in 1770, the same year as Beethoven, had been a fixture of Parisian society for a decade and had written more than three hundred compositions for the guitar before Carcassi arrived and stole his audience. Carcassi himself seems to have moved to Paris only after being hounded from Vienna by the arrival of Giuliani.

Niccolò Paganini was the greatest violin virtuoso in history. Yet a contemporary wrote that "it is hard to decide whether he is greater on the violin or guitar." Franz Schubert composed most of his songs on the guitar and only later transcribed them for piano accompaniment. Many of Schubert's songs were originally published with a guitar part, including "Ungeduld," "Das Wandern," "Heidenröslein," and "Lied der Mignon." At least three guitars once owned by Schubert have survived. And Schubert had company. In an era when composers were generally piano virtuosos, Hector Berlioz played the piano with one finger. As an impoverished student in 1820s Paris, he gave guitar lessons to earn his rent, and he used the guitar in several of his compositions, including "Mephisto's Serenade" and his last opera, *Béatrice et Bénédict*. A guitar once owned and autographed by both Berlioz and Paganini is now in the rare instrument collection at the Paris Conservatory. Martin Luther played the guitar, as did Benjamin Franklin and Richard Wagner. Giuseppe Verdi was a promoter of the instrument. Gustav Mahler composed for it, as did Arnold Schoenberg and Igor Stravinsky.

And yet for some reason, in the minds of the musical elite, the guitar was an instrument of sentiment, not of serious music. "The guitar is for the bower, or the boudoir, and to accompany tender tales of love," pronounced the British music journal *The Harmonicon* in an 1829 review of music by Giuliani. "But to give it brilliant compositions, requiring the execution of a violinist, and suited . . . to the concert room, it then becomes as ineffective as a piping bullfinch perched on a trombone in the midst of a military band." If Schubert played the guitar, this must be a sign of his poverty, not a musical preference. Imagine! He couldn't even afford a proper instrument. Certainly Berlioz was an unconventional composer. But according to Maurice Ravel, Berlioz was "the worst musician among the musical geniuses." How do we know? Well, he played the guitar . . . If the instrument demonstrated Schubert's poverty, for Berlioz, the guitar signaled wildness and lack of discipline.

Over and over I heard the same criticisms, until the repetition seemed too consistent to be a mistake. It had to reveal a flaw, a prejudice, some deep-rooted resistance that prevented critics from hearing the instrument itself. Regardless of the skill of its players, to the critics, the guitar remained the guitar. Too quiet. Too sweet. Not enough—*something*. But *what*? What was wrong with the guitar?

As I practiced furiously in a cramped room at the Conservatory, struggling with the limitations of my hands, these questions repeated in my head. Everywhere I turned, I felt confined. Something was lacking, and the pang of lack worked deeper and deeper into my playing until I couldn't hear the music anymore. What I heard, instead, was "The guitar remains the guitar." Nothing could have hurt me more. I was dissatisfied with myself and with my ability; I wanted to improve. But the voice of the critics insisted, "You will stay this way forever."

Playing Sor's étude in G major once more, I begin to teach myself a better way to move. It's slow, painful work. There's still a lot of history to overcome, conflicts buried deep in my playing. I'm struggling, but there's no other way. I want to change the way I play, to let the notes ring out as they should. But I can't dream these changes into being, can't escape my body or my history. Technique is at the crux of being a musician—of being a person, really—the place where what you imagine meets the reality of who you are, where your ideals meet your habits. Whether you're working to change, or working not to, you always return to technique.

tHe sweetest CHORDS
IN tHe WORLD

ONE WINTER afternoon in my second year at the Conservatory, my teacher held our lesson at his apartment in Boston. It was a viciously cold day, and as I walked the few blocks down Massachusetts Avenue to Boylston Street, the snow crunching underfoot sounded like bones cracking. Although I was wearing skier's gloves, by the time I arrived, my hands had frozen in the shape of my guitar case handle.

I rang the bell while stamping clots of ice from my boots. Aaron opened the door and laughed. He was wearing an old pair of jeans and a colorful, large wool sweater. The outfit contrasted with his usual sober attire at school, where he was never seen without a pressed button-down shirt and crisp, pleated slacks. I had never been to Aaron's apartment before, and I was nervous to meet outside our familiar context. Leaving my hat, coat, scarf, gloves, and boots by the hallway closet, I followed him past the living room, through the dining room, and into the kitchen. Compared with my dingy room, his apartment was a palace.

"I should have told you not to bring your guitar in the cold," Aaron said as he put water on the stove for tea. "I just wanted to listen to recordings with you today."

I rubbed my hands together next to the gas flame. It was a rite of passage to be invited to Aaron's apartment for a lesson. Normally a parade of guitarists lined up in the busy hall outside his room at school. But occasionally Aaron would pluck one student from the queue and schedule a session off campus. In quieter surroundings, and with more time to work, these special meetings signaled that Aaron heard something ripening in your playing. I had worked on études all summer and fall, and now, he promised, I could start building a repertoire. We carried our mugs into the living room and Aaron nodded me to the sofa. He sat by the stereo and started fingering through a crate full of LPs.

"Let's start with some Bach," he said, selecting an album and showing me the cover. It was John Williams's 1975 recording of the first lute suite, a piece I'd been nagging Aaron to let me play. I knew the recording well. I'd bought the album while still in high school, and for several years I'd thought that Williams was a better guitarist than Segovia. Williams's father, also a guitarist, had recognized his son's talent early and sent him to study with the Maestro, who promptly declared, "A prince of the guitar has arrived." Williams's first recording, issued when he was eighteen, was a Bach violin sonata. He was the first guitarist to record all of Bach's lute suites.

Aaron put the record on the turntable, then perched on the edge of a chair to listen. Williams charged through the first movement, a prelude followed by a presto. His technique was flawless, and he attacked each note with an engineer's precision. Bach's lines came through with complete clarity, allowing the musical structure to build in the air, a machine made of sound. But I'd grown increasingly critical of Williams since arriving at the Conservatory. Hearing him now, I thought the insistence of his technique often overwhelmed Bach's phrases. He measured each line so precisely, the music no longer felt alive.

At the end of the movement, Aaron put on a different record, the same piece recorded by Julian Bream in 1965. Like Williams, Bream was the son of a musician and had achieved recognition as a young man. Although never officially anointed by Segovia, he'd been the protégé of the British Philharmonic Society of Guitarists and had attended the Royal College of Music. During the 1960s and 1970s he and Williams were Segovia's heirs apparent. However, Bream's approach to Bach was a pole apart from Williams's. His technique was never as clean, but his sense of the music was much richer. Instead of racing through the notes, Bream lingered over each one. The guitar possesses an enormous palette of tonal variety, and Bream took advantage of this in his interpretation, perhaps too much so. He colored each note until the piece shimmered like a rainbow.

When we'd heard both recordings, Aaron asked me which I preferred.

I wasn't happy with the choices. Bream seemed to understand the music much better than Williams. Yet his coloring blurred the counterpoint, thrusting the instrument almost luridly into the foreground. Williams played coolly, and this lack of expression allowed the notes to emerge forcefully, independently. But his clarity dispensed with all subtlety. Williams played the notes, while Bream played the guitar, and neither quite captured the music.

"They each give half of a good performance," I said after a moment. "And neither one is as good as Glenn Gould."

A year earlier Gould had issued his final recording, Bach's *Goldberg Variations*. It was the best Bach I'd ever heard: lyrical and articulate, with an improvisatory openness, yet perfectly in control. Gould's piano playing had both color and clarity, I said. His lines were utterly free and independent, and each note was like a diamond, hard and faceted, yet warm, and exquisitely set within the piece's larger design. I grew excited trying to illustrate what I meant, leaning forward on the couch and shaping the air with my hands.

Maybe this was what Aaron was waiting for, to see how the music excited me and how I expressed my excitement. It was important to analyze different interpretations of Bach. But I don't think he was concerned with interpretation at that moment. Interpretation is just the theory of a performance, and the experience of music is more than this theory put into practice. Aaron didn't agree or disagree with my enthusiasm for Glenn Gould. He let me talk, asked me questions, and finally suggested we have more tea.

When we sat down again in the living room, he thought for a moment, then told me to close my eyes. There was one other piece he wanted to play. I heard him flip through the records in the crate, remove one, and slide it from its sleeve. I heard the album drop onto the platter, the needle find its groove. But I was unprepared for what I heard next.

> *Love, look at the two of us*
> *Strangers in many ways . . .*

My eyes sprang open in horror. "I can't believe you own a record by the Carpenters," I stammered. But instead of apologizing, Aaron told me to listen.

I gritted my teeth, closed my eyes, and listened. The anemic cheerfulness of the orchestration, the sappy strings, background singers bleating "looooove," and above it all Karen Carpenter's nasal alto, which was innocent and insinuating at the same time, like an insipid, commercial leer. After Bach, this felt like a desecration. I could find nothing in the music to listen to, just layer after layer of artificial sweetener. I couldn't keep my eyes closed; the song was too cloying. I wanted to escape, and I squirmed on the couch, looking out the window, staring at my hands, waiting for the song to end.

When it was finally over, Aaron asked me what I thought the lyrics were about.

I trusted Aaron, but I had no idea what he wanted to hear. "It's a bubble-gum pop song about a couple in love," I said.

"Really?" he asked. "Listen again." I groaned, but he paid no attention. With complete seriousness, he inflicted the song on me once more.

What was I supposed to hear? It still sounded like a candy-coated love song to me. Aaron looked at me with his eyebrows raised. He watched me silently until I threw my hands up in confusion. I couldn't think of anything to say.

Aaron nodded, then blew across the surface of his tea before taking a sip.

"Imagine that your guitar has been stolen," he said. "You go to the police. You hunt around the pawnshops. But it's nowhere to be found. It's just gone. A year goes by, two years. You find a new instrument. But it's not the same. Then one day you're walking past a music store in a strange city, and there it is in the window. You run inside, and this is really it, the guitar you'd lost."

Then he played the song again.

> *Love, look at the two of us*
> *Strangers in many ways . . .*

The feel of my guitar was in my hands, its weight and shape against me. I wrapped my arms around each other as if to hug the instrument, then caught myself in the middle of this gesture and began to laugh. I think I was blushing. The song still sounded saccharine, but now I was embarrassed by it, not angered, embarrassed to let Aaron see me responding to its trite and sappy sentiment. Maybe finding my lost guitar in a strange city after years of searching I would feel stupidly happy and have nothing but trite words to express my joy and relief. To anyone else, it might sound trivial. The words themselves had little meaning. I'd have to fill them, explaining how long I'd waited, how the theft had left me feeling naked and bereft.

Again I was squirming on the couch, trying to escape, but this time because I felt too much. The story had transformed the experience. Aaron let the song play to the end, then politely excused himself, leaving me to consider what had happened.

What did I care about? What makes a note, a phrase, or a series of words meaningful? "Figure it out," Aaron said to me with this song. "Find out what's important to you, and practice that."

A week later I was in one of the spacious practice rooms on the second floor of the Conservatory coming down with the flu. Flu epidemics were common in the winter. So many musicians breathing deeply must provide a rich breeding ground for disease. Selfishly, we string players looked forward to these waves of illness, since they hit the wind players hardest. If you could stay well enough to practice, it was much easier to find an empty room.

I was in the early stages of learning a "Theme and Variations" by Mauro Giuliani, wrestling with the simple, almost vapid theme. No matter how I played it, the theme wanted to skip. A dotted rhythm gave the melody its pronounced character. Each time I played it, I pictured skipping down a country lane trying to sing this song with a straight face. It was laughable.

Giuliani's music can be embarrassing. Even if you've never heard it before, the tunes sound familiar. I'd been working for almost two hours, and still the piece made me cringe. What was in it that mattered to me? How could I find something to make the notes meaningful?

I stopped playing for a moment and listened. If the theme skipped, it sounded silly. It didn't hold my attention. But the music didn't force me to play it this way. Skipping was my idea, my unthinking response to Giuliani's composition.

I played it again, listening, and heard Karen Carpenter singing along. I grimaced and shuddered with a sudden chill. And then it occurred to me that maybe Giuliani had thought the theme was silly too. He might have struggled with it, just as I was doing now, searching for some way to make the music interesting. The variations were his response. They showed the different moods, the different characters that he was able to draw out of the music. He was *playing* with the melody.

I tried the theme once more, and this time I heard something in the dotted rhythm I hadn't thought of before, a humor or impishness. Looking ahead, I found this mocking attitude everywhere in the variations. Suddenly the theme was full of attitude, full of opportunity. The dotted rhythm didn't skip, it sneaked. It occurred to me this was a thief's tune, a con man whistling in an alley. He was not skipping down a lane but laying a trap. The music was charming, mock heroic, sly, fearful of being found out.

Had I not heard this before? The whole piece told a story. The theme introduced a deceptively simple character, a charming deceiver. The first variation allowed him to show off in a dazzling sleight-of-hand display. The second variation sounded stern by contrast, almost reproachful. An alternation between treble and bass strings created a back-and-forth, like the wagging of a finger. It was as if this character had a bad conscience or was being harangued by the law. The third variation was defiant, full of bravado, with large, sweeping gestures. But the fourth variation was hushed, meditative, as if the bravado concealed anxiety. The final variation was a chase scene, and the music shook loose in a burst of animation. The thief was taunting the law, daring it to catch him. Flying across the fretboard, the thief and his plodding pursuer raced headlong into an expansive and surprising coda. The thief collapsed, winded and cornered. But the law had been transformed too, adopting some of the thief's attitude and mannerisms. The music ended in a kind of duet, the two characters standing arm in arm, together singing brightly of reconciliation.

I played through the music, enacting the drama as I'd imagined it. The story helped accentuate certain phrases. Rhythmic figures that I'd missed before leaped out. Each variation had character and movement. When I finished playing, however, I was surprised to feel annoyed by the music again. The story had helped me play better, I'd thought, but now it felt arbitrary and forced. I could make up a hundred different stories, twists on the same idea. The theme wasn't a con man but a girl pretending to be a boy, tripping from one adventure to another. I acted out the new scenario with the music, and it changed the sound, the effect. The rhythm, dynamics, and mood were all dramatically altered. But were they better? More musical? I couldn't tell. It didn't seem to matter. The whole piece made me feel a bit queasy. Or perhaps I was becoming feverish.

It struck me that I was alone. I poked my head into the hall and heard an eerie stillness. The rooms on either side of me were empty. I'd never before experienced such quiet in the music building. My eyes had begun stinging, and my stomach wobbled. I walked down the hall to a water fountain and splashed cold water on my face. The halls were empty, a ghost town. The sound of a lone pianist drifted up from somewhere far away, maybe Jordan Hall.

Back in my practice room, I couldn't concentrate on the Giuliani anymore. I definitely had the flu. But I didn't want to leave. I pushed the music stand away and thought of something easy to play, an anonymous *Romanza,* one of the first classical pieces I'd learned as a child. It was simple, and it wouldn't require much energy or attention. I just wanted to take advantage of the stillness, and this piece was deep in the reservoir of movements that I carried in my hands. I closed my eyes and performed it to the empty room.

Perhaps the fever had affected my hearing. Perhaps the mortuary silence in the building had spooked me. I felt the lick of fever climbing my spine and a chill in my head descending. I felt strange, dizzy. The sound of my guitar was distant, disembodied, but I felt it vibrating against me. I tried to remain calm, but I was shaking, shivering, and then seized by a sudden, uncontrollable urge to shout

out, to sob. The stillness was too much. I really felt this *Romanza*. It wasn't a story. It was the loneliest music I'd ever heard.

⌒

What makes music meaningful? I lay in bed for a week with the flu, deliriously reliving my experience of that lonely *Romanza*. I'd played the same piece a hundred times before, but it had never affected me the way it did that day. In the right moment, notes reveal powerful emotions, depths of feeling, whole worlds of meaning that seem expressible in no other way. Perhaps only a few minutes have elapsed. But something has *happened*. The time has been folded, shaped, an origami of time. And in this time these few notes hold sway over you, they get inside, and you feel exposed, wounded. But how does it happen? When I could sit up again, I began to read, searching for an answer.

Since ancient times, people have believed we live in a musical cosmos. Pythagoras imagined the solar system as a musical instrument, with strings stretched between the earth and the planets, their different lengths creating the tones of a musical scale. To him, music was the key to nature, making the intricate order of all things comprehensible. "There is geometry in the humming of the strings," he wrote. "There is music in the spacings of the spheres." For centuries afterward music seemed to express not just the truth of our hearts but truth itself. It was meaningful because it revealed to us God's magnificent plan.

No wonder we thrill to hear it. Musical harmony is just the audible form of the greater harmony of all creation. "The movements of the heavens are nothing except a certain everlasting polyphony, perceived by the intellect, not by the ear," wrote Johannes Kepler in *The Harmony of the Universe*. In fashioning the tones of the major scale, Kepler felt, we act merely as "the ape of God the Creator,

playing, as it were, a drama about the order of celestial motions."
Our hearts, our minds, and the throbbing of the stars all vibrate to
the same frequency. For Greek philosophers, Renaissance scientists, and New Age gurus, music proves the fundamental harmony
of nature. Even Isaac Newton, that most rational observer, thought
the seven colors of the rainbow corresponded in wavelength to the
seven tones of the Western major scale. Vibration is at the heart of
nature. Music allows us to feel it.

It made me feel better to read this. But when my head cleared a
little more, I knew that this was a metaphor, not an explanation.
Peering deeply into the night sky, poets, scientists, and philosophers
have always found there the harmony they sought. The world, for
them, was *like* music. But what does this prove? These thinkers
were all under the sway of a strange physical phenomenon known
as "sympathetic vibration." If you place two identically tuned
stringed instruments next to each other and pluck the first string of
one, the first string of the other will begin to sound too, as if by
magic. Removing the dampers from a piano and speaking next to it
produces the same effect. The tones of your voice will cause strings
of related pitches to resonate. If two things strike us as harmonious,
the philosophers seemed to believe, don't they *have* to be related?

From this common vibration, a whole musical cosmology was
born. Athanasius Kircher, a seventeenth-century Jesuit antiquarian,
gave us the theory's greatest elaboration. Kircher's job was to catalog the anthropological artifacts that missionaries from around the
world sent back to Rome. Struck by patterns he discerned across
cultures, he intuited a great order behind this apparent diversity.
According to him, the world embodied "a wondrous harmony of
one with all, and all with one." To illustrate his theory, Kircher
drew a series of "enneachords," nine-stringed instruments that represented the different orders of creation. Resonance among these
instruments showed how universal harmony arose. "If the string of
Saturn is struck," he explained, "then all of the saturnine things

(lead, topaz, hellebore, cypress, etc.) will vibrate sympathetically." For Kircher, sympathetic vibration—the ability of a vibrating string to cause related strings to vibrate—seemed to explain the coherence of all creation, the great web of relations that bound up all things great and small.

Each era of history has provided its own myth of music's power, its own explanation for why music moves us. Music "is so powerful a thing," wrote Robert Burton in a 1621 essay, "The Secret Power of Music," "that it ravisheth the soul, *regina sensuum,* the queen of the senses, by sweet pleasure." Jean-Jacques Rousseau called music "the originary language of the heart." For the sixth-century Roman philosopher Boethius, music was the force that knit together the spiritual and material realms. "For what unites the incorporeal existence of reason with the body," he asked, "except a certain harmony and, as it were, a careful tuning of low and high pitches?" For Ptolemy, music explained the nature of morality. "Virtue is a kind of consonance of the soul," he asserted, and "evil, a dissonance." Whole musical treatises were written to instruct composers in the science of curing the body and educating the soul with music. Andreas Werckmeister assured his readers in 1686 that "melancholic or passionate people very much appreciate the correct use of dissonance."

From my bed in the Conservatory dorm, I heard the wave of illness subside, as clarinets, oboes, bassoons, and brass again made the music building a riot of practicing. The noise convinced me that the theorists had all somehow missed the point. Still recuperating, I was grateful to the German poet Heinrich Heine, who declared, "Nothing is more futile than theorizing about music." Here finally was someone I agreed with, someone who'd been listening. Instead of offering a theory, Heine described an experience. "The essence of music," he said, "is revelation."

For all of these music lovers, music was something other than music. It might be different for each one. But it was always the thing they loved the most. To the astronomer, music is disguised astronomy. To the mathematician, it is disguised mathematics. Leibniz, who invented calculus, was quite certain that "music is an unconscious exercise in arithmetic in which the mind doesn't know it is counting." The philosopher Arthur Schopenhauer was equally convinced that "music is an unconscious exercise in metaphysics in which the mind does not know it is philosophizing." Among my friends at the Conservatory, we took for granted that music recounted the narrative of our emotional struggles. In Susanne Langer's phrase, music was "our myth of the inner life." Langer quotes the eighteenth-century theorist J. A. Hüller, who expressed our belief, writing, " 'Music has fulfilled its mission whenever our hearts are satisfied.' " This sounded right. It still didn't explain music's power. But it described how music comes to be the pure metaphor of our desire.

For each writer, music reveals whatever he most reveres. "Music," then, becomes the symbol of love, the medium in which desire is fulfilled. *How* this happens remains a mystery. But the "meaning" of music, its truth, depends on it. "The tones of the *Kithara*, although in themselves they signify nothing at all, often cast a wonderful spell over an audience," wrote Longinus in *On the Sublime*. Longinus must have been a musician, a performer and not just a theorist. He understood that it is not the notes but the performance that moves the listener. And whether you respond to order or to feeling, or to some mystic merging of the two, the impetus is the same, recognizable across centuries. Music enacts the highs and lows of our temperament; it demonstrates that lonely distances may be crossed, as if by magic; it proves that two things—two strings, two hearts—might vibrate as one. Music embodies the hope that the innumerable scattered facts of our existence conform beneath the surface to some meaningful plan. It expresses the grandeur, the sweet pleasure, of order. By sympathetic vibration, it shows us what we feel most deeply, proving to us that it *must* be true. And while it lasts, it casts a wonderful spell in which we believe that our hearts *can* be satisfied. "Whoever will consider this a little more deeply," wrote Athanasius Kircher, "will find that the seven planets sing with the Earth a perfect four-part harmony, in which dissonance is combined so artistically with consonance that it gives forth the sweetest chords in the world." We can't prove our theories of what music means. But each theory reveals what we long for; it proves the truth of our longing.

⌢

"Slower, slower—and now at tempo." Aaron hovered over me like a magician over his hat. He waved his arms, then crouched down in front of me and suddenly sprang up. "More! More!" he urged. "Now, *piano.*"

The spring sunshine was bright on the practice room walls, and music of all kinds filtered in through the windows. I was playing "Capricho Arabe," a swooping, romantic serenade by Francisco Tárrega. We'd been working already for half an hour, breaking the piece into small segments and going through it note by note. Now I'd started playing the whole piece from the beginning. Without warning, Aaron had risen from his chair and begun conducting, then acting out the music in front of me.

"The weight. Feel the weight," he whispered as he started hauling an imaginary chain across the floor. "Oh! So heavy."

I felt the burden of the line I was playing, the effort of making it move. It wasn't something made up. I felt it in my arms, my back, the pit of my stomach, as I watched Aaron struggle toward the window.

"Let it sink," Aaron said from the corner of the room. "Let it drop." He sank wearily into the corner, his back sliding down the wall to the floor. "Now take a breath," he said, sighing, "and leap into the air!" He leaped into the air, arms over his head, almost touching the ceiling.

What was happening? I had lost my place in the music and started laughing, but my fingers were still playing just what they needed to, and better than ever. I looked at them in astonishment as I tried to catch up in my mind.

"Leaping. Leaping. Flying through the air," Aaron piped, jumping around the room and flailing his arms.

He'd never behaved this way before. I froze for a moment when he tripped over a music stand and sent it hurtling to the floor.

"Don't stop. Let it go!" he shouted.

The music was off balance too. But it held together, whirling on the brink of a precipice. The lines were darting frenetically, heedlessly over the fretboard. Yet somehow they were effortlessly lofting an enormous weight. The phrases were flighty, openhearted in one instant, wounded and resigned in the next. I had never played like this, though I'd known this piece for years.

Aaron had fluttered into the far corner of the room by the door. He slowed to a creep, then sank to the floor. He didn't say anything. But he began to wind the opposite end of the imaginary chain around his arm, showing the strain in his muscles. He stood and, with bent back, began hauling it across the room again.

I concentrated on his movements while listening to myself play. It was as if his motions, not mine, made sounds emerge from the instrument. The music gathered strength and grew more intense. It rose up into a kind of fullness, then paused, slid back, and subsided. Aaron coaxed the phrases forward, then slowly let them die away.

We sat in silence for a few minutes. I drooped back into my chair, exhausted.

"Like that," Aaron said finally.

I laughed. I didn't know what to say.

The music felt greater than I had ever imagined. And all along I'd had it in me without knowing how to let it out.

⌒

Nearly ten thousand people were in the audience at Eisenhower State Park in East Meadow, Long Island. They'd brought blankets and picnic dinners and had colonized the great lawn to enjoy the final round of a teen talent competition sponsored by the Long Island newspaper *Newsday*. I held my guitar by the neck, straightened my tie, and shook out my shoulders and arms.

"How do you feel?" asked the stage manager.

I looked at her and tried to concentrate.

How did I feel? I felt the way I always felt before a performance: like I was about to be executed; like I was a fraud; like I was that infinitely compressed point, just before the big bang. The stage manager put her hand on my arm in an encouraging gesture. She had been a judge during the early rounds of the competition, and now she was responsible for keeping the show on schedule.

"You're next," she said.

Though the lighting backstage was very dim, I was pretty sure she winked at me. I shivered with stage fright and knelt behind the curtain for five more minutes of preparation.

I had auditioned a month earlier during a summer thunderstorm at a run-down community center in Robert Moses State Park. It was a long, low room, with glass doors leading onto the beach, and on other days it hosted bingo games and local beauty pageants. A long table had been set in the center of the room facing the narrow stage. Three women with clipboards sat behind it: an older woman, the director, who had an unchanging expression of unpleasant surprise, and two younger women, one of whom later became the stage manager. At the back of the room a scraggly man with a jangling wad of keys at his belt operated the spotlight and the sound system. One by one the contestants were invited onto the stage to perform—singers, dancers, baton twirlers, and musicians. When I arrived, more than a hundred competitors were milling around, along with a troop of pushy parents.

I'd chosen to perform the piece Aaron had acted out, "Capricho Arabe" by Francisco Tárrega. As a young man in Barcelona, Segovia had played this piece to seduce girls. It is music, he later said, "especially suited to reach the sensitive chords of a feminine heart." I'd never seduced anyone, at least not knowingly, though I was always hopeful. I thought the piece showed off the guitar's beauty. It was dramatic and accessible, a more sophisticated version of the *Romanza* that had become so meaningful to me.

When my name was called, I introduced myself, took my place on stage, and began to play. At the same instant a cataclysmic thunderclap shook the room and a bolt of lightning struck the beach just outside the glass doors. The lights went out and several people shrieked. I jumped off my chair, knocking it over backward, then stood perfectly still in the middle of the stage, afraid I'd fall over the edge if I moved. The lights came back on. Everyone laughed nervously. The middle woman at the judges' table called for quiet and said to me, "Would you like to start again? This time without pyrotechnics?" I righted my chair, sat down, and waited for my hands to stop shaking. I'd thought I was nervous before. Now it felt like God was listening.

I advanced to the second round and then to the finals, where the pool had been thinned to eight soloists. I was the only classical guitarist on the program, competing against a ballet dancer, an opera singer, a jazz pianist, and several other talented kids.

I peeked out from behind the curtain to the enormous crowd on the lawn. When I'd performed on *The Merv Griffin Show*, the audience had been in the millions. But that had been with a band, and the studio held just a few hundred people. This was by far my largest live audience. I knelt again in the wings and practiced gymnastic exercises and difficult passages, trying to concentrate on the notes, not the audience. I'd worked up a whole story to dramatize the music. A traveler, some Gulliver, awakens in a strange land, encounters people and music and customs he can't understand . . . All the details were clear in my mind. Then Ellen, the stage manager, put her hand on my shoulder again. She smiled and said, "One minute."

She was just a few years older than I, but a grown-up in my eyes and, since she'd been one of the judges, a figure of authority. At the audition she'd been very attentive, coming up to me after my performance to say the judges had liked me. Now I noticed that she kept her hand on my shoulder just a little longer than necessary to attract my attention. She was dressed simply, in jeans and a black linen blouse. And when she motioned silently to me that my moment had arrived, something in her shadowed eyes struck me like a thunderclap.

I walked through the curtains and crossed into the spotlight to the lone folding chair waiting at center stage. I heard a drizzle of applause as I tuned my instrument. Then I let my hands hang for a moment by my side and took a deep breath. Later my sister, who was out on the lawn with my parents, told me a microphone had picked up this sigh. It made people chuckle. But from the stage I didn't hear anything. I just felt the enormous open space in front of me, the receptive stillness.

The amplified sound of the guitar boomed, even when I played very quietly. An airplane rumbled overhead. The newspaper photographer in front of the stage snapped pictures. I'd meant to tell a story about travel and adventure, the discovery of a strange country. But as I played, I forgot everything I'd planned. Instead I listened to myself perform, hearing the notes take shape in the open air. I didn't add anything that wasn't already there. I just tried to play honestly what I heard, to make it feel genuine in my hands, satisfying. The piece felt expansive enough in that moment to include all these people listening, the airplane, and the photographer. But more, though I couldn't have found words then to express it. The sound reached out to the people before me and reached in to some equal expanse in my own experience that I hadn't known was there: as if the music were a single string, and I were at its center, where the vibrations are most pronounced. I seemed to change shape with the tones, growing and contracting, and to change color and mood as well. As if performing the piece I were physically showing what this music held, living through it for everyone to see and hear. But not as a solitary experience. We were all there in the music. I was just playing it.

The contestants stood on stage for a collective bow before they announced the winners. We held hands and attempted a modest kick line. Second place went to a comic singer who'd put words to Chopin's "Minute Waltz." First place—but I didn't hear the announcer very well. The girl next to me, a dancer, started jumping up and down and hugging me. I thought she had won. But then she didn't step forward, and everyone was looking at me. Finally she gave me a little push, and I walked to the front to collect the award, a tin trophy with a winged angel on the top.

Backstage was a jumble. The winner of the group competition was a girls' precision drill team, and every boy in the audience wanted an autograph and a telephone number. I ran a gauntlet of hugs and congratulations, spinning through knots of parents and friends of the contestants. At the edge of the tumult I saw Ellen the stage manager. She waved to me, then ran over and grabbed me. We hung motionless like that for a moment, and a bolt of absolute certainty shot through me. "Capricho Arabe" worked, and this was what I'd won. We were about to kiss.

Then my family arrived.

Ellen hugged me briskly, then stepped back to make way. "It's well deserved," she said, pointing to the trophy. After an awkward pause she disappeared into the crowd.

"We're so proud of you," my mother said, and my father slapped me on the back.

My family bundled into the car to celebrate. We drove to Baskin-Robbins, and everyone ordered a double scoop.

I ate my ice cream feeling ecstatic and cheated. The essence of music is revelation, I thought. The essence of life, however, seems to be disappointment. I'd played well. I'd won the competition by performing better than ever before. For the first time, music had let me express the sweetness of shared experience. But once the music ended, the experience slipped away. Harmony is not eternal, though our need for it may be.

At nineteen years old, I wanted something more. I wanted everything to be like music.

Invocation and Dance

M Y FINGERS are moving well, and I'm ready to begin work
on a new piece, "Invocación y Danza" by Joaquín Rodrigo. Rodrigo is famous for composing the *Concierto de Aranjuez*,
probably the most popular work in the guitar's repertoire. The
Concierto has been recorded dozens of times, and it is the only regularly performed concerto for guitar and orchestra. It's a piece you'll
hear at bookstores and restaurants. Miles Davis recorded a jazz version of its second movement on the album *Sketches of Spain*. "Invocación y Danza," by contrast, is not well known. Although it shares
the *Concierto*'s flamenco rhythms, this is guitarists' music, rarely performed, almost a secret. The music is unsettling, its mood always
shifting, by turns mischievous, vibrant, seething, eerie, elated. I sense
a dark vitality in these shifts, something in the depths that needs this
music to be heard. But the music is very demanding, calling out
extremes of feeling and technique at the edge of my ability to hold
together. It will be a reach for me.

Learning a new piece is like arriving in an unfamiliar city. The
language, the pace, the expressions on people's faces—everything
is exciting and bewildering. Simply to walk across the street can be
an adventure, and finding your bearings sometimes requires days or
weeks. The "Invocación" looms unexplored around me. My fingers

don't know where to go. And while every step shows me something new, the challenge of finding my way seems almost insurmountable.

"One phrase at a time," I tell myself, taking a long, deep breath. The "Invocación" begins with a sequence of harmonics punctuated by fretted bass notes. The effect is ethereal but with an anxious undertone. I play the first four notes so slowly they feel days apart. Nothing is difficult if you play it slowly enough. But taking the time to play this slowly can be excruciating. The mood, the sensation of the notes, is so close—right here at the tips of my fingers—and yet beyond me, seemingly inaccessible. I have to wait for it. But I don't want to wait. I want to know where I am right away. The pressure makes my hands tense, and I grip the guitar's neck as if I were wringing it.

The problem is not my fingers or technique—it's impatience. I shake out my hands and begin the "Invocación" again. Impatience has little to do with the notes themselves. Instead, it is a fight with time. Faced with a new piece of music, an unknown city, a difficult moment in your life, you want to leap over the anxiety and confusion, to be ahead of where you are. But most of the time the solutions you achieve in impatience are narrow and awkward. You establish your first response as a habit, then have to spend all your time trying to correct it, instead of waiting, listening, and learning more. I clear my head and try to fill myself with sound only. The music is *here*. It doesn't need to be captured, just released. Notes shimmer in the air around me. But they are foreign and indistinct. I begin again, tentatively adding the bass notes to the harmonics. Like catching a glimpse down an unknown alley, this passage hints at a different life, a world of experience and expression I've only just imagined. For a moment I plunge into this new life, the thrill of playing unfamiliar music. It is as if I could recompose myself from these notes. Every new piece of music offers this possibility. But then I catch myself racing ahead again. In eagerness, my fingers falter, or my mind wanders into fantasy, and I find that rather than arriving someplace unknown, I'm repeating myself. I haven't really gone anywhere.

"Step back," I say out loud as I put the guitar down, leaning it against the couch. Then I literally step back to look at it, my arms crossed against my chest. In these moments the guitar feels like a trap, and my impatience seems like fate, my old, inescapable story. Perhaps this piece is too difficult for me. Every musician has a boundary, some technical limit. Maybe this is mine. But the thought just makes me more impatient. I want to break out, break through, break *something*. Glaring at my guitar resting helplessly against the couch, a malicious image from *Animal House* comes to mind, John Belushi smashing a guitar against the wall. I look at my instrument again.

The urge passes. Smashing the guitar might feel good—for a moment. But it won't solve the problem. It's not the instrument's fault that I'm stuck; it's mine. The guitar is just a guitar, a thing of wood and string, an instrument. Yet so much gets tangled up in my relationship to it. Each curve of the wood, each vibrating note is knotted with my desire to improve and the fear that I cannot, that what I want is beyond me. The same story, over and over, like a bad habit. I have to slow down, suspend my anxiety, and just listen. Perhaps the music will recompose me someday, but only in its own time. Fighting with the tempo gets me nowhere. I pick up my guitar and settle into the work. As impatient as I am, something here longs for slowness. What is the music telling me? What life do these notes evoke?

"The guitar has its own particular spirit," wrote the guitarist and composer Dionisio Aguado in 1835. "It is *sweet, harmonious, melancholy*; sometimes it can even be *majestic*, although it lacks the grandiosity of the harp or the piano. But its sounds may be modified and combined to render it *mysterious,* and very appropriate for melody and expression."

When Aguado wrote this description, the violin and piano had come to dominate European musical taste. Hoping to distinguish the guitar from its rivals, Aguado claimed a realm of independence for the instrument with this characterization. How well he succeeded can be seen at your local CD store. Go out some afternoon and flip through the bin devoted to classical guitar. Segovia will certainly be there, as will his immediate heirs, John Williams and Julian Bream. Christopher Parkening, Sharon Isbin, and Pepe and Angel Romero might represent the guitar's third generation, along with Liona Boyd, Manuel Barrueco, and a handful of lesser-known artists. But whomever the store has in stock, you'll notice a strange monotony among the titles. You'll find *Guitar Magic* and *The Magic of the Guitar.* John Williams plays the *Romance of the Guitar,* while Angel Romero promises *A Touch of Romance.* Julian Bream has issued an album of "guitar favorites for romantic daydreams," and Sharon Isbin performs both *Dreams of a World* and *Latin Romances for Guitar.* A Deutsche Grammophon compilation, *Mad About Guitars,* sums up the others in its marketing copy: "From street corner musicians to the masters of the concert stage, the guitar's sweet, gentle sound and Spanish rhythms evoke romance, passion and mystery   all here in superb digital sound."

It doesn't matter what you play. More than 170 years after Aguado, the guitar is still sweet, nostalgic, and romantic. Dig deeper. Try to escape this image, this sticky sweet trap. Try to express your anger, your intelligence, your ambition or anguish. Play Bach, play Mendelssohn, play Mussorgsky, Hindemith, or Rodrigo. Revolutionize the instrument. Then listen again to how the reviewers respond, hear what they think you've played.

The guitar inspires its listeners to dream, and dreams, as Freud says, are the royal road to the unconscious. When Segovia stepped onstage in the 1920s, introducing the instrument to a concert audience, he did not enter a new world naked. The guitar was already steeped in the vocabulary of wish fulfillment. "Under the magic touch of Segovia, this poor Cinderella of musical instruments is changed into a princess and rides in a coach by his side," wrote a reviewer in *The New York Times*. Read on. The guitar is an instrument of fantasy as much as a medium of music. There's no end to what it can reveal. Bernard Gavoty, music critic for *Le Figaro* in Paris and author of a 1955 biography of Segovia, grows breathless imagining the guitarist and his guitar. Segovia, the critic writes, has a "prelate-like gravity," while his instrument is "an elderly queen whom he has unceremoniously laid across his knees: the gleaming light varnish disguises like greasepaint the face of a centenarian coquette who won't admit her age, a much-travelled woman no longer capable of surprise."

One worries about Mr. Gavoty. Yet in describing the guitar as an ancient whore about to get a spanking, he is no more florid than previous generations of writers. In 1674 the composer Gaspar Sanz, former organist at King's Chapel in Naples, published a method for guitar. Introducing his subject, he writes, "A guitar is a woman to whom the saying, 'Look but don't touch,' does not apply. Her rosette soundhole is the very opposite of a real rose bud, for she will not wither, no matter how much you touch her with your hands."

A guitar is a woman. Can this be a surprise? Just look at it. The guitar has an idealized feminine form. Just listen. It has an idealized feminine temperament too, moody, sentimental, and soft. It shouldn't come as a complete shock, then, to find the guitar a whore in fantasy but treated like music's little lady: as a sweet, gentle, mysterious instrument, excluded from the serious business of music because—regrettably—it lacks some essential quality. Perhaps in a rebellious, liberated age, the electric guitar can flaunt its wild sexuality. But listen once again to the classical guitar's detractors, with their insistence that it remain in its place, with its expressive limits and its inadequate repertoire. Listen even to Segovia, that sly Prince Charming, who sighs, "The guitar is the most unpredictable and least reliable musical instrument in existence—and also the sweetest, the warmest, the most delicate, whose melancholic voice awakes in our soul exquisite reveries." The guitar is a woman—or someone's peculiar fantasy of a woman. Grasping the details here is important. Because when you play on this instrument, it plays you too, and the dreams this relationship brings out may get to the bottom of who you are.

Once more I take a long, slow breath and play the "Invocación" from the beginning, this difficult, dark, and vital piece. Let me wrap my arms around the guitar and with the gentlest touch brush my fingers against its delicate strings. I feel its body vibrate with a full, singing tone. I hear this music; I feel it in my own body. The notes come from somewhere deep inside, filled with longing and bitterness and love. This is a guitar, not a woman. And yet it was in this relationship that I experienced and tried to express the urgency of what I felt, tried and was rebuffed, tried and responded with anger and resentment when the music I heard refused to yield to my touch. All the richness, all the joy and bittersweet warmth of music, was lost in struggle. All the music. Begin the piece again, ethereal harmonics and brooding bass tones together. Go back to the beginning and tell a better, fuller story this time, not dreaming the guitar but letting it be an instrument, not fighting with where I am but learning to live through it.

⌒

The origin is mythical, as all symbolic origins must be. Like ethereal harmonics, the guitar appears first in ghostly form, in a carving on the Sphinx Gate at Alaca Höyük, in central Turkey. Dating from about 1300 B.C., this so-called "Hittite guitar" is not a guitar but an unknown, lost instrument, a sphinx itself. We know nothing of its music or its significance to those who played it. For us, however, the sphinx is a prophet: the curvaceous, hourglass shape was new in recorded music history. Whatever it meant to these ancient musicians, this mute image establishes the guitar's association with the female form. But this is just the symbol. To arrive at the real guitar, we have to follow a longer, more sinuous path.

The Hittite instrument's feminine lines distinguish it from another stringed instrument, also plucked and strummed, but set on a teardrop- or pear-shaped body. A Mesopotamian cylinder seal from 2200 B.C. shows an early version of this older, rounder instrument with a short neck and a tortoise-shell body. A slightly different form, somewhat larger, with a long neck and a wooden soundbox, appears frequently in Egyptian art beginning around 2000 B.C. Tomb paintings from the reign of the Pharaoh Akhenaten depict musicians performing on this larger instrument using an eagle-feather plectrum to strike the strings.

The wooden body of the larger instrument may have given it its name: in Arabic, *al-oud* means "from wood." The oud would undergo a long development, emerging in the third century A.D. as a stable family of Arabic stringed instruments. Today the oud is known as *ut* or *ud* in Turkey, *laouta* in Greece, and *udi* in parts of Africa. The instrument spread across North Africa with the Muslims and appeared in Europe with the Moorish invasion of Spain in 711. There the *al-oud* became the lute.

Lutes and guitars are cousins, members of the family called chordophones, instruments with vibrating strings. The earliest ancestor of this family, and therefore of all stringed instruments, was a musical hunting bow, first depicted in a Paleolithic cave painting at Trois Frères, in southern France, dating from 15,000 B.C. In this image a priest or sorcerer dressed in a bison skin holds a bow to the mouth of his mask, using his own skull as a resonator. The musical hunting bow survives as the *okongo* or *kora*, used during rituals in sub-Saharan Africa. Similar musical bows are found in South America and among Native Americans. The Washambala tribe in eastern Africa believes that a man will not marry if a string of the musical bow breaks while he is making it. The Maidu tribe of California preferred the musical bow as the best instrument for contacting spirits.

From the musical hunting bow, it is a short step to the lyre. The lyre is a musical bow bent into a V- or U-shape with a crossbar added to form a triangle. Sumerian lyres of this type date from around 2800 B.C. and have up to eleven strings of identical length, tuned to different pitches with levers or pegs. The lyre has another feature, also derived from the musical hunting bow, that shows we are on the right path. In the search for greater volume, ancient bow players attached a gourd or tortoise shell to their instrument, giving the musical bow a body. The drive for greater volume would eventually lead to the Marshall amplifier stacks favored by Jimi Hendrix. ("Listen to me!" this body says. "I want to be heard.") Lacking electricity, early musicians experimented with a range of bowl-shaped fruits and shells. With the addition of a fixed, permanent resonator, the bow evolved into the arms of the lyre and, eventually, into the neck of the lute, guitar, and violin.

We are among ancestors then, even guiding spirits. I want to gather their powers, their secret histories, since these too belong to the guitar's birthright.

In Greek mythology the lyre was a magical instrument. Its discovery was attributed to Hermes, who attached wooden arms to a tortoise shell and strung them with the gut of a cow he had stolen from Apollo. When the theft was discovered, Hermes played so beautifully that Apollo forgave him and exchanged his whole herd for the instrument. Apollo thereafter became the god of music, while Hermes protected herdsmen and shepherds. Homer relates the story of Amphion, son of Zeus and Antiope, who built the walls of Thebes with a lyre. He played with such compelling skill that the stones laid themselves in place. When Orpheus descended to the underworld to seek his wife, Eurydice, his lyre-playing was so moving that the Fates permitted him to bring her back to life. As a result, the image of Orpheus holding a lyre signified immortality in early Orphic rites. The first Christians adapted this image by replacing Orpheus with Christ. This is why angels play the harp.

Homer refers to Hermes's lyre as a *kitharis*. Vase paintings show the kitharis as a light instrument made from the carapace of a tortoise with oxhide stretched over the bowl and two curved and slender arms. The instrument's name can be traced back to the Assyrian *chetarah* of the second millennium B.C., to the ancient Hebrew *kinnura* or *kinnor*, and to the Chaldean *qitra*. The common root of all of these instruments is likely found in the Sanskrit *chhatur-tar*, meaning "four strings." The Sanskrit terms came into Persian as *char* (four) and *tar* (string) and from there into Greek.

In the seventh century B.C., however, a new form of lyre supplanted the Greek kitharis, establishing a pattern that would repeat over and over. The new instrument possessed a large wooden resonator and was called a *kithara*. It was heavier, louder, and musically more versatile than the old kitharis, and it quickly replaced that instrument, warping its name in the process. The kitharis received a new name, *lyra*, and was relegated to the status of folk instrument, known to common Greeks as *chelys* (tortoise) and to the Romans as *testudo* (turtle). One instrument was for the nobility, the other for the people: the first represented power, intellect, poetry, and philosophy; the other became a symbol of weakness, peasant vulgarity, popular entertainment, and the body. Again and again the boundary will be drawn along the same lines. But here, in another moment of symbolic origin, the guitar comes out on top.

The new kithara—from which the guitar derives its name—was

the instrument of choice among professional musicians in Greece and Rome. With seven gut or sinew strings, plucked with the fingers of the left hand or with a plectrum held in the right, it was played at games and religious festivals, and its graceful form still serves as the symbol of classical music on concert halls, statues, and music stands everywhere. In the fifth century B.C. everyone wanted to play the kithara. Sappho was a virtuoso, as was Sophocles. Plutarch mentions that Themistocles invited the most fashionable kitharist in Athens to practice at his home, thus becoming the first politician to use a musical celebrity to attain office. Socrates studied the kithara in his later years under Damon, the teacher of Pericles, though it is not clear that the philosopher was a particularly good student. On his deathbed Socrates confessed to a recurrent dream in which a spirit tells him, "Cultivate music." It's a sad story. He died wishing he had philosophized less and practiced more.

The Romans adopted the kithara from the Greeks. In Roman Latin the instrument came to be called *fidicula*, a diminutive of *fides*, meaning "strings." As the Romans conquered Europe, they introduced the kithara or fidicula into the lives and languages of the conquered peoples. Fidicula became *fidula* or *vitula* in Medieval Latin, *vielle* in French, *viula* in Provençal, *viola* and *violino* in Italian, *vihuela* in Spanish, *videle* or *fiedel* in German, and *fithele* or *fiddle* in English. When Rome burned in A.D. 64, Emperor Nero fiddled on a kithara, not on a violin.

All this lies buried in the guitar's name. But the instrument itself remains formless, pure potential. Until the early part of the first millennium, the ancient kithara flourished in the shade of Roman imperial power. But the weakening and eventual collapse of the empire in Europe led to a period of cultural splintering. Roman influence became a memory, elided, yet kept alive in vestigial forms. This is reflected in the morphology of musical instruments. The kithara began a period of erratic and awkward change, like a shape-shifting spirit or a child entering adolescence. In 1957 archaeologists discovered a mosaic in Qasr el-Lebia, Libya, depicting a strange half-and-half instrument, with both a guitarlike neck and the arms of a kithara. The mosaic dates from after the conquest of Alexandria in 642 and is the earliest direct evidence of a kithara-guitar metamorphosis. The Utrecht Psalter, executed in the diocese of Reims around 850 but probably based on sources from the fifth or sixth centuries, shows both an ancient kithara as well as a kithara-shaped instrument with a fretted neck instead of a crossbar. The arms of the kithara remained as ornamental wings. (The kithara-shaped "lyre guitar" enjoyed a sudden vogue in the early nineteenth century, and Empress Marie-Louise presented such an instrument, given her by Napoleon, to Giuliani. In 1823 the virtuoso performed several concerts in Naples on this "Lira di Apollo.")

It could have become so many different things! By the twelfth century in Europe there had been a wild proliferation of stringed instruments somewhere in between the kithara and the guitar. The troubadours used these instruments to accompany their songs. However, it is often impossible to tell from the name what instrument is meant. In medieval writings we encounter the kithara, as well as the *kitaire, quitare, getern, gittern, guiterne,* and *guitarra.* The word *guitar* was not introduced into English until 1621, when Ben Jonson used it in a play called *The Gypsies Metamorphosed.* Thereafter the term referred to the instrument we know today, even if it was spelled variously *kittar, gittar, gytarrh, guytar, gitar,* and *ghittar.*

But as in most stories of development, the guitar was shaped primarily by competition. As the kithara fumbled for identity in Europe, the Moors in Spain patiently cultivated their ouds. The Moors, though despised by the Spanish natives, had brought with them the high culture of the Arabic world, which made the courts of Córdoba, Málaga, and Seville renowned centers of music and poetry. The most famous oud player in Arabic Spain was Abul-l-Hasan 'Ali ibn Nafi', known as Ziryāb, the Blackbird. He was a black slave, educated in Baghdad but expelled from court there by his teacher, who apparently feared the younger musician's greater talent. In 822 Ziryāb arrived in Córdoba, where he served the court of the Andalusian emir. His vibrant tone emanated from strings said to be made from the intestines of lion cubs.

Between the ninth and the thirteenth centuries oud music slowly radiated out from Moorish courts into the Spanish countryside and so to the rest of Europe. There it mingled and ultimately merged with the traditions of kithara-playing left behind by the Romans. Both the lute and the early guitar were thus played throughout Europe during the Middle Ages and the Renaissance. Both were popular and cultivated instruments, used to accompany love songs, work songs, sailing songs, and ballads of adventure. Yet by tricks of fate and language, and through the vagaries of human sentiment and prejudice, it was the lute that came to dominate European court music, while the guitar became an instrument of the common people. Like the kithara and the lyra, the guitar and lute tangled in the limbo of cultural symbolism, and this time the guitar lost.

In translating the works of Plato, Aristotle, and Pythagoras, Arab scholars used the words most familiar to them, rendering the Greek *lyre* with the Arabic *oud*. As classical learning passed into the cultures of Europe, therefore, the lute, and not the guitar, inherited the kithara's mystical aura. Throughout the Renaissance, European philosophers, poets, and musicians would attribute to the lute the magical powers of Apollo, Amphion, and Orpheus. The lute became the philosopher's instrument, the symbol of neoclassical humanism, of learning and courtly love, while the guitar—though more closely related to the kithara—inherited the aristocracy's disdain for peasants and the Christian philosophers' mistrust of the body, women, and pleasure. It could have become so many things. But in the end it became this.

By the middle of the fourteenth century, Petrarch and Boccaccio were singing the lute's praises as the instrument of divine love. In

contemporary texts and illustrations, by contrast, the guitar signified subversion, agitation, political and social protest, and scan-
dalous eroticism. A twelfth-century Passional, now in the Royal
Library in Stuttgart, shows Saint Pelagia of Antioch riding a don-
key, accompanied by two companions, one of whom holds a guitar.
The guitar is not an innocent prop. The illustration depicts Saint
Pelagia prior to her sainthood, when she lived the life of a dancer
and courtesan. The guitar signals that she is still a sinner. The lute
was elevated, pure; the guitar was common, debased. And so it
would remain for the next five hundred years.

In 1554 the Merchants Adventurers Company in Newcastle,
England, swore out a complaint against its own apprentices for their
"lewd liberty," which included "dicing, carding and mumming,
what tippling, dancing, and brazing of harlots . . . what use of guitars at night—what wearing of beards." When police broke up the
Beatles' rooftop concert in January 1969, the Fab Four might have
saluted John Swetenham, William Garlthorp, and John Pycard. In
1381 these three men became the first British musicians sent to jail
for making a disturbance with "giternes."

It was a harsh blow for the guitar to leave the home of its mythical
ancestors. And yet I can't help but feel grateful for this abrupt
expulsion. Freed of its conventional, neoclassical heritage, the
instrument remained polymorphous and perverse. The classical
guitar hasn't always been sweet. From the fifteenth to the seventeenth century, its image as the instrument of sin lent it great expressive freedom. Derided in one era as lascivious, the guitar became
appealing to the next for the same reason. It could shock, it could
scandalize, it could seduce. And each new affront to reigning styles
and morals gave the guitar greater musical complexity and range,
enabling it to mature, to grow into its body. If you wanted to test the
tolerance of your times, then, all you had to do was flirt with the

guitar. Whereas for the next few centuries, not a single lute player was arrested.

During the reign of Henri II in France, the guitar enjoyed a sudden vogue when the king used it to serenade his mistress, Diane de Poitiers. I see him kneeling beneath her window, singing the 1546 romance "Gárdame las Vacas," or "Watch the Cows," the first published music for guitar, and its first association with cowboy music since Hermes gave the instrument to Apollo.

> *Watch the cows for me, and I shall kiss you,*
> *If not, kiss me, and I will watch the cows for you.*

Mademoiselle Poitiers swooned picturesquely, and in 1556 an anonymous observer at court wrote, "We used to play the lute more than the guitar, but for twelve or fifteen years now everyone has been guitaring, and the lute is nearly forgotten."

The Renaissance guitar played at the French court was the size of a ukulele, and instead of six strings it had four pairs or "courses" of strings, each note doubled to increase the instrument's volume. (The same principle gives the twelve-string folk guitar its resonance.) Myth holds that the poet and con man Vincente Espinel introduced the guitar's fifth string. Espinel was a friend of Cervantes and seems to have led an unconventional life. He was expelled from university, became a priest but was removed from office, and ended up writing erotic poems that were banned in Spain. The legend that he created the five-course Baroque guitar is based on a line from Lope de Vega's play *Dorotea*, written in 1632, eight years after Espinel's death.

> May heaven forgive that Espinel! He has brought us those new verses, *décimas* or *espinelas*, and the five strings of the guitar, so that now everyone forgets the old noble instruments as well as the old dances, what with these wild gesticulations and lascivi-

ous movements of the *chaconne,* which are so offensive to the virtue, the chastity, and the seemly silence of the ladies.

The guitar is coming of age. It is for dancing, for sex; it is a voice raised against convention and social constraint. And therefore—it is a threat, something foreign, deplorable, requiring censure, yet secretly enticing.

Just two years earlier, in 1630, French theorist Pierre Trichet published a treatise on musical instruments in which he asked rhetorically: "For who is not aware that the lute is what is proper and suitable for the French, and the most delightful of all musical instruments? Still, there are some of our nation who leave everything behind in order to take up and study the guitar. Isn't this because it is much easier to perfect oneself in this than in lute playing . . . ? Or is it because it has a certain something which is feminine and pleasing to women, flattering their hearts and making them inclined to voluptuousness?"

Subversive, vulgar, and immoral, the guitar didn't need rock 'n' roll to become a public nuisance. (You can almost hear Trichet screaming upstairs to his kids, "Turn down that awful noise!") Like the electric guitar in the 1950s, the five-course Baroque guitar was an instrument of cultural transformation. It was played in a hodgepodge of styles, and in its songs and dances the Old World met the New, and the music of an underclass achieved mainstream success.

Like Espinel's *chaconne,* the sarabande or *zarabanda* originated as a dance among the indigenous peoples of Latin America. Brought to Europe by Spanish sailors, it was played on the guitar. In a treatise from the late sixteenth century condemning public entertainments, Juan de Mariana considered the sarabande "so lascivious in its words, so ugly in its movements, that it is enough to inflame even very honest people." In the 1590s in Spain, a public performance of the sarabande was punishable by two hundred lashes. By 1606, however, it had been sufficiently tempered to be included in books of guitar music, and by 1610 the sarabande was a dance craze throughout Europe. A hundred years later Bach routinely included a sarabande in his suites. Nevertheless, as late as 1789, Spain and Spanish dances had a reputation as severe threats to the self-discipline and moral rectitude of honest northern Europeans. The French traveler J. F. Bourgoing confronted this ambiguous challenge that year, writing, "a Spanish female dancing the *seguidilla* . . . is one of the most seducing objects which love can employ to extend its empire."

As a result, the five-course Baroque guitar was referred to as the "Spanish" guitar, though it would be Italians who spread the instrument across the continent. But since the Italians adopted the term, it came into general usage and continues to be used today to refer to the classical guitar. (In 1939, when the Gibson guitar company introduced its first hollow-body electric guitar, they dubbed it the ES-150, with *ES* standing for "electric Spanish.")

Still, it is not clear in what respect the "Spanish guitar" is really Spanish. The instrument and its repertoire emerged from a constant interchange among the cultures of Europe, beginning with the Greeks and Romans, continuing through the Spanish Moors, and then achieving modern form simultaneously in Italy, Germany, France, and Spain. In the late sixteenth and early seventeenth centuries, the center of guitar-building was in northern Italy, though all the surviving guitars from the period were made by Germans. After 1640, activity shifted to France, where the patronage of Louis XIV spurred a lively demand for new "Spanish" guitars. At the same time the Spanish preferred a different instrument, called a *vihuela*, which was guitarlike but not a guitar and was played solely in Spain. The guitar proper didn't become widespread there until late in the eighteenth century. It doesn't matter. Symbol layers upon symbol. Then as now, *Spanish* served as a code word for the exotic, the racy, the anxiety and allure of otherness. The "Spanish guitar" conveyed the emotional music of these things, the fear of assimilation and moral ambiguity, the thrill of creative fertility, and an intimation of unbridled expression.

I wonder how the guitar might have been different if it had been left to develop by itself at this time. All the essentials of its form and technique were present, though it still had a lot of growing up to do. But this was not to be. It's painful to look back on this moment of promise. Once again the instrument will be shaped by competition, and this time its image will suffer profound and enduring harm.

Louis XIV's guitar teacher was an Italian, Francesco Corbetta, the most famous guitarist of his day. By the time he arrived in Paris to teach the young king, Corbetta had already established himself as a leading virtuoso, serving in quick succession the Duke of Mantua and the Archduke of Austria. In Paris, his pupils included not only King Louis but also the temporarily deposed King Charles II of England. In 1660, when Charles was restored to the throne, Samuel Pepys was charged with escorting the royal guitar safely to London. Pepys noted in his diary, "I troubled much with the king's gittar. . . . Methinks it is but a bauble." On August 5, 1667, Pepys heard Corbetta perform at court. He confided after the concert, "I was mightily troubled that all that pains should have been taken up on so bad an instrument."

Pepys played the lute. We're used to this sort of thing by now. His arrogance might even enhance our pleasure in the fact that he was wrong. Alas, poor Pepys! Like your king, your instrument's time is running out.

"If a lutenist lives to be eighty years old," quipped Johann Mattheson, a German music critic, in 1713, "surely he has spent sixty years tuning." By 1700 the lute had evolved into highly complex form, with eight, eleven, and even thirteen courses of strings. The difficulty of managing an instrument with twenty-five or twenty-six gut strings created an insurmountable obstacle to its development. The expense alone was prohibitive. In Mattheson's calculations, "it costs as much to keep a lute in Paris as it does a horse." European tolerance for neoclassical ideals had also waned in a more rational age. And so, having gloried so long in the borrowed finery of the mythical lyre, the lute now became the symbol of everything old-fashioned. By 1800 it was virtually extinct. Another sad story, though it also makes me want to gloat. Say what you want about the guitar, no one would ever play the air lute; no one would ever set an electric lute on fire.

The guitar and the lute had divided the world between them, into physical and spiritual realms, the base and the cultured. Then, after a competition lasting nearly half a millennium, the lute faded from the scene. Did the guitar now finally receive its due? No. Instead, strangely, tragically, at the very moment the instrument emerged in its modern, six-string form; at the moment its greatest classical performers and composers arrived to carry it to musical perfection; at the moment its listeners seemed inclined toward enlightened objectivity, the guitar was blindsided by a new rival, and this collision sent it tumbling into fantasies of denial from which it still hasn't quite recovered.

In 1709 Bartolomeo Cristofori had published a description of his new invention, the pianoforte. Over the following decades this instrument —along with the increasing preference for bowed strings over plucked—rendered the conflict between the lute and the guitar moot. The guitar blossomed in its new freedom. But while triumphant over its uptight rival, the now fully developed classical guitar met a force it could not resist: Romanticism. Once more the symbolic wheel turns. The violin and piano, fueled by the demonic energies of Beethoven, Paganini, and Liszt, spirited away the guitar's role as the instrument of sex, subversion, and rebellion. In the same instant it achieved musical maturity, therefore, the guitar's symbolic development was stunted. "On occasions of boating, while sailing in calm tranquillity on the silvery bosom of some quiet or rippling lake, whilst the moon may lend its mild rays to the scene—at such a moment, what could be so sweet and touching as the music from this instrument?" Instead of symbolizing sin, the guitar became the new image of feminine virtue and sentimentality. Women and the guitar were made of the same stuff, musicians and critics now relentlessly asserted. The instrument "echoes their sportive gaiety, their little griefs, calm tranquillity and noble and elevated thoughts, with such nice precision, that it would seem to be a natural append-age and true barometer of the state of their own fair bosoms."

The music freezes in my hands. After six measures of ghostly har-monics and dark, probing bass notes, Rodrigo's "Invocación" pauses for breath, then urgently asserts the theme. Again, the lowest tones are moving, while the higher ones respond with nervous flut-tering. Here. Right here, my hands seize in panic. Holding the two lines together is too difficult; I can't do both things at once.

I can't. And yet I am. It's happening despite what I think. The lines reach in opposite directions, stretching me. This irresistible urgency of what is inside, and the resistance, the fear—worse, the condescension, trivialization, the blithe refusal to take this music seriously. This is where I have always frozen; this is what angered and frustrated and embittered me as nothing before in my life, and what no amount of practicing could seem to change: what I felt and heard, and the voice that always said "No, you can't, you *shouldn't*," a voice I found repeated with such authority throughout the guitar's history. This is what I seized on to express what I could not play. Not that the guitar was a woman but that it embodied denial, a repressive fantasy of how I *ought* to behave, what I was allowed to feel. This moment, when the guitar was strangled, suppressed, frozen in a solid block of domestic comfort and artificial sentiment. The guitar and women—both treated like children whom no one wants to grow up. And I, as a child dreaming the romantic dream of becoming an artist, a guitarist, a man, identified with and fought against this image, this fate, this confinement, because the other struggle was too overwhelming. "Their sportive gaiety, their little griefs." I clenched my fists; music froze in my hands. And this was what I practiced, the childhood battle for respect and acceptance all knotted up in six strings. I feel it still, this paralysis, right now as I reach for an adult's full range of emotion. An old, inescapable story, one that I never knew how to live through, never trusted my ability to release.

I let my hands relax, then try the passage again, the two lines together in Rodrigo's "Invocation and Dance." Is this work really too difficult? Perhaps it can be different now. The music is *here*, not beyond me. It just takes time to learn. Time, attention, patience, and forgiveness.

It takes practice.

At this great and tragic moment in the guitar's history, Dionisio Aguado stepped in, declaring the instrument "sweet, harmonious, and melancholy." Was he joining in the era's domestic fantasy? I don't think so. No, I see Aguado sitting up late at night with his friend Fernando Sor, discussing the fate of their beloved guitar. It is 1835 in Paris. Both men are renowned virtuosos at the height of their careers. They are sitting over a glass of absinthe reading this latest inanity from the pen of a priggish critic.

" 'The state of their own fair bosoms!' " the younger Aguado spits, tossing the paper into the fire. "How can we make them *listen*?"

And Sor, still smarting from every nasty review he's ever received, answers, "We can't."

"But these are just words," Aguado protests. "There are others. *Majestic . . . mysterious . . .*"

Sor shakes his head. He's had this discussion before, and it has never made sense to him. "Why must you find other words or compare the guitar with the piano or violin? Those are fine instruments too. But is one more perfect, more expressive, than the other?"

He puts his glass down and begins to play. It's just an étude, Opus 31, no. 4, in B Minor. Just thirty-two measures, less than a minute long. And yet while he plays, everything is there, a fullness of music.

"The guitar is greater than you are," he says to his friend. "Every instrument is. Give yourself to this greatness, let it open your heart and expand your imagination. But don't confine its spirit with your words. Make the music you can," he sighs, settling back in his chair, "and let the guitar be the guitar."

kitchen music

"WHAT IF MOZART had used Wagner's rhythms?" A month
into the new semester my composition teacher was sitting
at the piano. He was a short, cheerfully rotund man, and he leaned
back from the keyboard to give his belly adequate room for expression. He started to play a Mozart piano sonata in C major, a piece
nearly every beginning piano student plays. But instead of supporting the melody with a crisp arpeggio in the left hand, he puffed the
notes out in billowing clouds of harmony. His face contorted in
mock agony as he rocked back and forth over the keys.

"Now what if Wagner had used Mozart's rhythms?" he asked
after the class had stopped laughing. He played the overture to
Tristan and Isolde. But rather than clusters of tones unfurling like
cigarette smoke, he tapped a steady sixteenth-note pulse, like a
horse-drawn carriage crossing cobblestones. He sat straight-backed
and wide-eyed, looking at us with curiosity.

The performance was a criticism. We were studying "microtonal composition," and the teacher, Joseph Maneri, wanted us to
hear things we'd never heard before.

The Conservatory's curriculum, just like Juilliard's, had originally been designed for orchestral musicians, with the goal of per-

petuating the grand tradition from Bach to Mozart to Beethoven to Mahler. In my other classes—harmony, ear training, music history—I learned about the origins of Western musical conventions. But in Joe's composition class we had to throw that all away. In 1974 the Conservatory's president, Gunther Schuller, had pioneered a program called Third Stream, designed to explore new genres at the intersection of jazz, classical, and world music. The school continued to train orchestral players; after all, Beethoven still dominated the lobby. But wild and audacious experiments were taking place off in the corners of the music building. "Microtones" are notes smaller than a half-step in the Western musical scale. During the mid-seventeenth century in Europe, the musical scale was standardized with a system called equal temperament, which divided the octave into twelve evenly spaced notes: C, C sharp, D, and so on. But the well-tempered scale is not based on natural acoustics. Instead, it is a rational ordering of what, in nature, is a more disorderly reality. Other cultures—for example, Arabic, Indian, and Chinese—do not use the West's twelve tones.

In the early twentieth century a few composers experimented with quarter-tones, dividing the twelve tones in half, creating an octave of twenty-four notes. The Hungarian György Ligeti composed quarter-tonal music for string ensemble in 1968, though he is more famous for his eerie, otherworldly *Requiem*, which was used in the soundtrack for Stanley Kubrick's 1968 film *2001: A Space Odyssey*. In microtonal composition we worked with a vastly larger palette than quarter-tones: an octave of seventy-two notes. These were sounds literally unheard of in Western music.

"Look at this," Joe said, waving a stack of our assignments in front of him as he got up from the piano. "Da-de-da-de-da. Pages and pages of it."

He dropped the sheaf of music paper on a desk and wandered over to the chalkboard. He took a fresh white chalk stick and pressed it to the board until it cracked. Pieces bounced off the board's aluminum ledge and fell to the floor.

"Did you hear that?" he asked, turning suddenly toward the class. He imitated the sound. "Tch-kre-btshoff-duhnnnn." He wiped his mouth on the back of his hand. "There are new rhythms everywhere. Why are you still going 'da-de-da-de-da'?"

Joe had started his career as a saxophone and clarinet player, performing jazz and traditional Greek, Turkish, and Jewish music. In the 1950s, he studied composition with Joseph Schmid, a student of Alban Berg and Arnold Schoenberg. Since the seventies he had been composing with microtones, pushing into unknown territory. In class we were supposed to follow him, inventing a new mode of musical expression with this expanded scale. Faced with microtones, musical structure as we'd understood it—melody, harmony, rhythm, and notes themselves—disintegrated, revealing a bizarre quantum level of interaction. But we were being too conventional; we weren't listening carefully enough. Playing unheard-of harmonies to familiar rhythms was like setting Wagner's melodies to Mozart's phrases, Joe was saying. He hounded us to break the musical habits we were all working so hard to acquire.

"Listen to people talking," he said, twisting a plastic Baggie that he'd found on the floor into a knot, then holding it under his nose like a mustache. "They don't speak in Wagner."

We went back to our exercises. I was sitting next to my friend Patrick, the violist I'd met in my first year. We balanced notebooks on our knees, holding our pencils ready, waiting to conjure something new from the air. Then someone nearby laughed. We tried to notate the rhythm.

"Did you make that four-four or three-four?" Pat asked.

Microtones forced us to reconsider the basic materials of music. What's a microtonal time signature? What are microtonal dynamics? The first twenty minutes of class each day were devoted simply to learning to hear the notes. Using a primitive monochord—a single wire stretched along a piece of wood, the same instrument Pythagoras used to discover the mathematics of vibrating strings— Joe taught us the fine gradations, making us sing the five new tones between C and C sharp. When we got it right, we sounded wildly out of tune, like a junior high school orchestra. But it changed how we heard. After a month of Joe's radical ear training, everything *else* sounded harshly dissonant. Playing an ordinary scale felt like traveling between the planets, the distances had become so great. A violinist dropped the class, complaining that Joe had ruined his hearing. He could no longer find the correct intonation when he played with the orchestra. The rest of us stumbled around with the strained, pinched expressions that musicians wear when pitches are not quite right.

Debating how to notate a laugh with Pat, I sensed for a moment the vertiginous leap that Joe made every day. Everything we'd been taught to value in musical style fell away. The music that we loved and wanted to keep hearing forever suddenly sounded impossibly ancient. Beethoven, Bach, Mozart—they were hundreds of years old, from a time when fifteen miles was a good day's journey, when bleeding was at the forefront of medical technology. For a moment, I sensed the giddy weightlessness that Joe must feel, the freedom to begin again in each moment. Then I read back what Pat and I had written. A strange rhythm by itself meant nothing. The unfamiliar notes had to make it necessary. And the rhythm needed to inhabit the notes, until together they felt inevitable. To use this freedom and make it sound *right*—for this there were no guidelines. We were feeling our way forward, but all of us were afraid to fall.

"Brrr-ba-kwang-Zak-ga-zak!" Joe was waving his hands over his head and shaking his hips, demonstrating something to a group of students in the corner. He was a restless, sometimes goofy man pushing himself to create a whole new music.

Pat and I tapped our pencils against the desktop.

"It's very possible that this man is a genius," he whispered.

⌢

"Find your place among the great people," insisted Leopold Mozart in a letter to his twenty-two-year-old son. Wolfgang was dawdling in Mannheim, where he had a girlfriend but no job, instead of moving to Paris, the cultural capital of Europe. His father furiously exhorted him to have ambition commensurate with his gifts. *"Aut Caesar aut nihil!"* Leopold commanded, "Be Caesar or be nothing." This was a fine motto for Mozart. For most of us, though, it's a dismal threat.

I was in my third year at the Conservatory, trying to find my place among the great musicians there. I knew I wasn't going to become a microtonal composer; nor was Pat or any of the other students in the class. Microtones were Joe's medium. But I think everyone in that room shared Joe's ambition to hear what had never been heard before and to let others hear it too. Even the most conventional pianist was striving to make warhorses sound new, if only through the tiniest subtleties of interpretation. Joe wielded a strange and shocking palette in order to realize the music in his head. Yet played with an equally experimental sensibility, even the Moonlight Sonata could become shocking, could fly off the cliff and make your ears roar with the boundless openness of each moment. All it took was an imaginative leap, breaking through the comfortable habits of hearing that made the notes always sound the same. Each day Joe demonstrated that it could be done. Yet most of the time, when you take an imaginative leap, you fall, at least at first. There is a compelling safety to hearing the notes the way you've always heard them, to reproducing the music you love rather than risking something unknown. And in the end not many of us are Caesar.

Before returning to school that year, I'd gone with my parents to see Peter Shaffer's play *Amadeus* on Broadway. The Milos Forman movie based on the play hadn't been made yet, and we knew only the bare outline of the plot when we took our seats in the orchestra section of the Broadhurst Theater. In the play Ian McKellen starred as Antonio Salieri, the most successful musician of his day, court composer to the Emperor Joseph II of Austria. Salieri is a conscientious and competent musician. As a child, he had prayed for fame and honor, and his prayers were answered. Flourishing in the emperor's service, Salieri is prolific and popular. Soon his music is celebrated throughout Europe. Enter Mozart. Sublime, infantile Wolfgang Amadeus Mozart.

In Mozart's music, Salieri recognizes something divinely inspired, absolute, and perfect. But what he hears ruins him. Confronted by this beauty beyond his ability to achieve, Salieri suffers his own talent and success in agony. "Thirty years of being called 'distinguished' by people incapable of distinguishing!" he cries, as the Viennese cheer him, while casually disregarding the genius in their midst. "If I cannot be Mozart then I do not wish to be anything." He gets his wish. Mozart is posthumously declared immortal, and Salieri, still alive, is utterly forgotten, the patron saint of the undistinguished. In his last line, the old, discarded court composer addresses the modern audience directly, all those who, like him, are not worth listening to. "Mediocrities everywhere—now and to come—I absolve you all," he says, sympathizing with our failure to be Mozart.

Driving home from Manhattan, my parents talked excitedly about the powerful acting and the gripping story. For them, it was a satisfying night of theater. I felt shattered by it. For me, Salieri embodied what I feared the most, that my talent would condemn me to mediocrity. When we got home, after my parents went to bed, I shut myself in the kitchen and practiced.

Looking back, however, I think *Amadeus* tells a different story from the one I rejected then. The play's dramatic power comes from its most unrealistic element. The Salieri that Shaffer created hears with the ears of history; he knows all along what only later listeners could know. When Mozart arrived in Vienna in 1781, his talent was obvious and undeniable, but his genius was still a matter of opinion. He wasn't yet *Mozart*. Peter Shaffer stacked the deck against Salieri by giving his self-doubts the weight of historical certainty. Because Salieri knows Mozart is a genius, his own failure then seems inevitable. But the real weight that he and every artist— every person who strives for greatness—suffers is the weight of not knowing. You must find in yourself the courage to leap off the cliff. Yet it is not up to you whether you fly or fall.

Early in December, as the music building's heaters practiced clanking, a group of guitarists claimed the large rehearsal space across the hall from the Beethoven statue for an informal workshop. John and Manuel, friends from my first year, cleared away the heavy black music stands that cluttered the room like charred trees. Lila, Marcus, and I arranged the folding chairs into rows, while Damien and a few others rolled our coats into logs and lined the door and windowsills with them to stop the draft. We drew numbers to determine the order.

Marcus, the RA from my freshman year, was the unacknowledged leader of the younger guitarists. He was soft-spoken and generous, always willing to listen and offer advice. Not everyone liked his playing. But we respected his insight and his commitment to this forum for performance and critique. He had an abiding faith in the value of community to foster good playing. The reality, however, didn't always live up to his vision.

Lila, a master's student like Marcus, performed first, playing her own transcription of a harpsichord sonata by Domenico Scarlatti. She had the expressions of a mischievous child but was one of the most accomplished guitarists at the school. The music suited her personality. It was sprightly, with an unusual sequence of modulations in the middle that tweaked the listener's ears. Lila had been working on it all semester, revising the way it sat on the instrument. She played the sonata twice for the group, testing different tempos in front of an audience. As she read from her cramped and crossed-out manuscript, she conducted the phrases with her face, swooping upward with her chin while her eyes tightened into sharp, staccato points.

When she finished playing, the discussion focused on a particular passage where two contrasting phrases intersected. Something wasn't right, but we couldn't agree what. John, who had a wrestler's physique and favored music by South American composers, thought it was Lila's timing. Manuel, who seemed more like a basketball star, with lanky hands and a rhythmic drooping in his shoulders as he played, felt it was her articulation. For several minutes, we went back and forth inconclusively, as Lila tried out different ideas.

After listening silently to the debate for a little while, Damien got up with a show of impatience. He was a blond, sarcastic boy, two years ahead of me, whose fingers were endowed with a mysterious precision, like manual perfect pitch. It lent him an aura that intimidated younger players. When I'd first heard him play, I'd realized I could practice scales for the rest of my life and still never match Damien's fluency. But most imposing of all, Damien had taken lessons from Segovia. It had been many years ago, when Damien was a child. But he still gloried in it, and he walked through the Conservatory halls with a superior smirk, indifferent and self-satisfied, as if all this practicing didn't concern him. Standing over Lila, holding his instrument awkwardly and resting his foot on her chair, he read from her scrawled score. At sight, with no preparation, he played the troublesome passage.

"You're letting *this* finger push *this* one off the string," he said, demonstrating. "It's your fingering that's bad."

Then Damien sat down again, smiling in a sad, pitying way, as if to say, "You might as well give up, there's just no hope for you."

Lila tried the different fingering. The problem disappeared. She was happy with this solution. The flaw was just in her fingering after all, not her playing. But John and Manuel and the rest of us sat quietly, impressed and annoyed. Why hadn't we caught the problem? Was Damien really so much better?

Yet Damien's playing was not unassailable. The Conservatory was full of technical virtuosos who didn't understand the notes their fingers so infallibly played. When his turn came, he chose a showpiece we all wished we could play, "El Colibri" by Julio Sagreras, which imitates a hummingbird in flight and is among the most technically demanding works for the guitar. He played flawlessly, then took his seat again in the audience, almost daring us to find fault with his performance.

"It was kind of harsh," said Manuel bravely, speaking of Damien's tone and phrasing.

Several of us nodded in agreement. Naturally we envied Damien and his impeccable technique, but as one envies the insipid rich—all that money, and look what he wastes it on. "He's technically amazing," one of us was always saying, "but he isn't musical." I heard someone speak this criticism almost every day, leveled at one envied performer or another. It was a great equalizer, implying that no matter how swift or precise one's fingers, something essential yet intangible was lacking. Spectacular but shallow. It allowed us to shake our heads sadly, pityingly too, just like Damien himself, as if to say, "Such facile fingers, but still there's no hope for you. You might as well give up."

"Try making the melody lighter, more . . . like something living," said Marcus mildly, struggling to define the missing quality in Damien's playing. "Let the phrases breathe," he said, almost purring as he spoke. Then he picked up his guitar, crossed his legs, and played the first few measures of the piece just as fast, just as precisely as Damien had, but gracefully, as if the notes were hovering in the air, sensitive to the slightest disturbance. Marcus was doing what he always did, trying to be a good teacher. But I too sniggered silently along with the others, hearing the nasty, talented Damien put in his place.

In the drafty palace of the Hapsburgs, it had probably been the same with Salieri and Mozart. In 1781, without the distance of history, questions of interpretation and of the quality of musical ideas were equally matters of opinion. For us, as instrumentalists playing a standard repertoire, the differences were very slight. We were hardly on the knife's edge of music, like Joe Maneri was. He stood alone, outside the tradition, coaxing new sounds from nothingness. We were interpreters of a tradition, and so we vied with one another over obvious things, technique and tone, while defensively banding together to criticize those we disliked. Like a gang of sour children, we would greet a new recording by Eliot Fisk with upturned noses, commenting, "Too rushed," "Too anxious." Or we'd sit in the balcony of Jordan Hall listening to Julian Bream perform and conclude, "Sloppy; overwrought." The Conservatory was a place of intense ambitions. Our careers—our faith in ourselves—depended on hearing more *music* in the notes than others. But the intensity of our ambition found expression most often in pettiness. We listened for mistakes rather than for inspiration, as if saying, "If I'm not the best, then no one should be."

When it was my turn to play, I chose a piece as different from "El Colibri" as possible, Manuel de Falla's "Homage on the Death of Debussy." Rather than competing technically, I wanted to demonstrate how deeply I understood music. It is often much harder to play slow, spare music than something brilliant and chatty. With these brooding, articulate silences and mournful outbursts, I thought, I could shame the more facile and advanced players into acknowledging my superiority.

"It sounded kind of the same all the way through," said John hesitantly. "Maybe you could vary the dynamics and tone more." The others nodded.

"Especially here, in the middle," Damien said, pointing to the one fast passage in the piece. "You need to really let loose here to contrast with the beginning and end."

They were probably right. If it had been one of them performing, I would have said the same things. But instead of being helpful, these comments drained the freedom from my playing. I *heard* a profound range of emotion in the music. But expressing it, displaying it unprotected before this group of politely vicious friends, was too scary. The fear of not being good enough narrowed my performance, just as it sharpened our comments. If the music sounded the same all the way through, this meant, "You're boring." If the fast passage didn't let loose, it meant, "You're rigid." It was reassuring to say these things to others. We were all pretty good. But with no way to know who was really the best, we found our certainty in criticism. Whatever their musical merit, most of these comments really asserted, "If I can correct your mistakes, I must be better." Mozart probably felt the same way. And Salieri must have felt it just as much. The tragedy isn't that one was truly a genius. To know this, years must pass, and even then our judgments are usually subject to revision. No, the tragedy is that, for most of us, competition made our music feel smaller; what we heard ruined us.

Yet who decides what is musical? The composer when he conceives the notes as an abstract form? The musician when he realizes them on an instrument in performance? The audience when they sit silently listening?

⌢

"Believe me," Mozart assured his father in a letter from 1781, shortly after his arrival in Vienna, "my sole purpose is to make as much money as possible; for after good health, it is the best thing to have."

At the Conservatory, we would stay up all night debating whose performances were most musical. But we all agreed what it meant to succeed: to have a solo career; to tour the world giving concerts; to make great music. Naturally we expected some money to be involved. But money wasn't what we were after. That kind of success seemed paltry next to our artistic ambitions. Still, there was something undeniably satisfying in making money, and with only vague ideas about how to achieve artistic success, we peevishly accepted the objective clarity of financial success. We hated the values of the marketplace. Nevertheless, we wanted to succeed.

As students, it was difficult for us to arrange concert performances. I mostly performed for my fellow guitarists, and only once or twice each year did I participate in an outside concert at a church, a local library, or a school. But there was plenty of other work for us, if we wanted it. Every day the Conservatory received calls from people seeking music for a party, a wedding, or a gallery opening. Here the market for orchestral musicians was very small. Precious few people in Boston resembled Haydn's patron Prince Esterházy, who employed a private orchestra as part of his kitchen staff because he liked hearing symphonies after dinner. The jobs coming into the Gig Office were for harp, string quartet, perhaps a wine-and-cheese jazz group—and classical guitar. These are the best instruments for background music. They're pleasant, atmospheric, unobtrusive. Beginning in my second year I played one of these jobs almost every week. When you are an unknown artist, people want to listen to your concerts for free. But they will pay well for the privilege of not listening, if they can chat and sip a cocktail while you play.

Through the Gig Office, I worked at a private party in a Brookline mansion, where three drunken executives sang along to Billy Joel's "Just the Way You Are." I performed at the gala opening of a department store lingerie shop, complete with sashaying models and champagne, both serious impediments to good technique. As a last-minute replacement for an ailing friend, I accompanied a violinist at the Italian-American Friendship Society's annual luncheon in Boston's North End. Standing under a vine-wrapped trellis, we played opera arias for three hours, dressed in tuxedos with red bow ties and matching cummerbunds.

The high point of my commercial success as a musician at the Conservatory was a wedding in Newport, Rhode Island, in the spring of my third year. It was an overcast morning when I arrived at the small seaside chapel. The wedding party was preparing the space, setting flowers and laying place cards on the pews. Only after I'd taken a seat in the back did the bride's mother inform me that I was part of the service. The couple had asked me to prepare "their song" for the reception, but now it turned out they'd written the whole ceremony themselves and wanted the song as the grand conclusion. And so, after the quotations from Shakespeare on the endurance of love, I performed an arrangement of "Memory," from the musical *Cats*. When I finished, a kilted bagpipe player led the wedding party and their guests down to the shore, where we boarded a seventy-foot yacht and spent the rest of the day cruising around Newport Harbor.

All afternoon I played classical guitar on the fantail. The sky had cleared and the sun glinted blindingly on the water. A mariachi band was strolling somewhere in a forward compartment, and the wail of a trumpet escaped each time someone opened the door to come out on deck. I sat in the shade of an awning beneath a large American flag, which snapped percussively in the breeze. The engines rumbled beneath me, their vibrations rising through my footstool. I played every piece I knew, and when I ran out of repertoire, I sight-read from a book of études I'd bought a few days before. I took every repeat. When I got to the end of the book, I started over, playing each piece at a new tempo.

One middle-aged gentleman, tall and red-faced and quite distinguished in his formal tails, kept circling back to where I was sitting.

He'd stand listening for a few minutes, and then, before returning inside, he'd strike a rock 'n' roll pose and make electric guitar sounds with his mouth, "Neerw-neerw-neerw," helping me along as I played.

Later, as the sun began to set, I stood by the railing on a break. A glamorous, flirtatious woman approached me.

"Ah, the *geeter* player," she said, leaning back against the railing and looking up at the seagulls circling above. She found parties boring, she said. What could I play that would entertain her? I cut short my break and launched into "Capricho Arabe," hoping I'd found a receptive audience. She stood at the railing, staring dreamily across the water.

"Thank you," she sighed when I was finished. "That was so lovely I almost fell asleep."

In other respects, however, the afternoon was a great success. When we docked at sunset, the inebriated, elated bride added a forty percent tip on top of my regular wedding fee of fifty dollars an hour. The total was more than a month's rent and expenses for me at the time. At an art gallery opening I might make twenty or thirty dollars for a few hours. A holiday office party might be as much as a hundred, plus free drinks.

Driving home from the Newport wedding, I laughed at how easy it was to make money from people who couldn't distinguish good music from bad. As I passed the imposing mansions that lined the shore, I found myself thinking it might even be pleasant to live without the struggle, the competition, and this practicing, always practicing. If I wanted to, I could make a good living, lead a comfortable life like my parents. I didn't need to get better. I was already good enough to support myself. Few of my teachers at the Conservatory had achieved the kind of performing career I imagined for myself. Most of them had hybrid identities—musician-teacher, musician-musicologist. One of the best guitarists I knew was a locksmith. What would be so bad about making a living performing at weddings? I could be a professional guitarist right now, never improve, and never need to practice for another instant. Besides, what was the point of refinements that only other guitarists would hear and would probably criticize in any case? Gigs demanded so little. I could perform Beethoven, or I could play scales. Either way people would tell me that it sounded lovely. Maybe that was enough.

As I unpacked my music books at home that night, I had a vision of myself in two, three, ten years, having abandoned my path of practicing, playing these same pieces for these same people at their next wedding, making pretty, classical-sounding noise to decorate the occasion. I shuddered at the thought. A life of loveliness. This was the opposite of everything I wanted. "Lovely" was nothing. It described a prettified music, drained of all power, of everything that made music great. Salieri had grown rich writing lovely music for the Viennese. Still, for all his success, no one dreams of being Salieri. If there was still the chance I could make great music, then settling for a life of "lovely" would be an unbearable betrayal.

Sitting down again to practice after dinner, I worked on a prelude by Heitor Villa-Lobos, its long, heavy lines unwinding into darkness. I wasn't sure yet how to make it musical. There were months, years of work ahead of me; there was so much more that I hadn't yet been able to perform. I was in the middle somewhere, learning to take the leap. Yet somehow that was reassuring. What did it matter if I didn't make the kind of money that bought a fancy house, a yacht, or a night on Broadway? Wasn't an artist's life preferable to a merely pleasant one? It was better not to know the value of what I played than to know for sure that it would never rise beyond "lovely." Worse than living with the uncertainty of my skill, I feared a life of insignificance, in which I played the same pieces over and over for people who couldn't *hear*. That would ruin music for me, I thought. For this reason, I was certain that my career would be different, that I would succeed. I couldn't conceive that something I labored at so passionately could come to nothing, or that something I loved so dearly could hurt me. Instead, I dreaded a different fate, a nightmare of wasted time, in which I spent my days thinking, "If only I'd listened closer, studied harder, practiced more ..."

The Cathedral

WHEN ONE vibrating body causes another to vibrate — exciting it, as they say in acoustics—the effect is called "vibrational coupling." I'm tuning the low E-string back up to pitch. Like peeking into the instrument's shadowy basement, I'd dropped the guitar's lowest string by a whole step to practice Rodrigo's "Invocación y Danza." Now, as I turn the tuning peg, the string climbs back up the step, causing different sections of the instrument to vibrate. My right thumb strikes the string, and it boings E-ward, exciting the sliver of bone, called the bridge, on which it rests. The bridge in turn excites the saddle that holds it in place, the saddle communicating this motion to the guitar's face, which then vibrates with the string's frequency, producing an audible tone, which excites me.

I'm not sure what to play next. Practicing the "Invocación" has left me feeling jittery and strange. The guitar feels foreign in my hands, unfamiliar. My fingers' warmth is still on the wood, yet it almost seems as if I've never really held the guitar before. Has the instrument changed, or is it my hands? For a moment, I sit quietly, feeling disconcerted. Can the guitar really have become a different shape? Can I?

Putting the instrument down, I walk into the kitchen to make some tea. The tea is really just an excuse to move around. Every day

I tell myself I'll have a cup. But then I start practicing again and forget to fetch it until it is cold and undrinkable. Today I'm determined to pay attention. I stand at the stove while the water boils, then wait silently for the tea to steep.

Back at my worktable, tea steaming in the sunlight, I stand the guitar on my knees. I want to see if it looks different. The top is a deep honey-colored cedar, and the back and sides are Brazilian rosewood, its flaming grain shot through with a signature golden stripe. Fine guitars are typically made from the oldest sections of mature trees, wood that ceased carrying sap hundreds of years ago. This inner section, called heartwood, is the hardest, tightest-grained, most resonant wood in the tree. But my guitar has a burst of luminous sapwood around its sides. The maker, Miguel Rodriguez of Córdoba, claimed he'd built it from the door of a deconsecrated church. The story is probably false, and the burst of color, though striking, is mostly cosmetic. Neither one has much effect on the guitar's sound. If you close your eyes and listen, the stories and appearance drop away, and all you hear is the instrument's full, responsive, hearty tone.

I close my eyes and strum the open strings. The sound is exhilarating, though I don't have any words to describe it. All the words I'm used to seem wrong, laughably inadequate. I play a few chords, just to feel their vibration. The difference I sense can't be seen. But I hear it now, as if the notes were emerging from deeper in the instrument than before, gathering more of its body with each pulse. I feel it in my chest and down into my legs. The sound is touching, penetrating. But what do I do with this feeling?

Musical instruments, like people, can choke on their words. For decades after the death of Fernando Sor in 1839, the guitar was monotonously sweet, until finally it seemed like it might die of sweetness. In 1859 Hector Berlioz heard the Romantic era's greatest virtuoso, the Italian Marco Aurelio Zani di Ferranti, and feared the worst. "Under his fingers," Berlioz wrote, "the guitar dreams and weeps; one might say that it foretells its own imminent end; it pleads for life. That poor orphan of the lute and mandolin seems to say 'Listen how I sing the beautiful melodies of Oberon, the King of the Fairies; how well I know the accent of love, discreet and timid; how my trembling voice blends with the voice of mysterious caresses! The lute is dead; the mandolin is dead, do not let me now die as well.' "

But no matter how gently Zani di Ferranti's guitar wept, no matter how many fairies Berlioz invoked, words could not rescue the guitar from its romantic slumber. Amateurs and aficionados kept the instrument alive. But no amount of dreaming or pleading could wake it. Fantasies were not what the guitar needed. It already had enough of those. What was needed instead was someone to listen carefully, without a head full of symbolic distractions. The guitar had lacked not images, but someone who would take it for what it is, who could look beneath the surface to the life inside.

For centuries, critics and guitar makers alike had been obsessed with the guitar's sensuous curves. Very few bothered to study how it actually worked. Instead guitar makers copied their construction methods from the lute. This was a mistake. Renaissance lutes employed a complex system of cross-braces to counter the pressure of the strings. These braces were thin slats of wood glued across the grain on the underside of the soundboard to provide extra strength and stability. Cross-bracing adequately supported the soundboard against the pull of the strings. But it also dampened the soundboard's vibrations, restricting the lute's tone and sustain. Worse, cross-bracing interfered with the soundboard as it responded to changes in humidity. The stress from this uneven movement could cause the soundboard to crack, even if the instrument were left unstrung. This is why so few Renaissance lutes survive. The instrument's form contradicted its function.

After the demise of the lute, however, the guitar continued to evolve. In the 1820s and 1830s, a new technique, called fan-bracing, emerged in guitar construction, and this led directly to the modern concert guitar. Louis Panormo, a luthier who was acquainted with Fernando Sor in London, made early attempts at fan-bracing his instruments, as did José Pagés and Josef Benecdid in Cádiz. An instrument by Francisco Sanguino dated 1759 is the oldest-known guitar with fan-bracing. But it was Antonio Torres who first understood and fully exploited the implications and benefits of the new method.

In 1862, just three years after Berlioz's overwrought eulogy for the guitar, Torres demonstrated that what matters is not symbolism or shape but movement. The guitar's tone is determined not by its body but by how well the string communicates its motion to the top. The secret to this communication is bracing. The modern classical guitar's six strings exert approximately ninety pounds of pull on the soundboard, depending on the length and composition of the strings. Braces prevent the instrument from self-destructing under this pressure. At the same time, however, they must be flexible enough to allow the soundboard to resonate. The lute's cross-bracing prevented the wood from vibrating freely. Fan-bracing, by contrast, enhances vibration. It divides the soundboard into sections, creating an articulated diaphragm that allows the maker to "tune" the wood. Stiff wood naturally emphasizes treble tones, while more flexible wood emphasizes the bass. By manipulating the thickness of the top and adjusting the size, shape, and placement of the inside braces, Torres learned to balance his instruments so they were clear and resonant across all registers. Working in obscurity in provincial Spain, Torres proved his discovery with a papier-mâché guitar, built with a high-quality spruce top but with sides and back of cardboard. To everyone's surprise, the instrument—now preserved at the Barcelona Conservatory—had a warm, full sound. Like the lyre's tortoise shell and the kithara's wooden sound box, the guitar's body acts as a resonator, collecting and projecting its sound. The size, shape, and construction of the body affect the instrument's volume. But full, rich tone is the result of a well-balanced soundboard. The tone of a Torres guitar was so superior to all competitors that, by the end of the nineteenth century, no other form of bracing was used. Only then, with this innovation, did the guitar—descendant of the magical *kithara*, melting pot of European and Arabic cultures, of aristocratic and popular tastes, Old and New World styles—truly become a Spanish instrument. Despite centuries of prejudice associating the guitar's shape with feminine sensuousness, it turned out that the curves were secondary. Torres's guitars are beautifully formed, but they were revolutionary because of their inner strength and flexibility. They were strong enough to let themselves vibrate.

I reach for my cup of tea. Of course it's cold, but it doesn't matter. Now I know what to play, "La Catedral" by Agustín Barrios Mangoré. Like Miguel Llobet, Barrios had been an internationally known concert guitarist early in the twentieth century, when Segovia was still a local talent in Granada. But also like Llobet, he was later overshadowed by Segovia. Born in Paraguay, he was the first guitarist to perform an entire Bach lute suite and the first to issue a guitar recording. Between 1913 and 1929 Barrios recorded more than fifty pieces, mostly his own compositions, of which about half survive. In the 1920s and 1930s he performed throughout Latin America. He died in 1944 and was forgotten, until a few guitarists and scholars revived his music in the late 1970s. When I began playing "La Catedral" a few years later, it was like participating in the excavation of a lost temple.

Similar to the Rodrigo in form, "La Catedral" has a slow, atmospheric introduction, followed by an episodic, rhythmic dance. It is constructed around a simple figure, an arpeggio that Barrios pushes through a series of chord changes: a small gesture, undistinguished in itself, yet full of musical possibilities. I set the music stand aside and play it from memory. The first finger of my left hand holds a bass note while above the theme sways with a tentative rise and fall. My left hand feels secure and steady, the ground on which the music builds. My fingers make swift, pulsing motions that gain weight and mass when the sound is larger, louder. The arpeggio grows increasingly insistent and agitated. I feel every note, not just in my fingers but along my arms to the elbows, where the fingers' motions begin, and into my shoulders, neck, chest, and back. Everything is connected. My ear, my muscles, my flesh, these notes, and this wood and string—all are parts of a single vibrating structure, communicating their movement to each other.

Playing feels different now. For the first time this cathedral is really dancing. It's built on a questioning anxiety. But the structure develops a kind of reassurance, like pleading that becomes a prayer. This feeling is not notated on the page. It is something that takes place within the notes, or between them, and within my body, within the guitar's body. I first played this piece in my third year at the Conservatory, just about the time I bought my church door guitar. With so fine an instrument in my hands, I suddenly heard an unexplored dimension latent in everything I played, as if the guitar knew things I had never dreamed of. It was a moment of great promise for me. The guitar offered a quality of vibration beyond anything I had imagined before, bringing greater forces into motion than just the strings. But in those days I couldn't play it. I was braced too tightly. Playing now feels somehow simpler. I'm not practicing a fantasy of the guitar or of myself, but *this* instrument, this wood, these strings; I'm playing this music, letting these notes dance.

It's easy to forget how simple music is. I'm like a soundboard, whose job is to communicate excitement, to balance tension. Building the instrument and learning to play it involve complicated physics. But music is about vibration, about allowing myself to be moved.

THe music of wHat Happens

THERE WERE THREE secret entrances to Jordan Hall. Two were upstairs on the second floor, concealed behind doors that were supposed to resemble supply closets. Within a few months after arriving at the Conservatory, however, the attentive student learned that these doors led onto the concert hall's balcony and were left unlocked during concerts. They provided cheap and reliable access to all of the Conservatory's major events. Sneaking into the gallery, I heard some of the best concerts of my life: Seiji Ozawa conducting the Conservatory orchestra; the Guarneri String Quartet performing the complete Beethoven cycle; and jazz drummer Max Roach giving an astonishing solo recital.

The third unadvertised entrance to Jordan Hall was located in the Conservatory basement and led backstage. Early in the morning before orchestra rehearsal, or late at night after a concert, a stealthy dash down an unlit hallway brought you into the heart of the historic auditorium. I first discovered it at the end of my third year. By the fall of my fourth year, I was slinking along the hallway once a week, using the big stage to prepare for my senior recital. Occasionally I ran into a janitor, an electrician, or an audio engineer working in the building. But they rarely minded if I played for ten or fifteen minutes. Practice might be the only way to get to Carnegie Hall. You can get to Jordan Hall by befriending the maintenance staff.

The senior recital was the goal of my four years of study. It was a full-length solo concert, intended to prepare the instrumentalist for a professional debut, the performance that would launch a career. As I crept down the dark passage into the empty concert hall one October day in my last year, I imagined that it was eight in the evening, not eight in the morning, and I was waiting backstage for my performance. I pictured the hall full of people. Stately members of Boston's musical society dressed in tuxedos and sequined evening gowns filled the orchestra section. A motley but enthusiastic mob of fellow students crowded the balcony, whistling and stamping their feet in anticipation. I could see my parents in the audience, my friends, and Aaron, my teacher. They smiled or waved at me discreetly, full of encouragement, lending me their confidence. But I didn't need the assistance. I felt perfectly prepared, as if I'd been waiting for this moment my entire life. I could feel each note of the pieces I would perform glinting hard and clear in my mind.

In reality, the hall was deserted, and I wasn't sure yet what I'd perform, or how. I put down my case and backpack; they were heavy with books, music, and my folding metal footstool. From backstage I appropriated a piano bench and carried it to center stage. The soft thump as I placed it in position reverberated against the room's empty seats. The acoustics are so finely balanced that it is impossible to hide in Jordan Hall. When you're on stage, the audience can hear you blink. I muffled the latches on my guitar case with my palm as I opened them. Tuning my instrument, I listened anxiously for the doors. Only authorized students and staff were allowed into Jordan Hall, and I'd already been given two friendly warnings. The Conservatory's main entrance was just outside the hall. A security guard stood watch there, checking IDs and keeping order. In the usual morning din he was unlikely to notice the squeak of my sneakers or the whisper of my guitar. I wasn't the only one who ignored the rules. Still, I didn't want to be the first expelled from school for it.

The anxiety suited me. Stepping onto stage for my recital, I'd probably feel the same way, unsure if I belonged there, fearful of being found out. What I felt was just a variety of stage fright, and I'd have to perform as well as I could despite it. I closed my eyes and again imagined myself at the performance. I brought my hands into position, conscious that my gestures silenced the crowded hall. The audience held its breath and waited. A great, porous stillness descended, full of longing and expectation. I struck a low D, the first note of Bach's "Prelude, Fugue, and Allegro." The string slapped against the fretboard harshly. I looked up in surprise. Jordan Hall was empty. A dusty shaft of sunlight slipped between the double doors at the entrance. The only audience I could see was a green illuminated exit sign.

Although my degree was in Classical Guitar Performance, the Conservatory didn't cover performing in its coursework. In my lessons the emphasis was always on the tangible aspects of playing, and there was so much work to do. Building a repertoire, Aaron and I grappled with technique and interpretation. From week to week I practiced for him, not for performances. In classes I studied music theory, music history, composition, and conducting. We even had a smattering of liberal arts, literature, and science. But how to perform, how to sit confidently before an audience and make music— this was not discussed in class. The dynamics of performance were thought too personal, too subtle. They were left for each student to master alone, in the privacy of a practice room.

Sitting in Jordan Hall imagining my senior recital, I was trying to make music do what I wanted. To give a good performance, I felt, meant to demonstrate mastery, making the present moment respond to my touch. A performance ought to be something grand, something distinct from ordinary life, a kind of ecstasy, an explosion. In a performance the notes reached inside the audience and burst open the silenced emotion within them. The performer might be nervous or suffering from the flu. The audience might be lethargic or worried about their jobs, their families, their parking spots. But the performance should rise above these things, absorbing and transfiguring them. Nervousness, passing through the crucible of performance, would become a gripping tension, felt by the audience, making them lean forward in their seats, their hearts racing. Lethargy, injected with the performance's chemistry, would evolve, growing round and fat into a kind of noble contentment and majesty. Everything the audience felt before the concert, they would feel more deeply and honestly during the concert. The performance wasn't really separate from daily life but a profound exaggeration of it. I didn't know how to achieve this in my playing. But I'd heard it, I'd experienced it. And I knew that I didn't want the opposite, a boring performance, where time sank heavily over the audience, squeezing the life from them. I'd been to these concerts too, where the performer shrank the hall to the size of a practice room. The notes were all there, but the performance boxed them in. Instead of feeling ennobled or transformed by the music, I'd listened and felt squashed.

Many musicians are happiest practicing, at their best alone. Sneaking into Jordan Hall, I was trying to escape the practice room, to leap across the mental boundary between practicing and performing. I'd played for an audience many times over the years. But I'd never performed solo for more than half an hour. The senior recital would be two hours of music.

Recovering my composure, I filled the hall with people again and began the Bach once more. As the music began to move, I listened for the openings in each note. Sound unfolded in the space around me. I tried to hear the room as my instrument. Even if a green exit sign was my only audience, performing changed the experience of playing. Practicing, you can always play the music over again. Not in performance, and not in life. Performance is the real thing, unrecoverable, unrepeatable. In the end, I thought, it wouldn't matter how I'd practiced if I learned how to perform. Then I'd belong on stage.

⌢̇

"I am not the right person to give concerts," Chopin wrote in a letter to his friend Franz Liszt. "The public intimidates me. I feel asphyxiated by the breath of people in the audience, paralyzed by their curious stares and dumb before that sea of unknown faces."

Chopin was lucky. In 1830s Paris, he could thrive without public concerts, performing instead at private recitals before an exclusive circle of aristocratic friends. Nervous performers are not so fortunate today. A successful modern concert artist might give a hundred or more public performances in a year, while Chopin gave only thirty in his whole life. To be a professional musician now means to be a performer.

When I was fourteen, I took a performance class during the Guitar Workshop's summer session. Class was held in the school's tiny auditorium, which doubled as a cafeteria. The kitchen took up one end of the room. At the other end a stage rose three child-size steps above the linoleum floor. Sometimes three little steps are all that separate a performer from the audience. Yet crossing that boundary in a classroom can be as terrifying as at Carnegie Hall.

At one of the first classes, I climbed the steps to play a bourrée by Bach. I'd played the piece for a year or more, performing it for friends and for my family. But now, as I sat on stage, I became acutely conscious of sitting there, of holding a guitar and moving my fingers. The air seemed transformed into water. I had to keep playing to stay afloat. If I stopped, I was sure I would drown. The audience straightened in their seats. I felt their attention like invisible, slimy tentacles all over my skin. They wanted to hear something. They sat blank-faced and waiting. I heard dishes clacking together in the kitchen. My chair squeaked. The audience was still waiting. And all I had to offer was a little piece of music. It felt as if I'd lost half of my ability. My tone wobbled. I missed notes that I'd never missed before. I rushed to get finished. I stumbled at the end. When I was finished, I felt ashamed of my performance.

My fellow students offered encouragement. It was wonderful that I could play this music at all, they said. I was only fourteen years old, and even the older students complained of stage fright.

"Picture the audience naked," suggested a woman who sang songs about her two young children.

"I look at the back wall, over the heads of the audience," confessed a man in his twenties, an apprentice rock star, who always prefaced his songs by shouting, "How ya doin' out there?!" as if he expected a stadium audience to respond.

When it was my turn, I became intimidated, embarrassed. Sympathy and advice only made things worse. I felt the audience watching me, waiting, listening, expecting something, even if I undressed or avoided them. The next time I took the stage, I sheepishly tried to give it back, as if performing were bad manners.

"This isn't really ready, but I'll try it anyway," I mumbled. I played in a blur, racing to shake off the audience's attention.

Afterward Jeff, the burly man who had led the Guitar Workshop's midday "sings," made me repeat after him, " 'I will not apologize before I play.' "

"If you need to apologize," he said in his deep, oracular voice, "there's time enough later."

Over the course of the summer, I realized that everyone was ashamed of performing, though they hid it in different ways. If they didn't apologize for their performance, they apologized with it, finding some way to deflect the audience's attention from themselves, by giggling, fidgeting, or sneezing. Picturing the audience naked just acknowledged that performing was something naughty, and I thought the woman who suggested it covered her embarrassment by mentally embarrassing the audience too. The man who stared at the back wall, though he was tall and stylish and seemed at ease in front of people, could only be confident if he pretended to be alone or imagined himself surrounded by an audience so large that he felt anonymous. No one, it seemed, was able to sit on stage and just play. Instead, each in our own way, we pretended the performance was something other than what it was: fully clothed people paying close attention to you and the music you made.

To make it through my performances, I experimented with a variety of different roles. I pretended I was Segovia, glaring at a man with a white ponytail when he cleared his throat. I pretended I was just practicing, that it didn't matter how I played because I could always do it over. I imagined that the performance was already over and I was remembering how well it had gone. After a while I became proficient in removing myself from the immediacy of the moment, protecting myself from the sense of baffling expectation. And with experience my nervousness disappeared. For years afterward I thought pretending to be someone or somewhere else was the secret to being on stage. I thought this was what Jeff meant with another of his rules, repeated at least once every class.

"Either step on stage or don't," he would say. "But if you step on stage, give a performance."

I stepped onto stages all through high school and at the Conservatory, and each time I urged myself to give a performance. At nineteen years old I thought a good performance meant taking charge of the audience's experience, enacting a ritual of seduction. The audience wants to be swept away by the performer's authority and passion, I believed, which they interpret as virility, availability. The performer in turn draws strength and courage from the rapt, adoring gaze of an empathetic public. This was how it sounded in the music history I learned. "His bow, like an angel's sword, shot forth flames and rays from his prodigious instrument," a reviewer recalled of Paganini's Paris debut on March 9, 1831. "It threw off incandescent harmonies, it dispersed sweet melodies like the perfumes of the Orient, it let loose resounding thunderclaps like those of God."

It was Paganini, along with Chopin's friend Liszt, who created the modern solo recital in the late 1830s. Previously a performer like Mozart or Beethoven had hired an orchestra and presented a variety show of pieces—a symphony, a concerto, a collection of arias or operatic scenes. Then in 1832 Felix Mendelssohn had given Beethoven's *Waldstein* Sonata its first public performance. Five years later Clara Schumann premiered Beethoven's *Appassionata* Sonata, playing the piece from memory and so setting the standard for future recitalists. With Paganini and Liszt, however, the form and circumstances of the solo recital crystallized as a showcase for a lone artist's virtuosity and charisma. In May 1838 the *Allgemeine musikalische Zeitung* in Vienna had this to say about a solo concert by Liszt:

> He the Prometheus, who creates a form from every note, a magnetizer who conjures the electric fluid from every key, a gnome, an amiable monster, who now treats his beloved, the piano, tenderly, then tyrannically; caresses, pouts, scolds, strikes, drags by the hair, and then, all the more fervently, with all the fire and glow of love, throws his arms around her with a shout, and away with her through all space; he stands there, bowing his head, leaning languidly on a chair, with a strange smile; like an exclamation mark after the outburst of universal admiration: this is Franz Liszt!

This was what I wanted: a primal scene as sexually provocative and emotionally exhilarating as Beatlemania. Even though the classical recital had grown into a staid institution by the time I was performing, I felt these forces still lurked beneath the surface. The best performances brought them out. The audience was receptive, formless clay, which the performer shaped and put through the fire. Without the audience, the performance was mere rehearsal; but without the performer, the audience was just a crowd.

But these were the thoughts of someone who read too much and hadn't performed enough. Despite the success I'd had performing up till then, I still had an observer's ideas of performance, balcony seats. I hadn't yet found the passage backstage.

At the end of my third year at the Conservatory, I participated in a weeklong master class held by one of the greatest guitarists in the world, Pepe Romero. Pepe was the second of Celedonio Romero's three sons, each a virtuoso classical guitarist. The Romeros had achieved major concert careers, individually and as a quartet. Pepe had been performing and recording since he was a teenager, and while not as flashy as his younger brother Angel, he was the outstanding musician of the family. He seemed to understand the guitar from the inside. And his performances received wild ovations. That summer he accepted me as one of six students to participate in his annual master class. For five days each student received a one-hour lesson in front of the group and a paying audience. Then on Friday night the students would present a group recital. The week culminated with a concert by Pepe on Saturday.

In the sweltering July humidity I arrived at the campus of Rice University, in Houston, Texas. The lush grounds felt like an equatorial jungle, and on the short walk from the dorm, where I was housed, to the auditorium, I grew clammy and frazzled. The auditorium itself was a bright, whitewashed room, like the formal salon of a colonial mansion. Designed as a small concert hall for 150 people, it looked as if students used it as a study hall during the school year. Chairs were scattered in clumps around the space, and small worktables had been lined up against the wall. At the foot of the stage a long buffet table had been set with pads and pencils and a sweating pitcher of water. Pepe sat at the table's center, talking with the administrators of the class. A semicircle of students and admirers hovered nearby, waiting for their chance to approach him.

After a few minutes of handshakes and small talk, Pepe asked the performers to introduce themselves. Burt and Simon were professors of music in Florida, guitarists whose careers had settled comfortably into teaching. Old friends of Pepe's, they were both in their late thirties and had the moonlike glow of reflected brilliance. Rohan was also a professor of guitar. He'd traveled from his home in Manitoba, Canada, to attend the class. A gangly, weathered man in his fifties, he had an Abe Lincoln beard, and during every class break he loped outside to have a smoke on his pipe. Karen and Fernando were, like me, undergraduate music students, Karen from Texas and Fernando from southern California. The three of us gravitated toward one another, pressed together by the older, established performers' confidence. We were still unformed as musicians, and we were in awe of Pepe, his friends, and their achievements.

Pepe was a very pleasant, unassuming man with the soft features of a pastry chef. Yet something magical surrounded him. It was more than his fame or his talent, the things that made everyone want to get near him. Watching him during the first few lessons, I saw how carefully, how completely, he listened. Naturally he knew each piece and the technical challenges of performing it. But there was a deeper level of concentration in his listening, as if he heard past the guitar, past the performer's fingers, past even the composer's conceptions, to the source of musical feeling, some primal human impulse that we were all dumbly following. With a few comments he could produce stunning changes in a student's playing. By the time my turn arrived, therefore, I was terrified. It was impossible to get away with anything in front of him. He was like a seer who had the ability to divine the future. Did I want to know what my future held?

For my first lesson I chose a cautious piece, an étude by Carcassi. My hands were trembling and I couldn't seem to get comfortable on the chair. I performed in the form of a question, as if opening my palm and reluctantly asking, What do you see?

"You have great ability," Pepe said when I'd finished. "Play something else."

With an audible sigh of relief, I played "Capricho Arabe," the piece that had sent Aaron dancing around the room at the Conservatory and with which I'd won the *Newsday* competition. I pictured myself back on the outdoor stage on Long Island. The piece had been so successful then. I wanted to replicate the performance now, impressing Pepe as I'd apparently impressed the competition's judges. If he wanted to, Pepe could grant any of his students the mentoring and access to booking agents that would make a career possible.

When the piece ended, Pepe came on stage and sat in a chair opposite me.

"Play a chord," he said, "anything. But very quietly, *pianissimo.*"

I felt the warmth of his stare in my fingers.

"Now a little more, *piano,*" he instructed, leaning toward me to watch more intently. "Now *mezzoforte*. And *forte.*"

And then he looked at me in surprise. The notes had lost fullness with each increase in volume until they were brittle and harsh. Pepe stood and felt along the muscles of my right hand, my wrist and forearm, like a surgeon, a sculptor.

"Your performance breaks down here, between *mezzoforte* and *forte,*" he concluded, tapping his finger just inside my elbow. "Something's blocking the movement. Let's get rid of it and then hear how it sounds."

For the rest of the week we reached into my playing, into deep technique, the place where musical ideas become physical. I had practiced and practiced to get my hands on these notes. Yet in the moment when my intentions grew most intense—usually when the music grew louder or more forceful—I seized up, I resisted. There was a line to cross, another tiny step across an invisible boundary between playing and giving a performance. But I was afraid to cross it by myself. Instead, as I'd been doing since I was fourteen, at the moment of real performance, I turned inward, shielding myself from the audience with mental distance and physical tension.

On the last day of the class, I sat on stage in the orange light of late afternoon, with Pepe peering at me from behind his thick glasses. He held his guitar on his lap, supporting it against his chest.

"Watch my hands as you play," he said, and we started "Leyenda" by Isaac Albéniz, together. He played quietly, the tones from his instrument like a crystal at the center of my playing. As I watched his fingers, I imagined that the sounds I produced were coming from him. I had played this piece the previous day, struggling to keep myself as calm as possible. Today Pepe had wanted to hear it again, but freer, "with abandon," he'd said. My first attempt hadn't succeeded, and now Pepe was playing along, leading me somewhere I didn't know existed, somewhere I was afraid to go alone.

I concentrated on his fingers, losing the sense of my own movements. And then a strange jolt shook me, like two strings springing into tune. What we were playing was beautiful, and I couldn't tell whose fingers were responsible. I recoiled instantly in a panic more penetrating than any stage fright I'd known. My heart pounded; I felt a growing drone in my ears. Some unknown life squirmed in my hands. I wanted to yelp or gag in terror.

"Keep playing," Pepe said softly.

I brought myself back to his hands, as graceful and unconstrained as before. My panic subsided. And then something unexpected occurred. It started to feel good to let the music sound, without knowing how it sounded. It just felt good.

It is terrifying to step out of the practice room with its protective walls, to take the little steps that put you alone onstage in the full glare of attention and expectation and the clock ticking. The practice room excludes this terror, though it has risks of its own. But this step, summoning the audacity that places you before an audience, is the fuel, the spark of performance. Most of the time we experience fear at the prospect of performing, as if we weren't performing all the time, as if most moments in our lives didn't count. Faced with a sudden sense of significance, then, we panic. Being seen seems dangerous, and we hide ourselves; we protect what is most valuable and offer up only what we aren't afraid to lose. I'd thought I knew what the music should mean. So I held on to the notes instead of releasing them, trying to control them after they'd sounded, to shape how the audience heard me. As a consequence, however, instead of performing, instead of creating something living, what I held was stillborn. The tension in my elbow was just a cover, a defensive pose against the fear of giving music away and having nothing left for myself, the fear of being nothing. Holding my playing steady with his own, Pepe gently took the fear and tension away, leaving me sitting onstage, playing music, giving a performance.

When we finished "Leyenda," there was a murmur from the audience. I climbed down the steps overwhelmed by what had happened. I'd gotten it all wrong. Six years earlier at the Guitar Workshop, when Jeff told me to give a performance when I stepped onstage, I had heard his words entirely wrong. Performing isn't a ruse that protects you—just the opposite. It is a kind of freedom in your fear and excitement. Everything that practicing accumulates and protects, performing releases. It is a squandering of ability, the opposite of striving, the opposite of pretending. I sat in the audience listening to the other students and heard everything differently. Wherever the music went, to really perform it, I had to be willing to let it go.

Six months later Boston's winter wind hurtled down the street, driving a snowstorm against the windows of Goddard Chapel. Inside the church the sound of snowflakes striking the stained glass was like a thousand silver pins dropping on the floor. The building heaved with the gusts. But the storm outside accentuated the silence inside, making it feel warm and intimate. Twenty-five people had braved the weather to listen to me perform. They sat on the wooden pews beside mountains of coats and sweaters. Slushy puddles formed on the floor around their boots. I had prepared an hour's program as a trial run for my senior recital. But if the forecasters were correct, we might be trapped together in this church for days.

The concert was on the campus of Tufts University in Medford, a suburb of Boston. I'd arranged to hold my senior recital there the following spring and was fortunate to have this opportunity to give a practice concert. I'd selected the chapel because I liked the space. The acoustics were clear and flattering to the guitar, and the room was bright and comfortable. I'd given up sneaking into Jordan Hall. Only the very best pianists were allowed to hold their recitals there. Most students performed in the Conservatory's small recital hall or found a venue elsewhere in Boston. The small recital hall was dingy and neglected compared with the grandeur of Jordan Hall, I thought, and this seemed to reflect the Conservatory's ambivalent attitude toward the guitar. I didn't want to offer my concert in a hall that was second best. The senior recital was the culmination of four years of work. Goddard Chapel was a prime performance space at Tufts. I didn't need to sneak in to play there.

Aaron and I had planned a program of music from three centuries. I would begin with a "Theme and Variations" by Giuliani, a cheerful, frothy piece to welcome the audience and get comfortable on stage. Then I'd perform another "Theme and Variations" by the contemporary English composer Lennox Berkeley, a modern work contrasting starkly with the Giuliani. The concert's first half closed with a Partita by Bach, eight movements of concentrated counterpoint, very exacting to play and to listen to. After intermission I'd play two duets with another graduating senior, a violinist named Richard with whom I'd played several gigs. Finally, I would return alone to play Villa-Lobos's *Suite Popular Bresilienne,* a group of five contrasting movements in a jazz age, art deco style.

At this practice performance I had prepared all the solo pieces. I didn't want to be surprised in front of an audience. But I hadn't anticipated a blizzard. As I began the concert, settling into the Giuliani, the wind sliced through the music, sending the notes tumbling against the windows like the snowflakes outside. The creaking of the walls added an edge of danger to Giuliani's light melodies, as if the theme were fleeing ahead of the storm. Yet there was something solid in the music too that held its ground against the gusts. Like the church, the music gave the wind something to blow against, a point of reference and resistance.

"Listen to the storm," I said before beginning the Bach, cocking one ear toward the windows and the fine, glassy tinkling of snow.

The blizzard had created a holiday atmosphere, more powerful than the concert's aura. I felt there was no need to observe the formalities. And as I played, the notes were different than when I'd practiced, and the wind was something other than the wind. I'd prepared the music, but there was no way to prepare for the performance. The notes cascaded in the room, changing in my hands from self-contained, almost frozen balls of sound into a torrent, powerful and expansive. I had been afraid of losing my place, of stumbling. I'd been afraid of hearing myself through the audience's ears and finding that the interpretation I'd worked so hard to achieve was flawed and foolish. I was afraid that this perfect, profound music would turn ordinary in my hands.

Instead, as I played, the music seemed natural and inevitable, as if I were merely articulating the snowstorm. I was enveloped in the sound, the sensation. I had all the time, all the skill and experience necessary, to play these notes in this moment. The audience didn't scare me. They too seemed like part of the storm and the music. None of my friends from the Conservatory had made the ten-mile trek out to Medford. But these people might as well be my friends, I thought. The storm had made us comrades, not performer and audience. Sharing this experience, we understood each other. The interplay of music and the wind was our bond.

During the Villa-Lobos, though, my sense of the audience, the music, and myself changed into something at once more private and more inclusive. I lost my awareness of the storm outside, even of the audience in front of me. The boundaries between what I imagined, what I heard, and where I was dissolved. Yet without these boundaries, the storm, the room, the music, and the people listening didn't wash together, becoming indistinct. Rather, everything about the moment was present to me with penetrating clarity, not in thoughts or images but as sound, as the music. Concentrating as deeply and as pleasurably as I ever had before in my life, I felt an utter ease in the performance, as if the notes in their vibration created the physical space, the flow of time, and the relationships among us all. I felt the movement of sound throughout my body; I was an instrument of innumerable strings, resounding in sympathetic vibration to the fullness of the moment. There was no difference between me and the audience. The life of each sound shaped the texture of our experience, and this rise and fall was thrilling, heart-rending, suspenseful, and whole. We didn't know what would happen next, because in each moment the sound took us farther, and the music was everything we felt.

When the concert was over, the audience remained, reluctant to leave the warm chapel. A professor approached me, speaking excitedly in Italian. He was a small man, with wiry limbs and wiry hair, who gesticulated with his entire body, leaping in place as he spoke. I couldn't understand anything he said. But he kept talking, occasionally gripping my arm or singing a phrase from the music I'd played. He appeared to have enjoyed the concert, experiencing some urgent, illuminating idea during it, which he attributed to me. He stood for several minutes explaining it in Italian, then shook my hand vigorously, saying "Thank you, *grazie,* thank you."

As I put my instrument back in its heavy traveling case, a woman also stepped up to thank me.

"It was as if I could hear the violin," she said of the Bach Partita. "I'd closed my eyes and then was startled when I opened them again and saw you with a guitar."

Though she spoke English, I understood only a little of what she was saying. She was an imposing woman, perhaps forty years old, with dark hair piled on top of her head and deep rings under her eyes. She seemed deeply moved, on the verge of weeping. What had she heard? What had she imagined? Her associations with the violin were as obscure to me as the Italian professor's illumination. She shook my hand warmly, then left the church and was absorbed back into the swirl of her own thoughts.

I put on my jacket, scarf, and thick down gloves. I wanted to get back to my apartment while I still could. When I practiced, I was always trying to grasp something; I wanted to feel a sense of accomplishment. After this performance it felt like there was nothing left to accomplish. I had played as well as I knew how. But listening to these members of the audience express their responses, I couldn't tell how the performance had gone. I'd been absorbed by my own experience, by the storm and the music as it wove through the wind. But the audience had been living in their own thoughts, experiencing things I knew nothing about. It left me exhausted and spent, sad almost, but also strangely calm. For the first time as a solo performer, I'd given my performance to the audience.

When you sit on stage to perform, it feels as if the entire world were focused on the movements of your fingers and the sounds they produce. The warmth of the audience's attention fosters the illusion that, through this performance, our differences, our conflicting needs and divergent impressions, are all resolved into a single experience. But when you walk off stage, you find yourself back in a private world. Your senses may still jangle with the alertness and intensity of performance. Maybe it doesn't hit you until later, after the friends and well-wishers disperse, when you change your clothes or step into the shower. For the first time you're alone again. Now it will grip you in the stomach and squeeze, this loneliness of being finished. During the performance the many strands of your practice have come together, the hard work, the longing for listeners, the aching for connection. Now, the performance over, these strands unravel again. The music may have been deeply felt. But music doesn't stay felt. You have to begin again each time. Maybe the performance had achieved everything I'd dreamed of while practicing. But now it was over, and I was moving on. The next time I stepped onstage—at my senior recital—the music would be something entirely new.

The snow was light and floury and almost a foot deep when I left the church. My boots sank in, compacting the flakes with a heavy crunch. I balanced my guitar case against my chest with both arms wrapped around it to center my weight on the slippery path. The sidewalk lamps sparkled in the crystals. It was perfectly still, except for the sound of the snow falling. Though I'd held the concert, the performance was no longer mine.

⌒

May, springtime, sunlight, birds. Backstage at Goddard Chapel, it's ten minutes until eight and Aaron, my teacher, still hasn't arrived. He's never been to the Tufts campus before and is probably lost. But the concert, my senior recital, can't start without him. I'm warming up, watching the clock. The buttons on my suit jacket are buzzing against the back of the guitar. I have to remember to tuck them underneath the fabric when I sit down on stage.

My parents are already seated in the audience. They drove up from Long Island yesterday and spent the day today shopping for cheese and crackers, wine and beer for the reception at my apartment after the concert. All day they've been hovering quietly, politely, making me nervous. I peek at them through a side door. My father's fifty-ninth birthday was just a week ago. From my peephole, he appears relaxed, even cheerful. A year ago he moved his office from Manhattan to Great Neck and no longer has to commute an hour and a half each way. He seems younger, happier than I'd remembered. He's the only one in the audience properly dressed for a concert with a jacket and tie, just as if he were at the Philharmonic. Next to him my mother seems nervous. She's also nicely dressed, in a blue and cream silk blouse and navy blue slacks. But she keeps checking her watch, aware that my teacher is missing and that the concert is now late. She waves to someone across the room, then whispers to my father, and he waves too. Her gestures seem protective and helpless. There's nothing she can do except listen and silently pray that things go well. I recognize the careful, wary expression on her face. She'll search in my playing for the spark of inspiration, the sign that I'm closer to a career than I was a year ago, that this concert will lead to success.

Surrounding my parents are sixty people who have shown up to hear me on this bright, mild evening. Unknown faces are in every row. Friends of friends, indistinctly familiar, and strangers, people who love the classical guitar, or who support student musicians, or who have heard me before and have come back for more. Some are here out of love and responsibility; some out of friendship and solidarity. Maybe a few are here by accident, enticed by the lights in the chapel, throwing blue, red, green, and gold streaks onto the trees outside. Two older women sit in the second row, widows perhaps, friends or lovers, who attend all the free concerts on campus. Two couples in their thirties, perhaps acquaintances of Aaron. A professor of English and a professor of philosophy. They are here because they want to hear music. It's not me, not the notes, not my fingers or technique that matter to them, not the history of the guitar, its place in the world, or its importance to me. They're here for the music, for pleasure, for the peculiar joy and satisfaction that music offers. They've come here—

But really, I have no idea why they're here or what they expect. I only know they have come; they are my audience. I have to put myself in their hands.

John and Marcus, fellow guitarists, lean their heads through the doorway, then scramble into the room. Marcus's master's recital is in a few weeks. He grabs my shoulders and shakes, then climbs on an antique chair and jumps off, acting out the plunge we're both taking. John is an undergraduate, like me, though he still has another year before his recital.

"Break a nail," he laughs, observing a guitarist's superstition.

It's a nightmare to break a fingernail just before a concert. It changes the finger's relation to the string, throwing off all the careful calibration and threatening the whole performance. For three days I've been keeping anxious guard over my hands.

I try to laugh, and my strained attempt makes the two of them really laugh. We're friends, all reaching for the same goal. We've performed together, learned from each other, argued and celebrated together. Yet I know how they'll listen tonight, just as I have listened to them at other concerts, with mixed emotions, enthusiasm and comparison, hoping I do well but silently calculating the balance of my playing against their own. John wants to hear where I excel, where I falter. Am I better than he is? Better than he'll be in a year? Marcus, with more experience, will enjoy the concert, smiling at what I achieve and nodding knowingly at my lapses. He'll make a mental note for later, a week or a month from now, when he can gently suggest how I might improve.

It's ten minutes past eight. John and Marcus leave to take their seats. My hands are shaking and I feel a drumroll of nerves in my stomach. I've just noticed that the room has vaulted ceilings. Heavy bent-metal chandeliers hang from the thick wooden beams that support the roof. I decide to see how high I can jump. I take a running leap for the lights. I try three times, coming within a few inches. On the last try, as I'm flailing in midair, Aaron arrives.

"Remember to keep breathing," he says helpfully as I stand there panting. He straightens my tie. Then he shakes my hand and nods, as if he's said everything he can. My ability, in some sense, is a reflection on him. We've worked together for four years. He's rebuilt my technique and shaped my musicianship. But now I'm stepping before an audience as his student for the last time. And he's stepping back, distancing himself. The concert will show how much I was able to profit by his example, how much I've learned. The program holds enough music, enough variety, to demonstrate the scope, the maturity, of my imagination. Am I still a student, or have I truly begun to perform? The recital is a rite of passage, fleeting and revealing. He's done all he can for me now. He finds a seat in the audience, a row behind my parents.

For a last moment I'm alone. A welter of images crowds me— Aaron careening around a Conservatory practice room; a gang of guitarists sniggering at Julian Bream from the balcony of Jordan Hall; my family driving home from a Friday night dinner at Grandma's, my parents singing "Bye-Bye Blackbird" in the dark car. I want to include them all in my performance. I want to prove myself, to show off to strangers, to please and impress my parents and friends. I want to get through the whole program without humiliating myself. I want to triumph, to take my place among the great musicians. I want so many things, too many at once. Too much for any note to convey.

I take my instrument from its case, then strike a tuning fork against my knee and hold it to my ear. The guitar is perfectly in tune. I play two quick scales and then a gymnastic exercise to bring the blood back into motion. The instrument resounds full-bodied in the small back room. I strum the first chord of my first piece. The pressure of my fingers releases the strings' tension. The guitar's whole body swells and then contracts. I take a deep breath and let go of everything I want. Whatever happens will happen. It's like this, really, in every moment, though we rarely have the presence of mind to notice. Instead we're always planning, protecting, wishing, and wanting, as if we could spend our whole lives practicing. I've had enough of practicing. Holding the instrument by the neck, I open the door and step onto the stage to perform.

The Blue Guitar

ALL MORNING I've been reaching out for something intangible. My hands glow from inside, blood, bones, and muscles pulsating with delicate energy. A peculiar warmth purrs in the center of my forehead, the clarity and intensity that come from deep concentration. Almost three hours have passed, though often it's felt as if time has stopped. Now I look up from my fingers, and the day surprises me.

Brilliant noontime sunlight is spilling into the courtyard outside my window. Across the street students are flopped on the sidewalk, flirting, eating lunch, talking on their cell phones. Wisps of fog have begun to feather the roofs. I see the same scene every day, but now something is different. The distances seem altered, or the colors. I can't put my finger on it, yet the warmth, the breeze, the students' laughter, the sparkle of parked cars all penetrate my senses in an unexpected flaring up of pleasure. The passing moments feel full of life. My apartment is quiet and peaceful, yet now there is a roaring in my ears, a warmth beneath my skin. The day is rushing through me, burning itself up and generating this heat and noise inside me. Time hasn't stood still. Everything has changed.

Suddenly I have too much energy to sit with. I lay the guitar on the floor and shake out my shoulders and arms vigorously. It's not enough. I spring across the room, hugging myself, trying to contain the excitement, the bursting and burning I feel. I jump in place and squeeze my arms as tightly across my chest as I can. I'd thought I was sitting still, patiently starting over, correcting my mistakes. But all this time I've been on fire without realizing. Now it overwhelms me, the exhilaration and danger of this instant. I've been so cautious, protecting myself with a firewall of stories, saving myself for later. But like Joshua's trumpet, the notes of "La Catedral" have brought the walls tumbling down. Now the moment roars through me unchecked, igniting my senses with its freedom and uncertainty.

Picking up my guitar by the neck, I walk around the living room to collect myself. My stomach is jittery; my ears hiss. I sit down again and close my eyes, composing my senses on the guitar, until all that I'm feeling, all I've experienced today, concentrates with glowing urgency at the crown of my head. The guitar is changing in my hands, and I am changing as well. I have only this moment to play with, only this instrument to express the fullness of right now. I bring my hands to the strings. I wait. I listen. Silence brightens my senses. The music might step into the current of any of these moments. I wait for it. And then I've begun

/ ॑ \

An airy melodic figure swirls upward, outlining an E-major seventh chord. This is "Transforming," the first movement of Sir Michael Tippett's work *The Blue Guitar*. Written in 1983, it's loosely atonal, impulsive and edgy, with sharply juxtaposed textures, tone colors, and rhythms. The title refers to Wallace Stevens's 1937 poem "The Man with the Blue Guitar," itself inspired by Picasso's 1903 portrait of a blind street musician. I keep my eyes closed as the first notes dissipate. I'm feeling my way forward, drifting as the sound drifts.

A second airy chord reaches up. But before it rounds off, the notes are trampled. Three powerful impacts grind the melody down until only a gasp is left. Notes rise weakly, but the rhythmic pounding returns, more insistent now, with nine heavy attacks. Crystalline harmonics ascend like spirits to the top of the guitar's range, then plummet down the neck to stillness. This rising figure, ground down into a gasp—it's painful, it's pain, as if I were reaching out and violently repulsed. I don't *want* the melody to end like this, but it does. I don't want the notes to die away. But I can't help it. The notes pass through me, and their resonance comes back from the walls, the windows, the answering air of my room. The sound inside and the sound outside. I have to live with this division. Loss lingers in my body. But the music is always moving.

Rhythmic chords break loose in a flurry of sixteenth notes, a disjointed scattering of sounds. My fingers dart up, across, and back down the strings, on the edge of my ability to control them. Now shorter bursts, bright jabs from the first string to the sixth. Can I hold these sharp edges together? Do I have to? I've spent so much time practicing technique, disciplining my fingers. Why? Why should discipline make me a better musician? Always pulling inward, always rounding off the edges. There's wildness in this movement. I want to throw off the burden of playing it and flail about madly. The music absorbs my doubts, the resistance in my technique, consuming it, turning wildness into the greatest demand for freedom. Notes fall away, then punch out again, my hands and the music and the phrase's angular movement together building a wave of intensity that fills me, pushes me onward, past where I've always stopped before. Wildness is *in* the music, not beyond it. I didn't know I could play like this, could expand in such freedom.

When I almost can't bear it any longer, the line eases a little, pausing for just an instant to catch its breath and let me catch mine. The wave slides back into itself, having created an openness that now feels empty, a counterpoint to freedom, now so much emptier than before.

Then high on the fingerboard, my left hand finds a singing tone.

My thumb creeps from behind the neck to support my fingers, resting on the underside of the joint between the guitar's neck and body. Two distinct melodies play against each other, the higher one sustained and lilting, the lower one percussive yet ringing, like the tones of a xylophone. Two lines, distinct and intertwined. Playing clearly, without favoring one line over the other, I feel an impossible balance—two lines as one; one line as two. Then the positions reverse, the guitar's lower register now sustained and lilting, while the higher notes are sharp and rhythmic. The balance flips again, yet the melodies remain distinct and together with such exquisite poise, it takes my breath away.

A full measure of silence ends the passage, held outside time by a fermata, that open eye of stillness. My hands fall away from the instrument slightly as I listen. The silence intensifies, an unbearable weight of waiting. Can I live in this silence, this aching, uncounted time? Hear this moment filled with waiting. If the music begins again, it will feel like a miracle.

Eight strong, slowly strummed chords break the stillness, each leaving a trail of dissipating tones behind, the last of which wanders off pitch into microtones. Like a jazz or rock guitarist, I bend the string off center. Classical guitar strings are much heavier than jazz or rock strings, and the note shivers less than a quarter-tone from true. The effect is otherworldly, as if my whole room were melting, bending sideways. It is a small gesture. But the strangeness of the sound sends me reeling. Notes don't have to be true to feel necessary. I've never played this sound before, never heard it. Yet it belongs here, in this moment transfigured, as if the whole piece, all its tension and tenderness, were expressed in bending off center, as if a note that didn't bend could never be true.

And then falling. Notes careen away from themselves, the ground flying out from underneath them. A single line split in two, the same intervals, but on different beats and pitches, played against each other: a canon. In the rush of the moment, it's difficult to hear the relationship. But I feel it, an exhilarating tautness in the music, great swoops of sound propelling me forward. Yet something in the way the two lines move together has grown darker, deeper, conclusive. My fingers flick against the strings while all the force of this movement hurtles through the air, its reaching out, its wildness and emptiness, and these divisions held in a balance so delicately poised that just listening will shatter it or shatter you. As the opening, airy melody again meets sharp rhythmic resistance, the friction grates harshly. I feel how much life is in it. The urgency of it burns through my body, flaring up in sound, then dying away. The music subsides, achieving a new shape with its final chords. Vibrations fall to stillness, forging me and my instrument into something unknown and newly lived.

$$\frown$$

I sit with the final notes, feeling the surprising shape of this music. I've given everything I can give now, a performance. Perhaps I am my only audience today, and my attention alone makes this a performance and not just playing in my room. But attention changes everything.

I have to laugh in wonder. I've found a new story of practicing, though it is not the one I expected when I sat down this morning. Practicing, I might repeat a note, a section, a whole piece a hundred times, as if I had all the time in the world to play. This bit of pretending allows me to escape the urgency of each instant and improve slowly. Yet each instant *is* urgent, and in the end practicing is a lie. It is a necessary lie—a fiction that suspends time so we may examine and reflect on what we do or who we are—but still a lie.

Music lives only in performance; only then does what we hear become real. Performing reveals everything we are able to show, and yet for this reason, the first time through, we often perform badly. And we yearn so deeply to go back again and correct our mistakes. Few yearnings are as profound in us, because the truth is, we cannot go back. Yet the fiction of practicing makes it *seem* as if we can, and this is enough to change our lives.

Practice lets us grow in our own time, protected from the demands, the vitality and mortality, of each moment. Within the practice-room walls it often seems as if time really does stand still, as if we could always remain protected, practicing and improving forever. This illusion holds transformative power—but also a dangerous seduction. Practice, by itself, is a dream of perfection. Only performing can turn practice into shared life, where our own time may join with others', becoming musical. Yet practicing is the necessary lie that lets us pause to collect ourselves. It is the inner life of performance, the inward turn that allows us to develop, to grow, to move forward having learned.

a most misunderstood
instrument

WHAT DO YOU MEAN it's *gone?*" I stared uncomprehendingly at the hawklike woman behind the lost-baggage counter.

"I'm sorry, sir," she said crisply, "the plane has left."

I looked out the window of Vienna's pristine international airport. Cows grazed alongside the tarmac. A trail of jet exhaust was slowly dissipating in the east.

"But I have a claim ticket," I stammered, still not willing to believe that my guitar had vanished.

"If the item is on board the aircraft, it will be returned on the next flight from Bucharest," the agent said. "If not, you will have to file a claim with the airline." She pushed a slip of paper across the counter. "Where is your residence in Vienna?"

I dug in my backpack for a letter from the Institute for European Studies. But my hands were shaking too much to copy the address into the little boxes on the form. When I gave it back, she took the letter too and rewrote the street name in clear, round characters.

"We will contact you if the item arrives in Bucharest."

Bucharest! Just a few hours before, I'd been sitting on the thinly cushioned seat of an Ilyushin 62, the largest Soviet passenger jet, reveling in how exotic, how adventurous, how bohemian it was to

fly the national airline of Romania. In August 1984 East Bloc coun-
tries were offering great deals on airfare, especially if you paid in
cash. Everything had corresponded to my image of a young artist,
setting out on his own. Even the heavyset Romanian flight atten-
dant had delighted me, with her uniform fashioned after a folk cos-
tume, red trim and a smocklike apron. "Eat," she'd insisted as she
handed me a meal tray. That was half of her English vocabulary.
Later she'd returned holding a wicker basket over her arm. "Apple,"
she declared. But now the exotic fantasy turned against me. I saw my
instrument arriving in Romania, the poorest country in the Soviet
bloc, and my head filled with clichés from *Dracula*. A tiny mountain
village, peasants with pitchforks, smoking long, malignant pipes. And
there's my guitar, disappearing untraceably into the dark Romanian
interior. I saw it handed off to some Communist Party boss in
exchange for butter, for flour. I saw it sold to Gypsies, packed into a
wagon and driven off into the wild. I heard strange, mysterious
music; I heard wood being splintered for kindling.

My guitar! How could I be so stupid? When Segovia traveled,
he booked an extra seat for his instrument, reserving it under the
name "Miss Segovia." But even at Romanian prices I couldn't have
afforded such precautions. My guitar had flown as checked bag-
gage. Now it was gone.

There was nothing else to do. I glared at the woman behind the
counter, then found my way to the train and rode into the music
capital of the world.

My senior recital had been a success, demonstrating a new freedom and depth in my playing. But the senior recital was just one
concert, not a career. It begged the question of what to do next. I
needed more experience performing. But how? To get my name
out, I'd have to book concerts, enter competitions. And while I was
doing this, I'd also have to pay the rent, pay off student loans. I considered staying in Boston and hustling for wedding gigs. But weddings would just lead to more weddings. I wanted to be moving

forward, advancing toward a concert career. Only concerts would generate more concerts. The problem was getting started. And so I followed the path worn by so many aspiring but unknown artists. I let school lead to more school.

Marcus, after graduating with his master's degree, had auditioned for Konrad Ragossnig, head of the guitar department at the Musikhochschule in Vienna. Beth, a flute player I knew, had matriculated around the corner at the Vienna Conservatory. Why not follow them to Vienna? Vienna, home of Haydn, Mozart, Beethoven, Mahler, and Schoenberg! Vienna, a place, I'd imagined, where *The Magic Flute* was popular culture. If any city embodied the life I dreamed of leading, it was Vienna. I still had one academic requirement at the Conservatory. But I convinced the administration to let me satisfy it through an American study-abroad program. I could prepare myself for the next step while I finished my degree. Then, if I needed more time, I could audition at the Musikhochschule, like Marcus. This plan had practical advantages. Remaining a student would allow me to defer my loan payments. Austrian universities and graduate schools are essentially free. But I had a deeper, artistic goal. For the sake of my playing, I'd told myself, I needed to broaden my experience. Learning another language, absorbing another culture, would enrich me as a person, and living in Vienna would bring me closer to the music I loved. Really, I had no idea what my prospects for success were. But I needed to feel that I was moving forward, and moving made me feel I was.

The Austrian countryside lurched past the train window, the fields irregularly shaped, angular like German consonants. After a while farms gave way to suburbs and industrial buildings. I barely noticed as the old imperial city rose around me. All I saw were the awful images in my head. This was my grand entrance into Vienna. I had come here to live like a real musician, and the first thing I'd done was lose my guitar.

⌒

The Institute for European Studies rented two floors of a decaying city palace from the decaying Austrian duchess who owned it. The Baroque ballroom was now a lecture hall, where painted angels floated among puffy pink clouds in the elaborately decorated ceiling. Two enormous dusty chandeliers glittered above plastic school chairs, comma-shaped writing surfaces finished with imitation wood grain. College juniors thronged the hallways, excitedly beginning a semester abroad. As I wandered through the palace's twelve-foot-high carved-wood doors, lively American chatter about nightclubs and weekend trips to Venice greeted me. There were beer halls and wine gardens to explore, the giant Ferris wheel, and the famous white Lipizzaner horses. It all seemed so foreign, though not because this was a different country. In these students I recognized none of the intense focus and ambition that I was used to at the Conservatory. A boy from Kenyon College in Ohio was majoring in psychology but wasn't sure what he wanted to do. A girl from the University of Wisconsin, Madison, hoped to become an architect, unless she went to law school. No one had come here for the classes. They were nineteen or twenty years old and had only a grainy sense of themselves. I was a year older and very different in my own eyes. I hadn't come to Vienna for the classes, either. I thought I knew exactly what I wanted.

Two miserable days after I arrived, my guitar returned from Bucharest undamaged, delivered by a stooped, fleshy man who held the handle with one finger. I raced up the marble staircase to the ballroom and threw open the case. "Love, look at the two of us." I had wandered the old city like a sleepwalker, lost and desperate, half of me missing. Now it felt like all of me had arrived, a reunion with myself. When my heart stopped pounding, I played the "Theme and Variations" by Giuliani that I'd performed at my senior recital. In a room like this—perhaps in this very room—Giuliani had played for Beethoven, and Mozart had improvised for the Hapsburg nobility. As the elegant variations chased each other past the chandeliers and into the realm of angels, I saw myself reflected in the age-clouded mirrors that alternated with gilt woodwork along the walls. Closing my eyes, I leaped over the 175 years that separated me from the days when the guitar first emerged as a classical instrument and Giuliani had premièred this music in this city. *I have arrived*, I thought with a thrill of expectation.

"Hey, the bus is leaving."

Someone was standing at the door waving me out of the room. The Institute held its orientation for new students in a small alpine village two hours from Vienna. My guitar had returned only twenty minutes before. But I quickly packed it up and stored it in a closet in the school director's office. I took the bus to Mariazell with all the other kids. I'd never seen any place so beautiful. For the first time in ten years I didn't practice for a whole week.

As soon as I returned to Vienna, I sprang into a new life. Each morning I crossed the Danube River on the commuter train, riding from the little house on the outskirts of the city that I shared with three other American students to the Prater, Vienna's largest urban park. From there I took the U-bahn three stops to Stephansplatz, where I emerged at the foot of St. Stephan's Cathedral, first built in 1182. I bought a pastry at a café in the shadow of the magnificent 450-foot-tall spire, then sat through my classes at the old palace. My real day began in the evening. Just a few blocks down Kärntnerstrasse stood Vienna's world-famous concert halls, the Konzerthaus, the Musikverein, the Staatsoper. If you were willing to wait on line for a few hours, standing-room tickets cost about a dollar. And from a chatty Viennese music lover, a woman in her fifties who blew kisses at the artists on stage, I learned that if standing room was sold out, a fifty-schilling note pressed into the palm of the usher worked as well as a ticket. Three or four nights a week I heard the greatest musicians perform in the finest halls in the world. Leonard Bernstein and Herbert von Karajan conducting the Vienna Philharmonic, the Juilliard String Quartet, Richard Goode, André Watts, and Itzhak Perlman in recital. Even at the Conservatory I had never felt so immersed in music. It was the heart of the city.

Three weeks after arriving, I took my place on the sidewalk outside the opera house. It was four in the afternoon before a seven-thirty show. This was my first time at the Vienna opera; I had saved myself for Mozart. When I was in high school, *Don Giovanni* had been a magic carpet for me and my friend Stephen, carrying us away from our sheltered suburb to more adventurous, more fulfilling lives. Listening, we'd felt like revolutionaries. Now I was outside the opera house in the city where it was written, twenty-one years old, on my own for the first time. I shivered in anticipation, waiting to see and hear what would become of me.

The standing-room line snaked beneath the neo-Renaissance loggia, populated by students from all over, trading stories and tips. Two Italian boys ahead of me on line were trying to talk with a Spanish girl, who translated into French for a young couple on their honeymoon. The man spoke a little German and was talking with the girl next to me. Everyone knew a little English.

"Budapest is so beautiful. You have to go see it."

"I thought Prague was nicer."

"But so depressing!"

"When you come to Florence, we have to get together."

The circuits lit up on my imaginary map of Europe, rail lines connecting Vienna to everywhere. A whole continent of young people with backpacks and copies of *Let's Go,* seeing the sights, exploring.

"Do you know *Don Giovanni?*" I asked the German girl. She had a serious expression and long, graceful fingers.

"Not personally," she replied, though I had to consult my dictionary before I understood her. Her name was Christine and she was studying viola at the Musikhochschule. Her dinner was packed in neatly labeled plastic containers in her bag, and she ate it while comfortably perched on a small folding stool. She'd obviously done this before.

"Mozart loves the viola," I ventured, making the best use of my limited German. I'd seen Mozart's viola two days earlier at his former apartment, just half a mile from where we were sitting. With hand gestures and the frequent use of my dictionary, Christine explained that she had been out to Heiligenstadt, in the suburbs, to the house where Beethoven wrote a suicide note in 1802 after he realized his deafness was incurable.

" 'It was only my Art that held me back,' " she quoted dramatically. She had long brown hair tied back in a braid and fine amber flecks in her eyes. She gave a defiant tilt to her head as she spoke.

It was different to talk about Mozart and Beethoven while living in Vienna, to fumble in German about their music. The place, the language, lifted them out of the books I'd read and made their lives feel real. It had happened right here. The manuscripts were in the archives a few blocks away.

When the guards opened the opera house doors, the orderly line became a shoving mass. Standing room was arranged on a series of steps at the back of the orchestra section, just beneath the royal box where the Kaiser used to sit. Metal banisters ran lengthwise between the steps to create rows and to give weary listeners something to lean on. Everyone pushed for the best places. To secure a spot, all you had to do was tie a handkerchief or a scarf to the railing. People tossed their sweaters over the crowd to claim jump. I was carried along by the momentum but then got shunted off into the sixth row, squeezed in among the other novices. I didn't care. I was just a few feet from the most expensive seats in one of the world's most renowned opera houses. Gustav Mahler had earned the hatred of the Viennese public when he was director of the Opera here for turning the lights down during performances. He'd had the audacity to assert that the action on the stage was more important than the audience's fashions. As that night's loden-coated crowd arrived, I saw instead the splendor of the fin-de-siècle, filling the opera house in my imagination with Viennese aristocrats at the height of their glamour and brilliance.

When the opera was over, the two Italian boys, the Spanish girl, Christine, and I raced up Kärntnerstrasse into the old city, following in Mozart's footsteps. The opera had been a bit disappointing. All of the notes were there, but like the stone statue that appears at the end, the performance had seemed bloodless. The Vienna State Opera performed *Don Giovanni* twenty times that year. It was a major draw for the tourists but not what I'd hoped for. Still, if Mozart wasn't at the opera house, I suggested, maybe he was at home. The five of us galloped to Stephansplatz, past the building that had replaced the composer's final apartment. It was now a department store. A plaque on the fourth floor, near kitchenwares, showed where he had died. Threading through the narrow streets behind the cathedral, we came at last to Domgasse. Mozart had lived here in 1786, when he composed *The Marriage of Figaro*. His dashing librettist, Lorenzo da Ponte, supposedly lived across the street, and the two had used a clothing line to pass pages back and forth. The building was still residential, and a few lights were on in upper floors. Mozart's rooms, now a museum, were dark and empty. The few artifacts inside did little to bring you closer to the man. But the building's stone stairs were original. Worn smooth and deeply bowed, they must have been intimately familiar to him. He'd hurried up and down these steps for three years at the peak of his popularity. Here we could touch what he had touched, fit ourselves into the world he inhabited. We sat in the stairwell, looking up in reverence at Mozart's door.

Perhaps there really is a sympathetic vibration that reaches across centuries and languages, binding together like with like. Around the corner we found the Café Diglas occupying the site of Mozart's favorite restaurant. We drank a toast to him and to the chance encounters that had led us all to this spot, this moment. Celebrating Mozart for the tourists, Vienna had made a caricature of his reality. Yet his life was still here, if you knew how to find it. We stumbled excitedly through our mixed-up vocabularies, enchanted by our secret connection to genius, deadened in monuments, but still alive for us.

Vienna had been a foreign city to me, and German a foreign language. I'd stood on the shore in New York and peered across the ocean to some distant, alien land, home to things I wanted. But now I gripped the smooth marble edge of the table in the creamy glow of a Vienna café and smiled at the four strangers sitting there with me. It was as if I were getting to live my dream life. And as we laughed and drank the local wine, the continents spun around. Now I looked back across the ocean at myself on that distant shore. Those sounds, that person, began to feel foreign. One of the Italian boys had his arm around the Spanish girl. I put my arm around Christine and grinned at her through the freeing mask of a new language. I didn't have to be the same person I'd been. No one here knew me. I hardly knew myself. Christine smiled back at me. Later she even kissed me on the cheek.

Late one night in November I was standing outside the Café Hawelka airing cigarette smoke from my clothes. A plaque on the wall said something in German about Franz Kafka. I was sounding out the words when I heard a familiar voice behind me.

"I'll buy you a coffee if you can translate it."

It was Marcus, wearing a dark overcoat and concealed behind a new anarchic beard. He'd arrived in the city a few weeks before, but neither of us had telephones, and we hadn't crossed paths until now. We strolled through the backstreets to the Tirolerhof, a quieter, less smoke-filled café, to catch up. I bought the drinks.

Marcus was taking advantage of Vienna's low cost of living while applying for artist-in-residence programs back home. Although he'd been ahead of me at the Conservatory, we were in the same position now, finished with school, trying to figure out what to do next. He'd begun hunting in the Vienna state archives for manuscripts by Giuliani, Diabelli, and the other guitarists who clustered around them during the guitar's great classical period.

"You can make good money publishing facsimiles of the original editions," he said, pulling out a sheaf of photocopies. With his unruly beard and dark eyes, he looked like an ecstatic Russian mystic.

" 'Although it is already universal,' " he read from Simon Molitor's 1811 guitar method, " 'it is still not well understood; indeed, a most misunderstood instrument.' " He laughed, then held up his finger to underline the words. " 'Yet there could scarcely be another place where authentic guitar-playing is so widely practiced as here in our Vienna.' "

In the muted, wood-paneled warmth of the Tirolerhof, we were conspicuously lively. Two Americans in animated conversation is the Viennese definition of a riot. Marcus nodded toward an old couple sitting in a booth by the window, and they stared disapprovingly at us. They were characteristic of the elderly Viennese, neatly dressed in matching forest-green jackets. The man had a horsehair bristle in his hat, which he'd placed protectively by his side. Across the table his wife wore a cheerful red and white scarf around her neck, though it was the only cheerful thing about her. They must have been in their seventies, lifetime residents of Vienna, the monumental capital of an eight-hundred-year-old empire, now fallen. Their faces were plump but deeply lined, and they sat over their coffee cups staring bitterly at the tabletop, out the window, or at the other customers. In the two hours Marcus and I observed them, they never spoke a word.

Tourist brochures represented Vienna with a Strauss waltz, Klimt's *Kiss,* and a Sacher torte. In my first few weeks there it had not been much different for me: a Baroque ballroom, *Don Giovanni,* and a pastry. But after three months in the city I remembered that Vienna had also exiled Wittgenstein and Freud. Here Mozart and Schubert had died in poverty, and Schoenberg was hissed from the stage. The city sagged beneath its history. And now that the weather had grown overcast and cold, the palaces that sparkled gloriously when I'd arrived huddled massive and gray along the Ringstrasse.

Marcus and I lowered our voices. Sitting at an ornate marble table, we acknowledged that our career options were limited. Marcus was taking classes at the Musikhochschule. But he was just killing time. He didn't need another degree. I hadn't arranged any recitals. It was difficult to see what route led to Vienna's concert stages, crowded as they were with violinists and pianists playing Mozart, Beethoven, and Brahms. As guitarists, with no orchestras to join, we were on our own.

"The Viennese love music," Marcus said, "just not by living musicians."

He lit a cigarette, and I ordered another hot chocolate. In those days the Tirolerhof had the best hot chocolate anywhere in Austria.

It had been Segovia's life ambition to storm the concert hall, claiming a place for the guitar alongside the violin and piano. He'd succeeded fabulously. For sixty years Segovia had toured the world, playing the classical guitar in the homes of the great orchestras— New York's Avery Fisher Hall, Vienna's Musikverein. He'd revived the music of the lute and the Renaissance guitar, recovered the classical heritage of Sor and Giuliani, and commissioned music from dozens of composers—Joaquín Turina, Manuel Ponce, Federico Moreno Torroba. But like the Viennese, Segovia's taste had been essentially conservative. He avoided the twentieth century's most important composers, favoring those who emphasized the guitar's romantic image. Schoenberg's music he considered "a grievous punishment for the ear." At the Conservatory we had heard David Leisner, David Tanenbaum, and other guitarists just a generation ahead of us performing pieces by Philip Glass, Steve Reich, Virgil Thomson, and Ned Rorem. These were fine musicians playing works by celebrated contemporary composers. Yet they could claim only a fraction of Segovia's audience. Despite Segovia's achievement, the guitar remained a foreigner in classical music, present but never quite accepted. If Marcus and I were going to have careers, we needed to do something new, to play music that would distinguish us. We sat quietly in the heavy hush of the café.

"There must be some way to liven things up," I said.

We had to make a choice. We could continue to practice Giuliani and Sor, maintaining the guitar's classical repertoire but, like the Viennese, looking backward to a lost golden era. Or we could try to capture some spark of the present that the guitar, because of its polyglot heritage, was uniquely able to express. We agreed that the guitar was trapped in a classical world that didn't accept or respect it. But did we have to stay there, fighting against the instrument's sweet, romantic image for the rest of our careers? Why should we perpetuate Segovia's crusade? Why should we remain unwanted outsiders, when everywhere else the guitar was the epitome of cool?

We had been trained to dismiss so much popular music because it was shallow and inept. But we really knew how to play. I had experience as a jazz musician, and Marcus was a talented composer. Maybe we could turn the tables, embrace the guitar's mongrel character and experiment with it, mixing the immediacy of improvisation with the considered depth of composition. If we used our skill to integrate the guitar's many voices, maybe we'd discover something new.

Marcus slapped the tabletop in enthusiasm. The whole café froze in horror. If we broke with convention, it seemed, we could capture people's attention. After a hasty exit, we arranged to meet again in a few days to begin exploring new sounds, new ideas. Let the Viennese worship Mozart and Beethoven, turn them into stone! That music was worth hearing now because it had once been revolutionary. Even Segovia had rebelled against the musical establishment before he became part of it. This was our choice. Instead of repeating history, we would challenge it. For a few months, fresh with our new freedom, we thought we could rewrite the story of the classical guitar.

I didn't know then that I was quitting. After four months in Vienna I'd completed my last requirements and graduated from the Conservatory without ceremony. I found a small apartment in the city, not far from the Vienna University. It was a dark, run-down studio looking onto the building's interior courtyard. But it cost only eighty dollars a month. I told my parents—and I believed myself—that I could keep practicing, keep working with Marcus while preparing myself for a career. But the end of college is often an unacknowledged disaster for an aspiring artist. The horizon collapses, and now your career is a day-to-day question, even if you're not ready to answer it. Instead of practicing your art or probing your imagination, you rack your brains for some ambitious plan to put the question off.

All winter Marcus and I played and argued and rehearsed. Eventually we conceived a program of music that juxtaposed intricately composed counterpoint with rhythmic sections of improvisation. In March we began auditioning at nightclubs and cafés. Within a few weeks we'd arranged a series of concerts stretching into the summer. We had posters printed and contacted the newspapers and music journals. By the end of April we were performing two nights a week, sometimes more. The music was energetic and unpredictable, drawing on pop, jazz, rock, and classical styles. It was fun to play, and people seemed to like it. We got better, and the music grew more accomplished, more interesting. A group of fans started following us from gig to gig.

In June the pop star Falco headlined the gala opening of the Wiener Festwochen, performing his hit "Rock Me, Amadeus," beneath the spindly towers of the Rathaus. Late one night that same week Marcus and I were onstage at a popular café in one of Vienna's less fashionable districts. The café was located in an old factory. Steel beams and steam pipes ran along the brick walls. The bar was constructed from pieces of ancient machinery. It was crowded with university students and young, downtrodden-looking Viennese. The air was thickened with smoke, which created psychedelic swirlings in the shafts of colored light that illuminated the stage. Christine was sitting at a table in the front with Anna, a Swiss woman whom Marcus had been dating. They were talking and laughing while we played.

Marcus took a long drag on his cigarette, then stuck it between the strings at the head of his guitar. Counting off the next piece, he took a tempo much slower than usual. I played the melody line, holding back softly, just drifting over the beat. We sounded pretty good. Then Marcus motioned with his chin toward Christine and Anna. They both had their eyes closed. Suddenly I noticed that the audience was paying attention. Marcus took an improvised solo over a repeated sequence of chords that was spiked with irregular accents. Someone in the audience shouted "Go!" in English as we increased the pace, beginning to segue into the next piece. I could feel the change coming over us as the music metamorphosed and the audience began moving, standing up and crowding forward. They pushed in on all sides of the stage. Marcus and I were playing faster. Soaring arcs of melody that we'd carefully rehearsed felt improvised, and minute shadings that we composed on the spot struck the audience with visible power. I could see what we were playing on the faces of the people around me. A sudden curl at the corner of a woman's mouth, the momentary arch of her lips, held and then released. A large, puffy-faced man with a Nietzschean mustache squinted, then bulged his eyes, as if conducting the music with his eyelids. I looked at Marcus, and he rocked back and forth in his chair as the piece made a last surge upward before dropping down to where it had begun.

The audience stayed with us for the rest of the night, keeping us onstage more than an hour longer than we'd planned. Christine and Anna left to catch the last streetcars before the system shut down at one o'clock. Marcus and I stayed onstage playing, then had a few beers at the bar. We struggled to understand the Viennese dialect of the people congratulating us. It was not a concert hall audience. They didn't have to listen. But this seemed fair, now that we had abandoned the concert hall's image of the classical guitar. We had to earn our listeners instead of letting an empty reverence for the past provide them for us. We were testing ourselves against a living sensibility. And unlike playing at weddings, if we were good enough here, this music might take us to any concert hall in the world. We told ourselves this before every performance. After the show, however, it was harder to believe.

The bar owner was a thief. He was a short man, very broad, with a dark gap between his two front teeth. As we packed up our things, he congratulated us on a good performance. Then he handed each of us about ten dollars. We were supposed to get a hundred.

"Not enough drinking," he said, tossing a hand dismissively toward the bar. "Good music. But not enough drinking."

Two bartenders came over to escort us to the street. The owner, they implied, didn't like arguments.

"It takes courage to try something new," Christine said a few weeks later, as we sat on a bench overlooking the city. It was the end of

June, early evening, and summer light glimmered through a curtain of blue silk, painting St. Stephan's spire orange, silver, and black. "You just have to be patient."

She was right, of course. Ten dollars, a hundred dollars. It wasn't very much money. So what if fees were renegotiated after the fact, if someone bolted out the door with the hat we'd passed around? Mozart suffered the same sort of thing all the time. In October 1790, just a year before his death, he had left Vienna to attend the coronation of the new Austrian emperor, Leopold II. Mozart was thirty-four years old, deeply in debt, and still without an official appointment. "I hope you got my letter from Mainz," he wrote to his wife. "The day before we left, I played before the Elector and received a measly 15 Carolin." That's what happens with musicians. You get cheated, exploited. Everyone knows it's a hard life. That doesn't diminish the value of the music.

Christine and I sat holding hands, watching the day darken over vineyards and groves of nut trees, the Danube green and purple in the distance. She spoke sweetly, wanting to help. But I wondered if she understood what was bothering me. It wasn't the money or the dishonesty of club owners that felt so demoralizing. Something much deeper was wrong with the life I was leading. I had an idea of what I wanted, an image of great music, exalted expression, inspired performances. This ideal glowed so vividly in me that I needed only to close my eyes to live in it. But when I opened my eyes, I saw a barroom full of scruffy people getting drunk and a squat, deceitful impresario calculating his take. In this equation Marcus and I were incidental, mere entertainment. And even if the audience loved us, the scene was too small, too finite, too ordinary to feel like success. I enjoyed the music we were playing, and I knew we had just begun to perform. But the dissonance between this and my ideal was eviscerating; it wasn't at all the life I had imagined.

Christine shivered in the descending night air.

"Let's keep walking," she said, pulling me up by the hand.

I had no idea how to explain to her how I felt. I was too young and didn't understand it myself. She snuggled under my arm for warmth. But rather than feeling love, I envied and resented her. Her path forward was clear. She was a talented violist who had come to Vienna for professional training. With hard work, there was every reason to expect she would have a career as an orchestral musician. For her, becoming an artist wasn't a daring struggle but something natural, even practical.

"Doesn't that man look like Mick Jagger?" I'd asked earlier, after a group of tourists trooped past us down the hillside.

"Who?"

Christine had never heard of the Rolling Stones. It was astounding, endearing. She'd grown up in a small north German city famous for its university, sheltered from the cultural tensions that infused my childhood. In the evenings when she was little, her father had listened to songs by Schubert when he came home from his civil service job. Sometimes, if she'd been very good, he would let her listen with him. Music had always spoken to her with one voice. For me, it had always spoken in many, and I was struggling to resolve the cacophony into counterpoint.

We picked our way down the footpath known as Beethoven's Walk. Really, I had everything a young artist full of idealistic passion could hope for: a fabled, romantic city; steady if seedy gigs; a cheap though dingy apartment; and a talented, compassionate girl-friend. But the essence of that ideal is dissatisfaction, because it's impossible to live in its purity. Christine wanted to share with me the trials of a musician's life. Yet as we walked back to the city with our arms around each other, I felt myself elsewhere, living an imaginary life of art. If I couldn't have that entirely, then no part of it was satisfying.

In July, Christine left Vienna for two months. She had been accepted at a prestigious summer youth orchestra in Germany. Marcus left a few weeks later, heading home to begin a series of one-month residencies at small colleges in the Midwest. I resumed practicing on my own. I had written away for applications to guitar competitions in Milan, in Madrid. For four hours each morning I studied the pieces they required, the Sonata Opus 47 by Alberto Ginastera, Rodrigo's *Concierto de Aranjuez*. But as the fall deadlines approached, I didn't feel ready to send in a tape. I'd been working so much with Marcus that I hadn't left enough time to prepare.

It takes courage to try something new. In late August my apartment was an airless oven. With the windows open onto the courtyard, I heard my neighbors watching television, coughing, arguing. The baby next door squalled all day and night, and its mother endlessly repeated its name in exhausted, helpless tones. I'd been in Vienna for a year.

Just be patient, I told myself. *You're only twenty-two; you still have time.*

I worked for three more weeks. Then, like any kid just out of school and in Europe for the first time, I packed a change of clothes and a sleeping bag into my backpack and headed out on the trains. I didn't bring my guitar. It was too good an instrument to leave in youth hostels, and I'd already lost it once. Besides, I wanted to see the sights, not sit in my room alone all day. Courtesy of a student Eurailpass, I visited Budapest, Berlin, Paris, and Rome. A year before, I'd gone a whole week without practicing. Now for the first time since I was seven years old, I didn't touch the guitar for more than a month.

⌒

Was this when I quit? Back in Vienna in the fall, I found a job at a school that taught business English. Chester, the director, was an eccentric expatriate, with springlike gray hair. He followed the teachings of a Bulgarian psychologist who encouraged the use of live music in the classroom. While one of the instructors read out loud to the students, I played quietly in the background at a steady sixty beats per minute. This tempo was supposed to revive memories of the mother's heartbeat, lulling students into a womblike sleep so they could absorb the language unconsciously. Remarkably, it seemed to work. I played études or Bach preludes, watching my metronome blink on the music stand. During the week I audited classes at the university. When I had time off, I traveled to Warsaw, Prague, and Istanbul.

In Prague I met a woman my age whose father had translated Jack Kerouac and Allen Ginsberg into Czech. After the Prague Spring in 1968 he had been arrested, and he died when she was still a child. Now, seventeen years later, his daughter's application to the university had been rejected three times. In Warsaw, where the trade union Solidarity had been outlawed and martial law was still in effect, I witnessed four hundred thousand people march silently through the streets to mourn the murder of an activist priest. Red Solidarity pins were barely concealed beneath their black armbands. A soldier chased me for three blocks after I snapped a picture of the armored trucks that flanked the demonstration. I disappeared into the subway, feeling like a spy.

When Marcus returned to Austria later that winter, we hustled for more gigs. We sent an audition tape to booking agencies in England, France, Germany, and Denmark. But I kept my job at the language school. Without acknowledging it, without even recognizing it, I became a working musician, not a practicing one. It was going to take a long time for Marcus and me to land enough concerts to survive. Maybe it would never happen. In the meantime we had to scrounge for other sources of income, teaching, publishing, playing at art gallery openings.

I had thought it would be different for me, that my effort and devotion would set me apart. Now, despite my practiced resistance, the thought crept in that maybe I was the same, just like my friends and teachers who supported themselves as musicians by being something else, a musicologist, a locksmith. Marcus and I took whatever gigs we could get while we struggled to launch careers. But maybe *this* was our career. Against all my devotion, a desperate conviction grew in darkness inside me, nourished by years of doubt and struggle. I'd wake up at thirty, thirty-five, forty years old, in another cramped, dingy apartment, still dreaming of a different life, a life not on the periphery but at the center of the musical world. Dreaming of the concert hall; dreaming of being an artist. Gigs dribbled in, but never enough. We had no direction. I shut my eyes to see what I wanted; I concentrated all my effort on hearing what mattered. In February the agent in Denmark responded to our tape. Would we be interested in playing at weddings?

That May, in my second year in Austria, Marcus and I held our last concert. Together with Christine, we rode the train through fairytale mountains south of Vienna to Graz, where an art gallery had billed us as "The New Classical." Quaint alpine villages nested in valley folds, chimney smoke hanging over bright meadows. Christine had traveled this route on vacation once as a child. She watched excitedly out the window as long-forgotten impressions revived. It was a treat for her to get out of the city. She had become an understudy in Vienna's second orchestra, the Wiener Symphoniker, and was busy with rehearsals in addition to school. We didn't see each other as much as we had, though neither of us admitted what this meant. On the contrary, we all embarked on that trip in high spirits, Marcus and I taking our act on the road, and Christine tickled to be a groupie. We didn't know it was the last concert or that, by the time we returned to Vienna, something irreparable would be broken. The train cut through snow-covered passes, and Marcus and I cheerfully explained about Elsie the Cow and Heidi, those American symbols of alpine innocence. Christine related the folktale of Krampus, the Austrian anti–Santa Claus, a devil with a long tongue who whips bad children the night before Saint Nick arrives. Everything I'd come to Europe to experience seemed right here, friends and freedom, a new culture and language, in many ways a new identity. In some very concealed part of myself, I must have felt how precarious this identity was, how flimsily it contained the rage and anger and frustration that grew as the ideal that guided my practicing weakened. But if I sensed it, I ignored it. Or perhaps I mistook the feeling for something else, mixed as it was with the volatility of trying something new, the excitement of making my own way. So much was at stake, and the deepest things often hide in plain sight. When we arrived at the station in Graz, the gallery owner shepherded us with flattery to the gig. Everything seemed just as it ought to be.

Marcus and I gave a good performance, and the audience of seventy or more gave us a standing ovation. The owner was delighted and asked us to return in the fall. But Marcus had applied for another round of residencies, and I was determined to prepare for that year's competitions. We made vague promises, uncertain if we'd have time to fulfill them. After a couple of glasses of wine, we were back on the train, this time watching the sunset submerge the mountain valleys in ashes.

We sat quietly as darkness made the train compartment contract. Marcus stretched out on the bench seat and drifted off to sleep. Christine and I cuddled in the corner by the window, debating whether we'd have time for dinner back in the city. She had rehearsal early in the morning, and I was exhausted by the performance. We'd been together for a year and a half, though by that time maybe we were more familiar than close. She was establishing the foundations of her life, preparing for a career and, even at twenty years old, beginning to think of a family. This was only a distant fantasy to me, still so intent on the dream so close at hand. Our sympathy was based on music, on a sensitivity of listening that let us share the deepest feelings. Perhaps this is a pure kind of love.

But in music as in relationships, it is not enough for a life together. After a while I began to talk about the concert, about passages that had worked onstage but that now fell flat in memory. We'd done an adequate job, I said. But something was lacking. Marcus had seemed distracted, and I was dissatisfied with my solos.

"You sounded like a good musician who doesn't practice enough," Christine said, looking down.

It takes courage to play new music; it takes courage to be a musician at all. But it takes more, so much more, to remain a musician, to let yourself be shaped by music however it speaks to you. Since I was twelve years old, I'd dreamed of living the life I heard, living an artist's life. But I'd misunderstood myself, my desires, my ambitions. I misunderstood what it meant to be an artist.

In fact, I was just beginning, just learning how to conduct myself as an artist in the world. But this wasn't the world I'd been working toward. And in that moment I saw that the distance between where I was and where I wanted to be was impossibly long. It sank in that I wasn't ever going to arrive, and so it suddenly felt like I was nowhere. All the pent-up bitterness of a desire endlessly deferred broke loose. It devastated my dream world of music. My fingers hadn't failed me; my technique and talent were not to blame. I'd just imagined the artist's life naïvely, childishly, with too much longing, too much poetry and innocence and purity. And this image ruined music for me.

When I looked up at Christine to reply, I no longer knew why I was a musician. She was going to succeed. But I wasn't. I'd known it for years. All my work had come to nothing.

"I'm sorry," she whispered, leaning over next to me. "I shouldn't have said that."

The story of my practicing came to an end. The guitar had been the instrument of my dreams. Now the dream was over.

ςεttiΝς UP

The man who has music in his soul will be most in love with the loveliest.

—PLATO, *Republic*

Nothing is accomplished by writing a piece of music
Nothing is accomplished by hearing a piece of music
Nothing is accomplished by playing a piece of music.

—JOHN CAGE, "Silence"

One keeps on playing year by year.

—WALLACE STEVENS, "The Man with the Blue Guitar"

IT IS AFTERNOON NOW. The ocean breeze has strengthened into wind, and the sidewalk trees outside my window are swaying. Stray leaves skitter down the street. In the distance a foghorn signals from beneath the Golden Gate Bridge. The damp summer mist must be gathering. By tonight it will probably cover the whole city, a blizzard of fog swirling past the streetlamps. During the summer in San Francisco you sometimes get all four seasons in the course of a single day.

I'm tired, spent. I've practiced for three hours. But it's not the time practicing that exhausts me. I've barely noticed the hours, the clock time that's passed. Musical time has absorbed me, and then even a few moments can encompass years. Now I look around with curiosity. My living room seems just the same as it did this morning when I first sat down. It hasn't melted. Only the sunlight has moved across the floor.

I'm still holding the position the notes have left me in, my fingers poised above the strings. I let out a deep breath and relax. Performing has surprised me. Like waking from a dream, or falling into one, I look at my guitar, wondering what kind of instrument it really is. A musical instrument, of course, a simple wooden device, which releases the kinetic energy of vibrating strings as sound. But the guitar is also an unintended barometer, registering subtle changes in humidity and air pressure. For many people, it is an instrument of imagination and fantasy, a soundboard for unconscious desire. And now, considering it at arm's length, I think for me the guitar might be a navigational instrument, always pointing to where I am. I see my reflection in its face. My breath makes its strings move.

I don't want to stop. I strum a few last chords, adjusting the strings that have drifted out of tune. Just a little longer, I think, just one more piece. I shouldn't. My fingers have lost their focus, and my mind is wandering off into the rest of my day. There is other work I need to do. This is the time when bad habits slither back in, undoing all that I've accomplished today. Still, some childish voice inside me keeps begging, please, please, please, pleading to play for even another minute. I check the tuning and then allow myself a finale, "Weeping Willow Rag" by Scott Joplin.

"Weeping Willow" was one of the first pieces I really played back at the Guitar Workshop, the transition between singing folk songs and becoming a classical guitarist. I had remembered it as a bright, playful tune with syncopation and jazzy harmonies, the perfect music for a precocious eleven-year-old out to impress his teachers, friends, and family. Reading through the notes again a few months ago, however, I was stung by its mournfulness. Despite the major key, the music sounded melancholy, its flatted blue notes tilting the tune inward. As a child, "Weeping Willow" first got me to practice, providing a glimpse of what I might achieve with music. As I played it again, thirty years later, it seemed to show me what I'd learned, what I'd lost when I gave up.

I pull the sheet music from the pile next to my worktable and turn on my desk light. Like my edition of Bach's violin sonatas, the score has notes scribbled all over it, "go through slowly and evenly" and "ha cha-cha," to indicate a rhythmic effect. I remember the instant I understood what my teacher meant, the instant that passage came alive for me. This afternoon I feel again something of the thrill and delight of those days when I first learned how to turn notes into music. Settling myself around the instrument for the last time today, I hold the sound in my head until I hear the whole piece as if all at once. And then I begin to play.

⌢
·

Practicing is a story. Sitting down with your instrument, you imagine yourself into the future, better than you are now, having passed through a limbo of work that changes you. The story creates continuity in change, giving the work context, so that each day's small step adds up to a journey. As long as you keep practicing, almost any goal seems attainable, a matter of time and effort. Each day, each moment, might be fraught with frustration. Still, the story of your practicing absorbs your work, good or bad, showing you the way forward.

When I got back to Vienna after my last concert with Marcus, the story of my practice unraveled. Surrounded again by Vienna's monumental stone architecture, and by the realities of the musical culture it represented, I lost my way. Nothing prevented me from earning a living as a classical guitarist—I could teach, I could play at cafés and weddings, perform the occasional concert. But this was not the life I'd striven for. Time splintered. Exercises became agony; preparing for competitions seemed futile. I continued working out of habit, until one day I looked up and I no longer knew what to do. I no longer knew who I was.

In September, instead of seeking out more gigs, I left Vienna and returned to New York. My sister let me stay in the guestroom of her apartment on the Upper East Side. She had gone to work with my father, carrying on the family business. I stayed up late at night learning how to type from a book I'd borrowed from the New York Public Library. A month later I found a job at a publishing house, in the division dedicated to books about music. Each morning I walked the twenty blocks down Third Avenue to the office, stunned and heartbroken, a sleepwalker. For most of my life I had been on a path to Art. Now, without understanding how it had happened, I was nowhere, lost.

Annmarie, my new boss, was an energetic woman in her late thirties, feisty, independent, and eager to foster my career. She taught me how to prepare book proposals, how to wrangle the numbers so every project seemed assured of success. Along the way I learned how to live in office culture, to write memos and transfer calls, to maneuver around the red nosed, bilious publisher responsible for our division. He liked books about baseball, fishing, true crime. He didn't like Annmarie.

Time felt like sandpaper against my skin. I typed fifty words a minute and let correspondence accumulate for weeks before filing it all away. I felt no attachment to the books we published, scholarly dissertations on musicology, general textbooks of music appreciation. And without faith in the goal of the work, my job felt crushingly menial. I decorated my cubicle walls with pages from unsolicited manuscripts, which gathered like dust on my desk: A novel about mad King Ludwig; a cycle of biographies of the great composers in verse. "Hector Berlioz had troubles with women," the poet began, "it was this that helped to do him in." Every day felt like the waste of my entire life.

For fifteen years I had practiced to become an artist. But I'd misunderstood what that meant. The truth is, the greatness of music is not imaginary. It is specific, physical, practical. No matter how grand my vision of art or how deep my feelings for music, performance always comes down to how you play. The guitar is just an instrument. Others had mastered it, overcome its technique and history to become performing musicians. But I would not. Most people give up their fantasies of art, exploration, and invention. I was furious at myself for having believed I was different, and even more furious that I wasn't.

Walking home from my job at night, I let my eyes droop almost closed and listened to the drum of ten thousand commuters pounding the sidewalk. The city had emerged from the bankrupt doldrums of the 1970s, and now the subways were clean, the streets a bit safer, and the spark of commerce made the air crackle. There was more movement, more intense ambition and envy in one block of New York City than in all of Vienna. But I had no part in it. There was nothing here that I wanted. I was walking home from a boring job, lost in a crowd of blue, gray, and brown business suits, skirting oncoming cars like a scuttling pigeon, because I had given up. My fingers were not to blame; nor were my parents, my teachers, music history, or my instrument. With every step I felt more harshly how I had failed, how fundamentally I had betrayed myself. Out of fear of being mediocre, I'd listened to the wrong voices. I'd been practicing all the wrong things.

I walked the twenty blocks back up to East 79th Street, then another twenty blocks past my building, up to the northern tip of the Central Park reservoir. Then downtown again along Fifth Avenue, past the Metropolitan Museum of Art, past the building on

East 68th Street where my grandmother used to live. Every night I avoided going home. I didn't want to see my guitar. Touching it made me physically sick.

⁀

"Weeping Willow" has three contrasting sections, arranged like a rondo. The main theme punctuates the other two, serving as the beginning, middle, and end, with interludes in between. Yet each time it appears, the theme sounds different because of what has preceded it. The piece is a study in the power of context to change the experience of a melody, even if all the notes remain the same.

As I play through the opening section, I wonder what I heard in this music when I first learned it as an eleven-year-old. I have no recordings of myself playing it, no notebooks from that time to reveal what I thought. My fingers moved in the same patterns as they do now, reaching the same notes. I feel the return of a childlike pleasure in making the music swing. But how could it be the same? So much has happened since then. Stretching for a high D at the top of the neck, I'm impressed that I could play it at all. The piece isn't too difficult technically—not like Rodrigo's "Invocación y Danza." But "Weeping Willow" is a real piece of music, not for beginners. I shake my head as I begin the first interlude. If I heard an eleven-year-old playing this today, I'd believe he or she had the potential to become a great guitarist.

Everyone who gives up a serious childhood dream—of becoming an artist, a doctor, an engineer, an athlete—lives the rest of their life with a sense of loss, with nagging what ifs. Is that time and effort, that talent and ambition, truly wasted? The resonance of these notes brings it all out in me. What if I had started playing younger? What if I'd had better instruction? If only the Guitar Workshop hadn't taught technique with a cloth mute under the strings, training my hands to work too hard. If only my teachers had been less impressed by me and had caught my flaws earlier. What if my parents had been musicians? What if I'd practiced more? I hear myself playing "Weeping Willow" now, and it makes music feel like an unfinished story, the ending somehow concealed in my hands.

⌒

After a few months as an editorial assistant in New York, I began dejectedly searching for some escape, some other story I could believe in. I lost touch with my friends from the Conservatory, though occasionally I came across a CD by someone I'd known. Dave, the saxophone player from my freshman hall, became a success in New York. One of the cellists landed a job with the Philadelphia Orchestra. But from the alumni magazine I learned that most of my classmates became teachers at music schools or colleges, performing on the side with regional orchestras or with their own bands and ensembles. Marcus branched out, hosting a radio program and publishing a guitar method book. But I didn't want to think about music anymore. Very quickly I forgot the pieces that had been important to me. I lost the agility, the skill, and the sensitivity that I had worked so hard to develop. For a while I still thought of myself as a musician, just one who didn't practice, a lapsed musician. But then I really couldn't play anymore. That winter I secretly applied to graduate school for literature. When I was accepted and offered a fellowship that made it possible, I quit my job and moved to California to start something new.

California, land of the reinvented self. After four years in a Boston practice room and two years of Viennese grayness, the luminous northern California sky revealed a kind of blue I'd never known. It was the deepest, most penetrating blue I could bear, and it opened up the deepest, bluest part of me. As lost and dejected and furious with myself as I felt, slowly, gradually, quitting music began to seem freeing. It was a relief to accept being heartbroken, not to resist becoming someone new. I'd brought my guitar with me. But it sat untouched in the closet. Not practicing allowed another life to flourish. Without enthusiasm at first, but then over the course of several years, I discovered that studying music had taught me how to read. Perhaps I did not become a great musician, I consoled myself. But I had learned great things, and this was as valuable as any lesson in life.

Interpreting literature was like performing a piece of music. It was a matter of lines and phrases, of hearing the resonance and learning where the stress falls. The note *A* has little significance by itself, just like the words *love* and *yes*. Yet placed just right, surrounded by other notes, other words, even a single tone can absorb all the forcefulness of our need, returning it to us as meaning. We want to attribute this meaning to the music, the words, the composer, the author. Yet who determines what is musical, what is meaningful? The essence of literature is revelation, it seemed to me, but what it reveals is your desire, the relationship between toneless marks and the music of the reader's imagination.

As long as I could translate it into new skills, not all of my training had been wasted. I finished graduate school and gravitated toward the emerging field of digital media. What happens when a photograph suddenly becomes a mass of pixels? In 1994 the newspapers were full of frightening stories of manipulated images, of falsification and fraud. Yet to me this sounded like what Joe Maneri had taught in microtonal composition. The twelve fixed tones of traditional photography were now broken open, demanding a new aesthetic, a new vocabulary. People don't see in Paul Strand any more than they talk in Wagner, however much our schools and cultural institutions may depend on perpetuating that history. A digitally manipulated image was no more true or false than a chemically rendered one. Both were forms of composition. I had once taken the leap with microtones, allowing myself to experience the rush of anxious freedom as everything familiar melted in the air. It was no different with photography, or film, or painting, or commerce. The technology was just an instrument, the medium just a medium. What mattered—what alone could make it revolutionary—was imagination, opening our eyes and ears to what lay outside the grid of our habits.

After a few years consulting at the San Francisco Museum of Modern Art, and a brief, gravity-defying ride inside the Internet bubble, I began teaching at an art college. The eighteen- or nineteen-year-old artists in my classes seemed very much like me at their age, naïve, earnest, and bewildered by the roughness of their talent. Learning to teach these students, I pulled together the many strands of my experience, as a music student, a performer, a literature professor, a multimedia consultant, and a writer. What did these strands all have in common, except a restless reaching out, a creative dissatisfaction with where I was and what I'd been taught? In all these things I found myself striving for more—more meaning, more feeling, more expression—more than I could ever seem to grasp. In this way I was a student still, though my curriculum had often been confused and fragmented. In classes on modern literature, philosophy, and the theory of art, I sought to make sense of this blind reaching with my students. We read Freud and Nietzsche, Virginia Woolf and Kate Chopin, wondering what makes certain lines or images come alive with joy or anguish, a sense of fullness, even truth. As an artist, you risk everything you are in the search for forms that equal your experience, I told my students. Yet you suffer the anxiety of not knowing, never knowing, if what you grasp will support you, will ever feel like home.

I don't know if they believed me. It had taken me a long time to learn this for myself.

For a decade, a whole era of my life, I lived without music. My guitar stayed in the closet while I built a comfortable life, turning thirty, thirty-five. When my parents retired to Florida, I packed up my old room in Roslyn, with all my notebooks, records, and sheet music, and sent it into storage. I had no use for any of it. And when, after five or six years, I could finally tolerate listening to music again, I sought out other sounds than those I knew, West African drumming, Japanese shakuhachi. Classical music was an acid in my ears. Sometimes, unavoidably, a guitarist at a restaurant would play a piece I had played. Or late at night a melody would come into my head and drive down into my limbs. Then a quiver of longing would break out in my body, and I'd wonder, what if I started again? What if I devoted myself to reclaiming my talent? Isn't it possible that it would be different this time? I'd take out my guitar, just to feel it in my hands. But the feeling was awful. The strings were dead, the wood cold and closed. I couldn't get the instrument into tune. I'd play a few chords, try the first notes of a piece I thought I remembered. And then I'd look at my hands in disgust. Everything was gone. I could still picture myself playing. I could still hear music in my head. But my fingers no longer knew how. The flabby imprecision of my body made me feel old. I put the guitar away again, letting it sit untouched for another six months, another year, another two years.

Then about three years ago, when my parents were cleaning out their house, I had my old boxes shipped to me. Sorting through them, I found school reports from first grade and the script from a sixth-grade play. In the last box I found my notebooks and journals from the Conservatory and fifteen years' worth of sheet music.

On a cold night in March, with a fire in the fireplace of my cozy San Francisco apartment, I sat down with thirteen spiral-bound college notebooks that I'd bought at the Coop in Harvard Square twenty years before. The wire bindings had rusted in storage, and they left flaky stains on my hands, like dried blood. I arranged them in a chronological stack on the wooden trunk that I used as a coffee table. Then I began to read, lighted by nostalgia, expecting the serene pleasure of safely looking back.

Instead I felt a deep, physical wound tearing open. In these notes I met myself as I had been at seventeen, at twenty-one: a young man, inexperienced with himself, struggling for expression. The big talk and the childish opinions embarrassed me, the bad writing, the immaturity. Yet I could feel again how passionately in pursuit of beautiful ideals I was, how full of great purpose. As I retraced my stumbling, innocent progress, I was seized again by the excitement, anxiety, and surging creativity of that time. Stunned by this vitality of feeling, I realized how much I'd lost when I quit music. The life I had built was interesting and rewarding. But the one I encountered here had consumed and inspired me. Suddenly I felt the years spent practicing had not been wasted. But all the time since then had been. What might I have accomplished with these ten years, if I had traversed them still striving, still burning with desire? I left the stack of notebooks lying on my coffee table, pulled my guitar from the closet, and impulsively opened my music books like a long-lost cache of love letters.

Holding the instrument again, I felt the rush of pleasure and possibility that had bubbled inside me each morning at the Conservatory as I set to work. This warmth in my hands—I hadn't realized how deeply I'd missed it. I read through forgotten, familiar pieces in an ecstasy of recollection. It didn't matter that I couldn't play. I resolved to practice every day, to regain my old ability. If I worked for a year, I thought, I could be better than I was when I quit. I dreamed of picking up the story where I'd left it, hoping to give it a happier ending.

Inspired, I hunted in the boxes for a bundle of cassette tapes, recordings of my concerts, the heart of my experience, which I'd packed away in storage. Going to Vienna and then quitting had been a tragic wrong turn, I concluded. My proper path had been suspended at my senior recital. Then, as I'd performed at Goddard Chapel, I'd felt exultant. I hadn't played as well as I could have—I still had a lifetime of work ahead of me. But my playing had made a surprising leap forward. This was the moment, the momentum I sought to recover. I found the recordings wrapped in a Guitar Workshop T-shirt, six tapes including my senior recital. I put it on the stereo and sat on the couch to listen.

Beneath the hiss of the tape and the shuffling of the audience, I heard myself playing at the height of my ability. I no longer felt like the performer. I couldn't play these pieces now. I didn't even remember how some of them went. Instead I listened like an anxious parent watching his child at the spring concert. *Please make it all the way through!* I prayed, even though the performance was long past. I wanted it to go well, to have gone well. I wanted to have given a good performance.

But as I listened, my heart sank. Rather than great potential lost to circumstance, I heard a harsh justice. The performance was not as good as I'd remembered. There were mistakes, of course. These were not what bothered me. Recordings accentuate finger slips. Few listeners who aren't also guitarists would hear them during the performance. The mistakes that bothered me now were botched phrases, garbled lines that interfered with the music. The performance was full of musical ideas. But no piece was good from start to finish. No whole movement sustained its mood. Almost every crescendo grew thin and brittle. The softer passages were rushed. Very little was left to build by itself. These were mistakes that everyone would hear, everyone would feel. The music had my hands all over it, holding on to every note, trying to keep from losing myself by giving too much away. Instead of playing the music, I'd strangled it.

A sense of squandered opportunity might have justified my longing for that time. It would have allowed me to believe that I had something to recover and so fueled my revived desire to practice.

But instead it now seemed as if my whole life as a musician had been a mistake. I listened, and I knew that the time, my effort, and my dreams of music were not waiting to be reclaimed but were irretrievably lost. I put my guitar back in the closet and left it there. I had to let the whole story go.

After ten years I'd finally quit. I became a former musician.

⌒

"Weeping Willow" hangs suspended over a D^7 chord before returning to the main theme for the final chorus. On the sheet music my teacher at the Guitar Workshop had written the word *sigh* over the chord, describing how the moment should feel. As the notes of the chord expire in the air, I let out a deep breath too, feeling it interlace with the music. I wait as long as I can stand it. Then, with a clear, silent pick-up breath, I play the first notes of the theme, now for the third time, launching the long arc to the end.

I was wrong about "Weeping Willow." The main theme is not mournful, or not just mournful. There is a deep, dark joyousness in it that I don't think I've ever heard, or have ever been ready to hear before. This music knows how much is at stake, how close to heartbreak we are in every moment. It knows how fragile are the great moments in our lives, how quickly our most profound experiences are lost in the grasping pettiness of every day. These are the same notes as earlier, the same fingerings and phrases. And yet the familiar music unfolds in revelation. This is the last time the theme will sound. It holds everything that has come before, letting it go with such sorrow, such poignant regret, with such grace and acceptance. The music knows that each moment is irretrievably lost. And yet paradoxically, loss makes the music whole.

I play as simply as I can. The notes emerge and die away. This is the moment I've been working toward all day. Practicing, I recognize myself. Performance, however, always surprises me. If I play truly and honestly, I hear things I never knew I could hear, feel things I never knew I could feel.

Six months after listening to the tape of my senior recital, I started to practice again. Finally, truly quitting had somehow opened the way. Almost nothing remained of my earlier skill. All those years of work, the devotion and solitude, were like a lost faith, impossible to recover. But I was no longer seeking to restore my old ability. I returned to practicing not as a young, aspiring artist, but as a former musician, with a different sense of what it means to play the guitar. I'm trying not to repeat myself. My first time through, I practiced badly, chasing an ideal that ruined music for me, turning what I had loved the most into torture. Now I'm pursuing not an ideal but the reality of my own experience. I began to practice again because I felt I could do it better this time.

How do you return to a love that has broken your heart? As I play the theme of "Weeping Willow" one last time, all my fantasies of success and all the flaws in my character rise again to the surface, my ambition and despair, concentrated in my fingertips. Each impulse, each need and doubt, clamors for expression, a little tyrant demanding its own way. And with each note these urgent demands collide with the limitations of my hands, my instrument, and my imagination. It is the same thing every day, the same as it always was. Yet everything has changed.

Making music—doing anything we really love—we are always at the limits of our ability. Despite what Salieri in *Amadeus* believes, no one is singled out for disdain because he hears and feels more than he can express. Every musician, every artist, every person suffers this disappointment. Even Yo-Yo Ma must sometimes wish he were better, wish he could capture a fleeting nuance that glimmers so clearly before him yet refuses to yield to his touch. Limitation is the condition of our lives. What matters—what allows us to reach beyond ourselves, as we are, and push at the boundaries of our ability—is that we continue. But then everything depends on how we practice, what we practice.

Beginning again, I became my own teacher, finally absorbing the best of what I had learned. At first I played just half an hour each day. My hands were stiff and clumsy, and pieces that had once felt easy now seemed impossibly beyond my reach. But I knew this wouldn't last. I kept playing the simplest études, letting the music teach my fingers how to move. I read method books and tried out their suggestions. Most of all I listened to the instrument. After a few months, though it still wasn't easy, I had learned how to play again. It took longer to admit I was practicing. The word itself evoked so much that was painful. When it struck me, I felt paralyzed and would skip a few days or a week. But then I'd miss the pleasure of simply playing, and I saw that I'd punished myself for calling this pleasure "practice."

Why should practice be painful, I wondered, when playing was such a joy? I let the question sink in, while continuing with simple études and little pieces that sounded good. Yet as I progressed, even with the simplest music, my old frustrations reemerged, impatience with my fingers and dissatisfaction with myself. I sought comfort in the methods and in books by respected musicians. But nothing I read gave me what I needed. My hands began to tense again until, over the course of a year, I gradually understood that I wasn't practicing to play the guitar, but playing the guitar to learn about practicing.

As a young man, impassioned and impatient, I played badly. Overwhelmed by what I felt, I wanted each note to embody everything. And I succeeded. With every fingerstroke I enacted the conflict between what I imagined and what I could achieve. Listening so intently, I heard only what was beyond me. The deeper into music I delved, the more obstacles and resistance I discovered. My hands, my instrument, its history, and the attitudes of those who heard me, my audiences—all seemed to stand between me and the perfect music in my head. I fought as hard as I could to close the distance, until finally practicing became a struggle leading nowhere. Each day was more of the same; each moment proved again that I would never arrive. Perhaps in the end you do perfect what you practice, though it may be years before you know what this is. Unable to find a way out of this conflict, I repeated it over and over, perfecting my grip on what blocked me. There was no escape but to give up.

Only a very few loves can disappoint you so fundamentally that you feel you've lost yourself when they're gone. Quitting music wounded me as deeply as any relationship in my life. It was my first great loss, this innocent, awkward failure to live with what I heard and felt. For more than ten years I avoided music. It hurt too much. My anger went as deep as my love had gone. I suppose this is natural. In the aftermath of something so painful, we subsist on bitterness, which sustains us against even greater loss. For most of the following years I practiced disappointment, even without touching the guitar. I pursued what interested me, but not what I loved. It has taken all this work, all this dredging through my history and habits, to accept this response to my failure, to reveal the deep flaw in my technique.

Practicing is different now because I am different. Quitting, I lived through what I had been afraid of feeling, what I had struggled against all those hours, all those years in the practice room. My dream of music had expressed what I wanted, what I hoped for. But when I quit, the underside of my practice, everything I didn't want, everything I dreaded, finally broke loose: the anger and bitterness and rage, the fear that I wasn't good enough, that without music I was nothing. I had been unable to accept these feelings *in* music, and so I had to experience them outside, as life. It was the harshest lesson I'd ever learned. And yet paradoxically the loss of music made me whole.

I may never again play as well as I did when I was seventeen or twenty-one, may never play as well as I think I could. My hands are not as flexible, and I've lost so much time not practicing. But each day now when I sit down, I try to give a performance, opening myself over and over again to what I love the most, knowing each time that I will have to let it go. To play better now means learning to continue, living through what slips away.

Practicing can be a dream world in which you escape the reality of time. You believe that you have everything to do over again, that you have all the time in the world to achieve perfection. And every day we must practice. There is no other way to improve. Still, practicing, by itself, cheats you of half your life. Even if you are your only audience, music lives fully only in performance. Performance brings all the strands together, for a moment, joining the many conflicting voices with which music speaks—the joy, the frustration and anger, the loneliness, regret, and sudden elation. But unlike practice, every performance has an end. And without an end, music is just a fantasy. Now, returning to music, I hear how these tones equal my experience. Ringing and dying; my dream and its loss— together these define the boundaries of my ability, the high and the low, the edges I will always push against. Together they describe what music is for me, what "music" is, the full measure of my love.

The losses we suffer are real and cannot be wished away. But the beauty of music is that it embodies our love and our disappointment together, moving us forward and not repeating. With every passage, it teaches us the sweet, bittersweet joy of development, of growth, of change. Because playing music, you are constantly leaving home, constantly leaving where you are comfortable and secure, giving up what you have loved and striven for, loved and settled for. You give it up, not knowing whether there is more ahead, whether what you will find next—what you will be next—will satisfy you.

Yet you give it up anyway, because you must, because time moves you forward, and life moves you forward, and the sound of *your* music is not what it was yesterday or last year or twenty years ago. You must make the music of today. You have to perform what you hear, what you feel, what you can grasp, today.

At least this is what I tell myself. It's taken me more than ten years to let go of the story of my failure and find a new one I could believe in, this myth of growth and return that helps me continue. I started practicing again because I felt I could do it better this time. Now, whatever my fingers allow me to play, I sit down to practice the fullness of my doubts and desire, my fantasies and flaws. Each day I follow them as far as I can bear it, for now. This is what teaches me my limits; this is what enables me to improve.

I think it is the same with anything you seriously practice, anything you deeply love. For me, it was music. The guitar. But whatever "music" is for you, if you practice for real, eventually it will show you everything that is within you. Because as accomplished or as disappointed as you may feel now, you don't know what remains concealed in your hands. Maybe you'll never grasp it all. What you want may never yield to your touch. And yet maybe one day a performance will surprise you. Maybe today your music will reveal all the joy and disappointment, all the love and the fear you are capable of, your whole life, the true concord of your own heart.

⌒

With the last notes of "Weeping Willow" still ringing in my ears, I take a dark blue dustcloth from the case and wipe the back and sides of the guitar. Oils from my fingers and from my body as it encircles the instrument wear away at the varnish. To slow the process, I clean the surfaces each day, tracing the cedar top and the rosewood back and sides with the soft cloth, making them shine. I slide the cloth underneath the strings by the soundhole, where dust from my fingernails accumulates. My hands follow the graceful contours, along the church door's blond stripe, across the fiery grain. The guitar has grown warm with my touch. Now it will lie still for the rest of the day, contracting as it cools and at the same time expanding with the fog. The wood will grow confused, and in the morning I'll have to remind it how it feels to be in tune. I'll have to remember how it feels myself.

The guitar fits snugly in the heavily padded, maroon interior of its case. This is the same fiberglass travel case that took a solo flight to Bucharest. I bought it when I thought I would be flying from city to city giving concerts. My name is stenciled in indelible ink on the side. There are scuffs and scratches all around the edges, even though it never went on tour. Now the case and my instrument mostly stay at home. I shut the top and secure its three latches.

I move the music stand to its place against the wall and stow my folding footstool beneath it. My music books are strewn on the desk—Bach, Rodrigo, Barrios, and Joplin. I gather them in a pile, squaring the edges against the desktop, then set them on the music stand. Finally I lift my chair by its backrest and swing it around so it slides under my desk.

There is so much left to express, so much still to practice. But I'm finished for now. I've worked hard and well—as well as I can, today. I turn out the light, letting music and my guitar rest until tomorrow. In the morning, like every morning, I'll begin again.

LISTENING

Like learning to play an instrument, becoming a good listener takes time and effort. Listening is a practice. Listening is also a great pleasure. In the course of writing, I've had the pleasure of listening to more guitar music than ever before. But I've still only sampled the vast repertoire of recordings. In the following recommendations, I've selected just a few performances of music mentioned in *Practicing*, emphasizing contemporary guitarists and readily available recordings.

J. S. BACH

In 1935, when Segovia premiered the Chaconne from Bach's Violin Partita no. 2 in D Minor in Paris, it was a daring experiment. Today Bach is probably the guitar's most performed composer. Recordings of Bach's lute, cello, flute, and violin music on guitar are too numerous to list. Every major recording artist and every aspiring performer plays Bach. There are transcriptions of *The Well-Tempered Clavier, The Art of the Fugue, The Goldberg Variations,* and even selected movements from *The Brandenburg Concertos.* But the recorded history of Bach on the guitar begins with Segovia.

Andrés Segovia, *Segovia Collection,* vol. 1. *Bach* (MCA, 1990)

This CD contains the most important of Segovia's Bach recordings, including the Chaconne, and the only complete suite recorded by Segovia, Cello Suite no. 3 in C Major (BWV 1009). The third cello suite provides an excellent opportunity for comparison, since numerous performers have recorded it. Compare Segovia's performance with those by Celedonio Romero, Pepe Romero, and David Leisner.

Celedonio Romero, *Bach and Gaspar Sanẓ* (Delos, 1986)
Pepe Romero, *Bach* (Philips, 1981)
David Leisner, *J. S. Bach* (Azica Records, 1999)

The Romeros perform an unadorned transcription of the cello music, while Leisner, like Segovia, has added bass notes and filled out the harmony, making the piece more guitaristic.

Recordings of the lute suites are numerous. I've recently been listening to Paul Galbraith, who has arranged them for eight-string guitar.

Paul Galbraith, *Bach Lute Suites* (Delos, 2000)

Other recordings of the complete lute suites include:

John Williams, *Bach: The Four Lute Suites* (Sony, 1990)
Sharon Isbin, *J. S. Bach: Complete Lute Suites* (EMI, 1989)

I prefer the guitar. But the lute is a fine instrument too. To hear Bach's lute music performed in the original keys and tunings, listen to Lutz Kirchhof.

Lutz Kirchhof, *Johann Sebastian Bach: The Works for Lute in Original Keys and Tunings* (Sony Classical, 1990)

Among the many recordings of individual lute and cello suites and violin sonatas, my favorites include:

Julian Bream, *Bach Guitar Recital* (EMI, 1994)
Manuel Barrueco, *J. S. Bach Sonatas* (EMI, 1997) (Barrueco also plays Bach on *300 Years of Guitar Masterpieces*, a three-

disc set with a wide range of music, including Villa-Lobos, *Suite Populaire Bresilienne* [Vox Box 3, 1991].)
Scott Tennant, *Guitar Recital* (GHA, 1994)
Martha Masters, *Guitar Recital* (Naxos, 2001)

FERNANDO SOR

Sor's concert pieces have been widely performed, and selected études appear scattered throughout the recordings. However, there are only a few recordings of the larger groups of études. David Tanenbaum has issued an exceptionally clear, unadorned performance as a guide for students, containing the twenty "Segovia" études by Sor, as well as twenty-five by Carcassi and twenty by Leo Brouwer.

David Tanenbaum, *Estudios: The Essential Recordings* (Guitar Solo Publications, 1990)

The Naxos label has issued the complete works of Fernando Sor, performed by a suite of guitarists, including Adam Holzman, Marc Teicholz, and John Holmquist. Nicholas Goluses performs the Study in G.

Nicholas Goluses, *Sor: 25 Progressive Studies, Op. 60* (Naxos, 1996)

Among performers of Sor's concert pieces, I enjoy Pepe Romero and Manuel Barrueco.

Pepe Romero, *Guitar Solos* (Philips, 1993) (This recording also includes Tárrega's "Capricho Arabe.")
Manuel Barrueco, *Mozart & Sor* (EMI, 1988)

Also of particular interest is a two-volume set by José Miguel Moreno, who performs on period instruments.

José Miguel Moreno, *La Guitarra Española*, vol. 1, 1536–1836 (Glossa, 1994), vol. 2, 1818–1918 (Glossa, 1996)

David Starobin reaches into the catalog and performs lesser-known works by Sor and Giuliani.

> David Starobin, *Sor & Giuliani* (Bridge, 2001) and *The Music of Fernando Sor: Les plus belles pages* (Bridge, 2005)

JOAQUÍN RODRIGO, "INVOCACIÓN Y DANZA"

After Bach, Rodrigo is probably the guitar's best-known composer. Numerous recordings of "Invocación y Danza" have emerged recently, offering another opportunity to compare performance styles and interpretation. Start with Scott Tennant, who has issued Rodrigo's complete guitar music on two CDs.

> Scott Tennant, *Joaquín Rodrigo: The Complete Guitar Works,* vol. 1 (GHA, 1994), vol. 2 (GHA, 2002)

Then compare Tennant's performance with:

> Pepe Romero, *Concierto de Aranjuez,* with Sir Neville Marriner and the Academy of St. Martin in the Fields (Philips, 1994)
> Sharon Isbin, *Road to the Sun: Latin Romances for Guitar* (Virgin Classics, 1992) (This recording also contains Barrios, "La Catedral," and Tárrega, "Capricho Arabe.")
> Dale Kavanagh, *Lyrical and Virtuosic Guitar Music* (Hanssler Classics, 1999)
> Antigoni Goni, *Rodrigo, Bomeniconi, Mompou, Barrios, Brouwer* (Naxos, 1996)

AGUSTÍN BARRIOS, "LA CATEDRAL"

We are fortunate that many of Barrios's recordings survive and have been reissued on CD.

Agustín Barrios, *The Complete Guitar Recordings* (Chanterelle Historical Recordings, 1997)

Numerous contemporary performers have recorded Barrios's music.

David Russell, *Music of Barrios* (Telarc, 1995)
John Williams, *The Great Paraguayan: Guitar Music of Barrios* (Sony, 2005)
Antigoni Goni, *Barrios Guitar Music*, vol. 1 (Naxos, 2001)
Enno Voorhorst, *Barrios Guitar Music*, vol. 2 (Naxos, 2004)

SIR MICHAEL TIPPETT, *THE BLUE GUITAR*

The Blue Guitar was written for Julian Bream, who gave the first performance in 1983.

Julian Bream, *Guitar Recital* (Testament, 2005)

Several younger guitarists have given fine performances of the piece. David Tanenbaum was the first to restore the original order of the movements, which had been transposed in the published edition.

David Tanenbaum, *Acoustic Counterpoint: Classical Guitar Music from the '80s* (New Albion Records, 1990)
Craig Ogden, *Tippett The Blue Guitar—20th Century Guitar Classics* (Nimbus Records, 1995)
Eleftheria Kotzia, *The Blue Guitar* (Pavillion Recordings, 2001)

SCOTT JOPLIN, "WEEPING WILLOW RAG"

Scott Joplin achieves a moodiness on guitar that I find lacking in many of the modern piano versions of his music. There are numerous recordings of "The Entertainer." "Weeping Willow" may be heard in

Listening

two very different performances. Giovanni De Chiaro gives a clean, bright rendition; Carlos Barbosa-Lima plays in a sassy swing time.

Giovanni De Chiaro, *Scott Joplin on Guitar* (Centaur, 1993)
Carlos Barbosa-Lima, *The Entertainer & Selected Works by Scott Joplin* (Concord Records, 1990)

READING

*"While we are practicing we must know what we are doing;
otherwise we will waste most of our time."*

When practicing, it certainly helps to know what you are doing. But if
you're at all like me, you frequently only figure it out along the way. As
I learned what I was doing, I sought information and guidance in
many quarters, consulting technical methods for the guitar, general
advice on the topic of practice, and histories of the instrument. The
following references are what I found to be most helpful. It is an idio-
syncratic and partial record, a list of starting points. The real work—
and the real pleasure—of practice lies in discovering how to do it
yourself. In my experience, if you keep practicing, you rarely waste
your time.

GUITAR METHODS

Guitar methods are an invaluable source of information about the
instrument, its history, and its musicality. Serious authors of a method
have thought about the instrument deeply, and even if you don't follow
their fingerings, you can learn what the guitar is in their hands. No
method book can substitute for a good teacher. But a method can serve
as a friend: its suggestions are worth considering, though in the end
you must decide what's best.

Among the many modern methods, I've found Scott Tennant's especially helpful.

> Scott Tennant, *Pumping Nylon: The Classical Guitarist's Technique Handbook* (Van Nuys, Calif.: Alfred Publishing Co., 1995)
> Scott Tennant, *Basic Classical Guitar Method* (Van Nuys, Calif.: Alfred Publishing Co., 2004) This book provides information for beginners.

For many years Frederick Noad's methods have been standards:

> Frederick M. Noad, *Playing the Guitar: A Self-Instruction Guide to Technique and Theory,* 3rd ed. (New York: Schirmer Books, 1981)
> Frederick M. Noad, *Solo Guitar Playing: A Complete Course of Instruction in the Techniques of Guitar Performance* (New York: Collier Books, 1994 [1968])

Other method books of interest include:

> John Mills, *The John Mills Classical Guitar Tutor* (London: Music Sales, 1992)
> Aaron Shearer, *Classic Guitar Technique* (Van Nuys, Calif.: Alfred Publishing Co., 1987)

We are in a golden age of guitar research. Many historically significant guitar methods have recently been reprinted, both in facsimile editions as well as in translation. Although modern technique contradicts what you'll find here, the serious student will certainly benefit from the insights of Sor, Aguado, and Pujol/Tárrega. No one has considered the instrument more thoroughly.

Fernando Sor, *Method for the Spanish Guitar*, A complete reprint of the 1832 English translation with a preface by Brian Jeffrey (London: Tecla Editions, 1995)

Dionisio Aguado, *New Guitar Method*, edited by Brian Jeffrey, translated by Louise Bigwood (London: Tecla Editions, 2004)

Emilio Pujol, *Guitar School: A Theoretical, Practical Method for the Guitar Based on the Principles of Francisco Tárrega*, translated by Brian Jeffrey, edited by Matanya Orphee (Columbus, Ohio: Editions Orphée, 1983)

Other historical methods that I have consulted for their studies and exercises include:

Matteo Carcassi (1792–1853), *Méthode complète pour la guitare* (Geneva: Éditions Minkoff, 1988): Facsimile of the 1925 edition, published by Carli (Paris). In French.

English edition: *The Complete Carcassi Guitar Method*, edited by Mel Bay and Joseph Chastle (Pacific, Mo.: Mel Bay Publications, 1974)

Ferdinando Carulli (1770–1841), *Méthode complète pour parvenir à pincer de la guitare, cinquième édition, op. 241* (Paris, 1810) (Geneva: Éditions Minkoff, 1987). Facsimile of the 1925 Carli edition (Paris). In French with a brief English introduction.

Charles Doisy (d. 1807), *Principes généraux de la guitare* (Geneva: Éditions Minkoff, 1978): Facsimile. In French.

Gaspar Sanz (1640–1710), *Instrucción de música sobre la guitarra española*, translated into English as *The Complete Guitar Works of Gaspar Sanz*, transcribed and edited for classical guitar by Robert Strizich (Saint-Nicolas, Québec: Doberman-Yppan, 1999)

Paul Wathen Cox has written a doctoral dissertation comparing the different methods for guitar published between 1770 and 1850. See *Classic Guitar Technique and Its Evolution as Reflected in the Method Books ca. 1770–1850* (PhD dissertation, Indiana University, 1978). This book contains excellent references and bibliography.

ABOUT PRACTICING

Strange as it may seem, "practicing" is rarely an item in the index of a musician's autobiography. You will find much of interest in the memoirs of famous performers, but almost never information about how they learned to perform. Pablo Casals, so articulate on other matters, is characteristic for the genre. "I was constantly practicing on my cello," he tells us, but not how. Never how.

For a discussion of the techniques of practicing itself, you must turn to practicing theory. But thinking about music can be as seductive as making it. Almost every philosopher succumbs to this temptation. "How much nobler is the study of music as a rational science than as a laborious skill of manufacturing sounds," exclaims Boethius. "It is nobler to the degree that the mind is nobler than the body." Musicians, by contrast, frequently fall in love with their fingers, confusing practicing with the invention of exercises.

In general, books about practicing address the in-between, the messy interface of the mind and the body. Even the most balanced, however, walks a tightrope between the wise and the banal, with the difference being a matter of the reader's temperament.

For me, Madeline Bruser's book was exceptionally helpful and enjoyable to read.

Madeline Bruser, *The Art of Practicing: A Guide to Making Music from the Heart* (New York: Bell Tower, 1997)

Other books and articles on the topic of practicing an instrument, not necessarily the guitar, include:

Alice Artzt, *The Art of Practicing* (Westport, Conn.: Bold Strummer, 1993)

Boris Berman, *Notes from the Pianist's Bench*, rev. ed. (New Haven, Conn.: Yale University Press, 2002)

Gordon Epperson, "How to Practice," *American String Teacher* 28, no. 3 (Summer 1978), pp. 24–25

Barry Green, with W. Timothy Gallwey, *The Inner Game of Music* (New York: Doubleday, 1986)

Ricardo Iznaola, *On Practicing: A Manual for Students of Guitar Performance* (Pacific, Mo.: Mel Bay Publications, 2000)

Richard Provost, *The Art and Technique of Practice* (San Francisco: Guitar Solo Publications, 1992)

Eric Rosenblith, "On Practicing," *American String Teacher* 34, no. 1 (Winter 1984), pp. 52–54

György Sandor, *On Piano Playing: Motion, Sound, and Expression* (New York: Schirmer Books, 1995)

Philip Toshio Sudo, *Zen Guitar* (New York: Simon and Schuster, 1998)

Musicians, of course, are not the only artists who practice. Sometimes an outside perspective shows the work in a new light. I found two classic books on acting particularly illuminating.

Uta Hagen and Haskel Frankel, *Respect for Acting* (New York: Wiley Publishing, 1973)

Constantin Stanislavski, *An Actor Prepares*, translated by Elizabeth Reynolds Hapgood (New York: Theater Arts Books, 1973)

GUITAR HISTORY

The 1908 Sears and Roebuck catalog advertises a full line of classical guitars, including a midpriced instrument, called "The Toreador," for

$3.15. The Toreador's soundboard is spruce, a traditional tonewood; the unidentified material for its back and sides is "finished in a perfect imitation of finely grained mahogany."

Like the Toreador, my history of the guitar is modeled after the finest examples, while satisfying needs other than history. I have described my relation to the instrument, supported by what information I have learned, received, or believed to be true. Many important developments and personalities are simply absent, and some are here in mere cameo. Still, I don't want my materials to go unidentified.

For information about the history of the guitar, I have relied heavily on the indispensable *The New Grove Dictionary of Music and Musicians*, edited by Stanley Sadie, 20 vols. (London: Macmillan, 1980), as well as on several general histories of the guitar, and numerous sources on specific aspects of the instrument.

GENERAL HISTORIES

Tom Evans and Mary Evans, *Guitars: Music, History, Construction and Players from the Renaissance to Rock* (New York: Paddington Press, 1977)

Frederic V. Grunfeld, *The Art and Times of the Guitar: An Illustrated History of Guitars and Guitarists* (New York: Collier Books, 1969)

John Morrish, ed., *The Classical Guitar: A Complete History*, 2nd rev. ed. (San Francisco: Backbeat Books, 2002)

Harvey Turnbull, *The Guitar from the Renaissance to the Present Day* (New York: Charles Scribner's Sons, 1974)

James Tyler and Paul Sparks, *The Guitar and Its Music from the Renaissance to the Classical Era* (Oxford: Oxford University Press, 2002)

Graham Wade, *Traditions of the Classical Guitar* (London: John Calder, 1980)

SPECIFIC TOPICS

William R. Cumpiano and Jonathan D. Natelson, *Guitarmaking: Tradition and Technology* (Hadley, Mass.: Rosewood Press, 1987)

Thomas Heck, *Mauro Giuliani: Virtuoso Guitarist and Composer* (Columbus, Ohio: Éditions Orphée, October 1995). Based on the author's *The Birth of the Classic Guitar and Its Cultivation in Vienna, Reflected in the Career and Compositions of Mauro Giuliani (d. 1829)* (PhD dissertation, Yale University, 1970).

Brian Jeffrey, *Fernando Sor, Guitarist and Composer* (London: Tecla Editions, 1977). Jeffrey is one of the most important figures in guitar scholarship, and his Tecla Editions publishes the complete works of many of the instrument's most significant composers in facsimile, including Fernando Sor and Mauro Giuliani.

Neil D. Pennington, *The Spanish Baroque Guitar* (Ann Arbor, Mich.: UMI Research Press, 1981)

Manuel Rodríguez, *The Art and Craft of Making Classical Guitars* (Milwaukee, Wis.: Hal Leonard, 2003)

José L. Romanillos, *Antonio de Torres: Guitar Maker—His Life and Work* (Longmead, Shaftesbury, Dorset: Element Books, 1987)

Andrés Segovia, *An Autobiography of the Years 1893–1920* (New York: Macmillan, 1976)

Douglas Alton Smith, *A History of the Lute from Antiquity to the Renaissance* (Lute Society of America, 2002)

Graham Wade, *A New Look at Segovia—His Life, His Music* (Pacific, Mo.: Mel Bay Publications, 1997)

Emanuel Winternitz, *Musical Instruments and Their Symbolism in Western Art* (New York: W. W. Norton & Co., 1967)

NOTES

SITTING DOWN

4. "rough edges that might impede the execution . . .": Antonio Abreu is quoted in Neil D. Pennington, *The Spanish Baroque Guitar* (Ann Arbor, Mich.: UMI Research Press, 1981), 62.

4. "to strike with the nails is imperfection . . .": Miguel Fuenllana is quoted in Tom Evans and Mary Evans, *Guitars: Music, History, Construction and Players from the Renaissance to Rock* (New York: Paddington Press, 1977), 102.

5. "by imitating this harmony on stringed instruments": Cicero, *De Republica* VI, quoted in Joscelyn Godwin, *Music, Mysticism, and Magic: A Sourcebook* (New York: Routledge & Kegan Paul, 1986), 10; quotation modified.

6. "For the past eighty years . . .": Pablo Casals, *Joys and Sorrows* (New York: Simon and Schuster, 1970), 17.

7. "[Practicing] is the search for ever greater joy": Yehudi Menuhin, "foreword" to Madeline Bruser, *The Art of Practicing: A Guide to Making Music from the Heart* (New York: Bell Tower, 1997), xiii.

7. "it is impossible to feign mastery . . .": Andrés Segovia, letter to Bernard Gavoty, December 20, 1954, quoted in Graham Wade, *Segovia: A Celebration of the Man and His Music* (London: Allison and Busby, 1983), 81.

8. "I was obliged to work hard . . .": J. S. Bach is quoted in Ian Crofton and Donald Fraser, *A Dictionary of Musical Quotations* (New York: Schirmer Books, 1985), 11.

8. "Whatever efforts we may make . . .": Jean-Jacques Rousseau, *Dictionary of Music*, quoted in Richard Taruskin and Piero Weiss, *Music in the Western World: A History in Documents* (New York: Schirmer Books, 1984), 283.

8. "The capacity for melody is a gift . . .": Igor Stravinsky, *Poetics of Music in the Form of Six Lessons*, trans. Arthur Knodel and Ingolf Dahl (Cambridge: Harvard University Press, 1977), 39.

8. "only mediocrities develop": Oscar Wilde is quoted in Adam Phillips, *On Kissing, Tickling, and Being Bored* (Cambridge: Harvard University Press, 1994), 74.

11. "Ariel to Miranda:—Take . . ." Percy Shelley, "With a Guitar, to Jane," in *Romantic Poetry and Prose*, ed. Harold Bloom and Lionel Trilling (New York: Oxford University Press, 1973), 474.

11. "If everyone knew how to work . . .": Wanda Landowska, *Wanda Landowska on Music*, ed. Denise Restout (New York: Stein and Day, 1965), 367.

12. "Guided by his own inexperience . . .": Johann Nikolas Forkel, "The Genius of Bach," in *German Essays on Music*, ed. Jost Hermand and Michael Gilbert (New York: Continuum, 1994), 57.

13. "in music, nothing is worse than *playing wrong notes*": Carl Czerny, *Letters to a Young Lady on the Art of Playing the Pianoforte* (New York: Da Capo Press, 1982 [1837]), 5.

13. "Whatever you may have to do in a piece . . .": Alice Artzt, *The Art of Practicing* (Westport, Conn.: Bold Strummer, 1993), 14.

13. "listen carefully to your playing all the time": John Mills, *The John Mills Classical Guitar Tutor* (London: Music Sales, 1992), 19.

13. "always practice with a purpose": Scott Tennant, *Pumping Nylon: The Classical Guitarist's Technique Handbook* (Van Nuys, Calif.: Alfred Publishing Company, 1995), 93.

13. "I believe that learning to play the guitar . . .": Philip Toshio Sudo, *Zen Guitar* (New York: Simon and Schuster, 1998), 15.

13. "In this school . . .": Ibid., 35.

13. "a clear and relaxed mind, an open heart . . .": Bruser, *Art of Practicing*, 4.

14. "your natural creativity and genius . . .": Barry Green, with W. Timothy Gallwey, *The Inner Game of Music* (New York: Doubleday, 1986), 7.

14. "The value of an exercise depends on your state of mind": Bruser, *Art of Practicing*, 17.

14. "We must give up excessive ambition . . .": Ibid., 14.

16. "each session of work being divided . . .": Andrés Segovia is quoted in Wade, *Segovia*, 81.

17. "I never practice; I always play": Wanda Landowska is quoted in *Time*, December 1, 1952.

17. "Thus passes the morning . . .": Emilio Pujol on Francisco Tárrega is quoted in Evans and Evans, *Guitars*, 161.

17. "There is no satisfaction . . .": Martha Graham is quoted in Agnes de Mille, *Dance to the Piper* (Boston: Atlantic Monthly Press, 1952), 335.

18. "[A circus elephant] was discovered at midnight . . .": Pliny the Elder, *Natural History* (New York: Penguin Books, 1991), 108–9.

18. "Men have practiced music at all times . . .": Arthur Schopenhauer, *The World as Will and Representation*, trans. E. F. J. Payne (New York: Dover, 1969), bk. 1, 256.

21. "The mastery of any art is the work of a lifetime . . .": Ezra Pound, "A Retrospect," *Literary Essays* (New York: New Directions, 1968), 10.

SETTING THE STRINGS IN MOTION

35. "[The poet is] destined to set in motion supreme forces . . .": Rainer Maria Rilke, "The Young Poet" (1913/1931), in *Where Silence Reigns: Selected Prose by Rainer Maria Rilke,* trans. G. Craig Housong (New York: New Directions, 1978), 63.

36. "He belongs to the very small group of musicians . . ." Olin Downes, writing in *The New York Times,* January 9, 1928.

37. "[Segovia] exacts a religious silence": Domingo Prat is quoted in Graham Wade, *A New Look at Segovia—His Life, His Music* (Pacific, Mo.: Mel Bay Publications, 1997), 84.

40. On Harpo Marx learning Bach from Segovia, see Oscar Levant, *A Smattering of Ignorance* (New York: Doubleday, Doran & Co., 1940), 77.

42. *The Merv Griffin Show* aired in New York on May 31, 1980.

ADAGIO AND FUGUE

47. "It isn't just education and discipline . . .": Rainer Maria Rilke, *Letters on Cézanne,* ed. Clara Rilke, trans. Joel Agee (New York: Fromm International, 1985), 22.

48. "the result, interesting as it is, is hardly Bach . . .": *The Gramophone* is quoted in Wade, *New Look,* 68.

49. "the world's greatest guitarist": Miguel Llobet is quoted in ibid., 78–79.

49. On Llobet as the first guitarist to make recordings, see ibid., 68.

49. "[Tárrega was] more saint than musician": Andrés Segovia is quoted in Graham Wade, *Segovia: A Celebration of the Man and His Music* (London: Allison and Busby, 1983), 51.

49. "[Llobet is] a serious, noble interpreter of Bach . . .": Andrés Segovia, *An Autobiography of the Years 1893–1920* (New York: Macmillan, 1976), 101.

PERFECTING MY MISTAKES

67. Biographical material about Fernando Sor comes from Brian Jeffrey, *Fernando Sor, Guitarist and Composer* (London: Tecla Editions, 1977).

67. "Mr. Sor's vocal compositions have gained such favour . . .": Ackermann's *Repository of Arts*, London, March 1, 1820, is quoted in ibid., 49.

68. "[Sor] astonished the audience . . .": George Hogarth is quoted in Graham Wade, *Segovia: A Celebration of the Man and His Music* (London: Allison and Busby, 1983), 112.

69. "We must be honest. Fernando Sor . . .": Andrés Segovia is quoted in *Guitar Review*, no. 7 (1948), and in Wade, *Segovia*, 51.

69. Biographical material about Mauro Giuliani comes from Thomas Heck, *The Birth of the Classic Guitar and Its Cultivation in Vienna, Reflected in the Career and Compositions of Mauro Giuliani (d. 1829)* (PhD dissertation, Yale University, 1970).

69. "the standard by which virtuosos . . .": *Allgemeine musikalische Zeitung* is quoted in Richard Taruskin and Piero Weiss, *Music in the Western World: A History in Documents* (New York: Schirmer Books, 1984), 324–25.

69. "[Giuliani] has become . . .": *Allgemeine musikalische Zeitung* is quoted in Heck, *Birth*, 70.

70. "with the famous guitarist Giuliani": Karl Benyovsky, *J. N. Hummel, der Mensch und Künstler* (Bratislava, 1834), quoted in Heck, *Birth*, 103.

70. "Ober-Kapellmeister Salieri . . .": Ludwig van Beethoven is quoted in Heck, *Birth*, 105; translation modified.

70. "The guitar was transformed in his hands . . .": *Giornale delle Due Sicilie* is quoted in Wade, *Segovia*, 119.

STUDY IN G

76. "The guitar is like an orchestra . . .": Andrés Segovia is quoted in Graham Wade, *Segovia: A Celebration of the Man and His Music* (London: Allison and Busby, 1983), 72.

77. "The elfin wizardry of his playing . . .": Lawrence Gilman, writing in the *New York Herald Tribune,* January 9, 1928.

77. "did not and cannot succeed . . .": Olin Downes, writing in *The New York Times,* January 9, 1928.

77. "M. Sor does very pretty things on the guitar . . .": François-Joseph Fétis is quoted in Brian Jeffrey, *Fernando Sor, Guitarist and Composer* (London: Tecla Editions, 1977), 106.

78. "it is hard to decide whether he is greater on the violin or guitar": George C. Krick, "Nicolo Paganini, Guitarist," *Étude* 63, no. 8 (August 1940).

78. On Franz Schubert composing most of his songs on the guitar, see George C. Krick, "Franz Schubert, Guitarist," *Étude* 56, no. 10 (October 1938).

78. "The guitar is for the bower . . .": *The Harmonicon* is quoted in Harvey Turnbull, *The Guitar from the Renaissance to the Present Day* (New York: Charles Scribner's Sons, 1974), 94.

79. "[Berlioz was] the worst musician . . .": Maurice Ravel is quoted in Ian Crofton and Donald Fraser, *A Dictionary of Musical Quotations* (New York: Schirmer Books, 1985), 20.

THE SWEETEST CHORDS IN THE WORLD

84. "For All We Know (Love, Look at the Two of Us)": Words and music by Fred Karlin, Robb Wilson, and Arthur James.

89. "There is geometry in the humming of the strings . . .": Pythagoras is quoted in Ian Crofton and Donald Fraser, *A Dictionary of Musical Quotations* (New York: Schirmer Books, 1985), 140.

89. "The movements of the heavens . . .": Johannes Kepler is quoted in

Jamie James, *The Music of the Spheres: Music, Science, and the Natural Order of the Universe* (New York: Grove Press, 1993), 149.

89. "the ape of God the Creator . . .": Kepler is quoted in Joscelyn Godwin, *The Harmony of the Spheres: A Sourcebook of the Pythagorean Tradition in Music* (Rochester, Vt.: Inner Traditions International, 1993), 232.

90. "a wondrous harmony . . .": Athanasius Kircher is quoted in ibid., 157. See also James, *Music of Spheres*, 134.

90. "If the string of Saturn is struck . . .": Kircher is quoted in James, *Music of Spheres*, 137–38.

91. "[Music] is so powerful a thing . . .": Robert Burton, "The Secret Power of Music," in Jacques Barzun, *Pleasures of Music* (New York: Viking Press, 1951), 166–67.

91. "the originary language of the heart": Jean-Jacques Rousseau is quoted in Susan Bernstein, *Virtuosity of the Nineteenth Century: Performing Music and Language in Heine, Liszt, and Baudelaire* (Stanford, Calif.: Stanford University Press, 1998), 4.

91. "For what unites the incorporeal existence of reason . . .": Boethius, "The Principles of Music," quoted in Richard Taruskin and Piero Weiss, *Music in the Western World: A History in Documents* (New York: Schirmer Books, 1984), 35.

91. "Virtue is a kind of consonance of the soul . . .": Ptolemy is quoted in Godwin, *Harmony of Spheres*, 26.

91. "melancholic or passionate people . . .": Andreas Werckmeister is quoted in Dietrich Bartel, *Musica Poetica: Musical-Rhetorical Figures in German Baroque Music* (Lincoln, Neb.: University of Nebraska Press, 1997), 39; translation modified.

91. "Nothing is more futile . . .": Heinrich Heine is quoted in Crofton and Fraser, *Dictionary*, 1.

92. "music is an unconscious exercise in arithmetic . . .": Leibniz, letter to Christian Goldbach, April 27, 1712, in the *Grove Dictionary of Music and Musicians.*

92. "music is an unconscious exercise in metaphysics . . .": Arthur

Schopenhauer, *The World as Will and Representation*, trans. E. F. J. Payne (New York: Dover, 1969), bk. 1, 204.

92. Music as "our myth of the inner life": Susanne Langer, *Philosophy in a New Key* (Cambridge, Mass.: Harvard University Press, 1957), 245.

92. " 'Music has fulfilled its mission . . .' ": J. A. Hüller, "Abhandlung von der Nachahmung der Natur in der Music," quoted in ibid., 235.

92. "The tones of the *Kithara* . . .": Longinus, *On the Sublime*, ed. and trans. W. Rhys Roberts (New York: AMS Press, 1979), 143.

93. "Whoever will consider this a little more deeply . . .": Athanasius Kircher is quoted in Godwin, *Harmony of Spheres*, 274.

96. A piece "especially suited to reach the sensitive chords . . .": Andrés Segovia, *An Autobiography of the Years 1893–1920* (New York: Macmillan, 1976), 10.

INVOCATION AND DANCE

102. "The guitar has its own particular spirit . . .": Dionysio Aguado is quoted in Frederic V. Grunfeld, *The Art and Times of the Guitar: An Illustrated History of Guitars and Guitarists* (New York: Collier Books, 1969), 194; translation modified.

103. "From street-corner musicians to the masters of the concert stage": *Mad About Guitars* (Deutsche Grammophon, 1993).

104. "Under the magic touch of Segovia . . .": The quotation is found on William Cumpiano's Segovia website, http://www.cumpiano. com/Home/Articles/Transcriptions/Segovia/Segtransc/Segovia TH.html. I have been unable to trace it to its source.

104. Segovia has a "prelate-like gravity . . .": Bernard Gavoty is quoted in Graham Wade, *A New Look at Segovia—His Life, His Music* (Pacific, Mo.: Mel Bay Publications, 1997), 161.

104. "A guitar is a woman . . .": Gaspar Sanz is quoted in Grunfeld, *Art and Times*, 127; translation modified.

105. "The guitar is the most unpredictable . . .": Andrés Segovia is

quoted in José L. Romanillos, *Antonio de Torres: Guitar Maker—His Life and Work* (Longmead, Shaftesbury, Dorset: Element Books, 1987), 78.

105. This guitar history has been synthesized from various sources, especially Grunfeld, *Art and Times*; Harvey Turnbull, *The Guitar from the Renaissance to the Present Day* (New York: Charles Scribner's Sons, 1974); and *The New Grove Dictionary of Music and Musicians*, ed. Stanley Sadie, 20 vols. (London: Macmillan, 1980).

110. On the Empress Marie-Louise presenting a lyre guitar to Giuliani, see Thomas Heck, *The Birth of the Classic Guitar and Its Cultivation in Vienna, Reflected in the Career and Compositions of Mauro Giuliani (d. 1829)* (PhD dissertation, Yale University, 1970).

110. On Giuliani's performing on the lyre guitar in Naples, see Turnbull, *Renaissance to Present*, 85.

112. "lewd liberty . . .": The Merchants Adventurers Company is quoted in Evans and Evans, *Guitar*, 135.

113. "We used to play the lute more than the guitar . . .": The anonymous observer is quoted in ibid., 132–33.

113. "May heaven forgive that Espinel! . . .": Lope de Vega is quoted in ibid., 131.

114. "For who is not aware that the lute . . .": Pierre Trichet is quoted in ibid., 136.

114. "so lascivious in its words . . .": Juan de Mariana is quoted in ibid., 111.

115. "a Spanish female dancing the *seguidilla* . . .": J. F. Bourgoing is quoted in Neil D. Pennington, *The Spanish Baroque Guitar* (Ann Arbor, Mich.: UMI Research Press, 1981), 178.

116. "I troubled much with the king's gittar . . .": Samuel Pepys is quoted in Evans and Evans, *Guitar*, 139–40.

116. "If a lutenist lives to be eighty years old . . .": Johann Mattheson is quoted in Graham Wade, *Traditions of the Classical Guitar* (London: John Calder, 1980), 87. See Ernst Gottlieb Baron, *Study of the*

Lute [Historisch-theoretisch und praktische Untersuchung des Instruments der Lauten] (Redondo Beach, Calif.: Instrumenta Antiqua Publications, 1976 [1727]), 95–96; translation modified.

117. "On occasions of boating, while sailing in calm tranquillity . . .": *The Giulianiad* is quoted in Turnbull, *Renaissance to Present*, 98.

118. The guitar "echoes their sportive gaiety, their little griefs . . .": *The Giulianiad* is quoted in Grunfeld, *Art and Times*, 174.

KITCHEN MUSIC

125. "Find your place among the great people": Leopold Mozart to Wolfgang Amadeus Mozart, February 12, 1778, in *The Letters of Mozart and His Family*, ed. Emily Anderson (London: Macmillan, 1985), 478.

126. "Thirty years of being called 'distinguished' . . .": Peter Shaffer, *Amadeus* (New York: Samuel French, 1981), 111.

126. "If I cannot be Mozart then I do not wish to be anything": Ibid., 113.

126. "Mediocrities everywhere . . .": Ibid., 115.

131. "Believe me, my sole purpose . . .": Wolfgang Amadeus Mozart, April 4, 1781, in Anderson, *Letters*, 721.

THE CATHEDRAL

139. "Under his fingers the guitar dreams and weeps . . .' ": Hector Berlioz is quoted in Simon Wynberg, *Marco Aurelio Zani de Ferranti, Guitarist (1801–1878)* (Heidelberg, Germany: Chanterelle, 1989), 48.

140. On the instrument by Francisco Sanguino dated 1759, see James Tyler and Paul Sparks, *The Guitar and Its Music from the Renaissance to the Classical Era* (New York: Oxford University Press, 2002), 195.

140. On Antonio Torres, see José L. Romanillos, *Antonio de Torres: Guitar Maker—His Life and Work* (Longmead, Shaftesbury, Dorset: Element Books, 1987).

THE MUSIC OF WHAT HAPPENS

148. "I am not the right person to give concerts": Frédéric Chopin, letter to Franz Liszt, quoted in Graham Wade, *Segovia: A Celebration of the Man and His Music* (London: Allison and Busby, 1983), 74.

151. "His bow, like an angel's sword . . .": "The Wandering Soul," quoted in Marc Pincherle, *The World of the Virtuoso* (New York: W. W. Norton & Co., 1963), 159.

151. Felix Mendelssohn and Clara Schumann's performances of Beethoven are discussed in Wade, *Segovia*, 75.

151. "He the Prometheus, who creates a form from every note . . .": *Allgemeine musikalische Zeitung* is quoted in Richard Taruskin and Piero Weiss, *Music in the Western World: A History in Documents* (New York: Schirmer Books, 1984), 365.

A MOST MISUNDERSTOOD INSTRUMENT

173. On Segovia booking an extra seat for his instrument, see Graham Wade, *A New Look at Segovia—His Life, His Music* (Pacific, Mo.: Mel Bay Publications, 1997), 2:112.

181. " 'Although it is already universal . . .' ": Simon Molitor is quoted in Frederic V. Grunfeld, *The Art and Times of the Guitar: An Illustrated History of Guitars and Guitarists* (New York: Collier Books, 1969), 169; translation modified.

181. "there could scarcely be another place. . . .": Simon Molitor is quoted in Thomas Heck, *The Birth of the Classic Guitar and Its Cultivation in Vienna, Reflected in the Career and Compositions of Mauro Giuliani (d. 1829)* (PhD dissertation, Yale University, 1970), 87.

183. "a grievous punishment for the ear": Andrés Segovia is quoted in Brian Hodel, "Twentieth Century Music and the Guitar, Part I: 1900–1945," *Guitar Review*, no. 117 (Summer 1999), 13.

187. "I hope you got my letter from Mainz . . .": Wolfgang Amadeus

Mozart, October 23, 1790, in *Mozart's Letters, Mozart's Life,* ed. Robert Spaethling (New York: W. W. Norton & Co., 2000).

READING

219. "While we are practicing we must know what we are doing . . .": György Sandor, *On Piano Playing: Motion, Sound, and Expression* (New York: Schirmer Books, 1995), x.

222. "I was constantly practicing on my cello": Pablo Casals, *Joys and Sorrows* (New York: Simon and Schuster, 1970), 59.

222. "How much nobler is the study of music as a rational . . .": Boethius, "The Principles of Music," quoted in Richard Taruskin and Piero Weiss, *Music in the Western World: A History in Documents* (New York: Schirmer Books, 1984), 37.

ACKNOWLEDGMENTS

While writing *Practicing* I was fortunate to have the help of many people. I am especially grateful to Howard Junker and *ZYZZYVA* for publishing an early version of the story, and to Erica Olsen for her patience, good advice, and great care. Kim Todd and Jay Stevens generously shared their comments and their work. Jay Cantor, David Tanenbaum, Mark Salzman, Julie Orringer, Mark Bittner, and Katherine Fraser, each in his or her own way, offered just the right words at just the right moments. I would like to thank the Ucross Foundation for the privilege of a one-month residency, and Debra Gitterman, for numerous, shorter-term residencies. I could not have persevered without the love and encouragement of John W. Lowell, Michael Rhodes, Tony Travostino, Carl Pritzkat, Alan Emtage, Randy Briggs, Elaine McCarthy, Janice Gitterman, Steven Kirchner, Jessica Mihaly, Jim McCarthy, Kit Schulte, Markus Guehrs, Rob Mackenzie, Shirley Mandel, Francine Barkan, Toby Hobish, Cynthia Kurtz, and Alys X. George. To me, you are music. Malaga Baldi has been an agent of wonders. Alena Graedon, Peter Mendelsund, Sarah Gelman, Gabrielle Brooks, and the production staff at Knopf have been a delight. Finally, I'm indebted to my editor, Robin Desser, who showed me in what I wrote the book I meant to write. Thank you all.

Glenn Kurtz graduated from the Tufts University–New England Conservatory of Music double-degree program in 1985 and subsequently earned a PhD in German Studies and Comparative Literature from Stanford University. He has taught at San Francisco State University, California College of the Arts, and Stanford University and has written extensively on art and digital media. He divides his time between San Francisco and New York.

A NOTE ON THE TYPE

Pierre Simon Fournier *le jeune*, who designed the type used in this book, was both an originator and a collector of types. His services to the art of printing were his design of letters, his creation of ornaments and initials, and his standardization of type sizes. His types are old style in character and sharply cut. In 1764 and 1766 he published his *Manuel typographique*, a treatise on the history of French types and printing, on typefounding in all its details, and on what many consider his most important contribution to typography—the measurement of type by the point system.

Composed by Creative Graphics, Allentown, Pennsylvania

Printed and bound by R. R. Donnelley & Sons, Harrisonburg, Virginia

Book design by Robert C. Olsson